EVERYTHING IS CHANGING

EVERYTHING

IS CHANGING

Contemporary U.S. Movements in Historical Perspective

DAVID De LEON

PRAEGER

New York
Westport, Connecticut
London

Library of Congress Cataloging-in-Publication Data

De Leon, David.
  Everything is changing.

  Includes bibliographies and index.
  1. Social change—United States.   2. Social
movements—United States.   3. Minorities—United
States—Social conditions.   4. United States—
Social conditions—1980–   . I. Title.
HN65.D339   1988   303.4'0973   87–7323
ISBN 0–275–92892–6 (lib. bdg. : alk. paper)
ISBN 0–275–92893–4 (pbk. : alk. paper)

British Library Cataloguing in Publication Data is available.

Library of Congress Catalog Card Number: 87–7323
ISBN: 0–275–92892–6
ISBN: 0–275–92893–4 (pbk.)

First published in 1988

Praeger Publishers, One Madison Avenue, New York, NY 10010
A division of Greenwood Press, Inc.

Printed in the United States of America

The paper used in this book complies with the
Permanent Paper Standard issued by the National
Information Standards Organization (Z39.48-1984).

10 9 8 7 6 5 4 3 2 1

To Mary Frances Berry, colleague

If there is no struggle, there is no progress. Those who profess to favor freedom, and yet deprecate agitation, are men who want crops without plowing up the ground. They want rain without thunder and lightning. They want the ocean without the awful roar of its many waters. This struggle may be a moral one; or it may be a physical one; or it may be both moral and physical; but it must be a struggle. Power concedes nothing without a demand. It never did, and it never will. Find out just what people will submit to, and you have found out the exact amount of injustice and wrong which will be imposed upon them; and these will continue till they are resisted with either words or blows, or with both. The limits of tyrants are prescribed by the endurance of those who they oppress.

FREDERICK DOUGLASS, American black leader, 1857

It is the minorities who have made the history of the world. It is the few who have had the courage to take their places at the front; who have been true enough to themselves to speak the truth that was in them; who have dared to oppose the established order of things; who have espoused the cause of the suffering, struggling poor; who have upheld without regard to personal consequences the cause of freedom and righteousness. It is they, the heroic, self-sacrificing few who have made the history of the race and who have paved the way from barbarism to civilization. The many prefer to remain upon the popular side. They lack the courage and vision to join a despised minority that stands for a principle; they have not the moral fiber that understands, endures and finally conquers. They are to be pitied and not treated with contempt for they cannot help their cowardice. But thank God, in every age there have been the brave and self-reliant few, and they have been sufficient to their historic task, and we, who are here today, are under infinite obligations to them because they suffered, they sacrificed . . .

EUGENE DEBS, socialist leader,
from a 1918 speech against World War I
that sent him to prison with a ten-year sentence

THE BOX

Contents

The Past in Our Lives

Our lives were fundamentally defined before we were born.

We were born male or female, but our society provided the essential models of how to "act like a man" or "act like a woman."

We were born of a particular class. Our early homelife, our childhood experiences, our schooling, our job opportunities, and the boundaries of our hopes were powerfully shaped by this.

We were born of a certain race. Even today, American society is not color-blind. The meaning of the color of our skin is a social prejudice.

We were born Democrats or Republicans; Anglos or Hispanics; Jews, Catholics, or Protestants; Northerners, Westerners, or Southerners. These communities gave us partial answers to the fundamental question, "Who are we?" They gave us the basic patterns of perception through which most of us will see the world for a lifetime. If we had begun our lives in some other part of the world or in some other culture, we would be quite different.

Whether we accept, modify, or reject our inherited roles, we cannot avoid the fact that we grew up in a particular time, a spot of geography, and a socioeconomic system. The past of our society is the foundation of our individual lives. The study of our society's history, then, is also the study of ourselves, because we are a part of what has happened.

It is also true that our lives are not totally programmed. Although every society has a kind of mass production of standard brands of people, there are variations and alternatives. Human beings are the only animals who can ask why things are not different from what they are, or who may attempt to change life.

Many of the changes in our society, whether the American Revolution, the abolition of slavery, or women's rights, were advocated first by people whom the majority feared as extreme. Because these reforms were successful, we now honor those who were once persecuted. William O. Douglas, when he was a justice of the U.S. Supreme Court, observed:

Americans revere Roger Williams, not those who drove him out of the Bay Colony; Thomas Jefferson, not George III; Henry David Thoreau, not those who jailed him for nonpayment of a poll tax. And it is John Brown whose "soul goes marching on," not that of the judge who imposed the death penalty on him.

In recent years, there have been changes that have reverberated through the lives of all of us. Because of alterations in the U.S. economy, and because of the activity of organizations and individuals, many essential elements of the present and of the future are in doubt.

Our environment can no longer be taken for granted. Will we finally pollute the wellsprings of life? What kind of world will our children inherit? Can the quality of our life be maintained, or even improved?

Can the principles of our religions and our democracy include peoples of all races and of both sexes? Or will our experiment toward a more equitable society fail?

Do Jesus and the prophets look that comfortable dressed up in pin-striped suits, speaking scornfully of the poor, and endorsing increased military spending?

What do many conservatives mean when they say that they want America to be number one in the world? We are not number one in personal income. We are not number one in health care. We are not number one in literacy. We are not number one in how long our citizens live. We are, however, the number one debtor nation in the world, because of our loans from foreigners. We are also number one in our power to kill. Such distinctions raise many questions.

Will the United States go the way of great empires of the past, spending ever-greater sums of money on the supposed strength of armies and navies, and on buying friends abroad, while its society rots from within?

Why aren't there jobs for everyone? Is it because the jobless are all ignorant, stupid, and inferior beings who deserve only our comfortable contempt? Why are there so many poor people in the United States?

Do we honor and respect the elderly, including our parents, in their later years? Will our own last days be happy and secure?

Can we plan realistically for the future? Is the hope that none of our atomic weapons will ever fail, or if any fail, that the error will be corrected without disaster a childish one? Isn't it more likely that the thousands of years of civilization may end within a single hour?

These are some of the inescapable questions of our time. Large majorities of Americans are worried also about additives in their food, pollutants in the air that they breathe, contamination of the water they drink, and health hazards where they work. Racial minorities continue to demand equal treatment, whether at the level of local jobs and school boards, or within presidential politics. The majority of women—even those who refuse to call themselves feminists—have expectations of careers, salaries, or other life opportunities that would have been radical several decades ago. The general public is wary of another Vietnam. It favors reduced military spending and increased negotiations for arms control. In summary, the 1980s have not resembled the bland mediocrity and dominant complacency of the 1920s or the 1950s.

Movements that would increase democratic rights and liberties have remained powerful because of their principles and because of their work to achieve those principles. While a realist may criticize such reformers for building castles in the sky, Henry David Thoreau once declared that castles in the sky are where they belong. It is only necessary to put foundations under them.

This book is an introduction to some of these castle builders. Each of the nine chapters is an outline of a contemporary movement for a more humane and productive society. Why did a specific movement begin? Where and when did it emerge? Who were its major leaders? What have been the most influential organizations?

The first two essays discuss modern controversies over ecology and energy, and how they have expanded our understanding of our many ties to the rest of nature.

The next three chapters cover several of the ethnic and cultural groups of our diverse society: Indians, blacks, and Hispanics.

This is followed by two chapters on how basic sex roles have changed so that both men and women are no longer as programmed and limited in their lives.

Finally, there are two examples of communities based upon vital questions most likely to be addressed at the end of our lives: the religious significance (if any) of our existence, and social and personal responses to aging. This book closes with such issues, as it began with the environment into which we were born.

It could be argued that this topical history of U.S. reform movements may isolate them from the interconnectedness that would be found if they were part of a larger narrative. Still, many of them are separate entities, with their members focused on their own interests. Whites may support reforms that are sponsored by blacks, but it will be primarily blacks who are concerned about their own community. Men may endorse feminist proposals, but their major proponents will be women. Jews will be affected most by Jewish issues; Catholics by Catholic issues; Protestants by Protestant issues. Although each group may have links to other groups, it is naive to suppose that people outside a particular community will be as deeply involved in its problems and in proposed solutions. Unified narratives are often "unified" by the author's consciously or unconsciously expressed values, which are generally white, male, middle-class, and middle-of-the-road. A topical survey of U.S. reforms is more honest, more detailed, and more illuminating.

Another objection might be that these movements are all of minorities. If we add them together, however, they are a large majority of our population. A history that did not include these minorities would be severely restricted.

The relative comprehensiveness of this approach allows me to claim that this is the first wide-ranging history of U.S. reform to be published in about a quarter of a century. Much has changed since the writing of such literary landmarks as Eric Goldman's *Rendezvous with Destiny: A History of Modern American Reform* (1952; revised 1965), Richard Hofstadter's *Age of Reform: From Bryan to F.D.R.* (1955), Louis Hartz's *The Liberal Tradition in America* (1955), and Sidney Lens's *Radicalism in America* (1966; updated in 1969). The cosmetic addition of a new introduction or a new epilogue to some of these books does not conceal the ravages of age. These narrative histories should be compared to the table of contents for *Everything Is Changing*. Modern ecology is much broader and deeper than the first conservation movements that they mention. Nuclear power was not an issue for most of them. "Negroes" were treated minimally, Indians were historical curiosities, and Spanish-speaking people were ignored. Women and the sexually "deviant" were almost invisible. The elderly had no major voice. Radical religion was lightly mentioned. Earlier conventional histories of reform, seen by the standards of today, are remarkably narrow.

Later books tend to be even more specialized. They frequently cover brief periods of time. They are restricted often to subject matter that is very white, very political (not cultural or sexual), and very conventional in their definitions of "left" and "right." *Everything Is Changing* encompasses subjects that are neglected in surveys of reform, and it includes both liberal and radical concepts of social change into the late 1980s.

Intelligent liberals and conservatives both realize that now and then it is necessary to reform the system in order to conserve it. Radicals, on the other hand, are concerned more with changes in the fundamental structure of society.

Since the turn of this century liberal and conservative reform has produced the welfare-warfare state or the corporate state. Large-scale business required a more aggressive central government as a gyroscope domestically to alleviate massive and obvious injustices that would promote social unrest and to protect business interests abroad militarily and diplomatically. The poor now have their minimal safety net, and the rich have a powerful enforcer. While reformers may see the problems of this society—Jimmy Walker, a mayor of New York City, said that "a reformer is a man who rides through a sewer in a glass boat"—the existing order is not challenged systematically.

Other movements, however, are radical. This word derives from the Latin *radix*, meaning "root." A radical analysis "goes to the root" of an issue. The term *radicalism* was first used in England in 1797 by Charles James Fox. He called for the radical reform that all men in England would be able to vote; at that time Englishmen could vote only if they owned a certain amount of property. A Radical, then, was someone who favored a wider suffrage. Only later did the concept of radicalism expand from politics to social and economic rights, as in the term *social democracy*.

In the United States, *radicalism* often has been used to mean extremes of any kind. Communism has been called the radicalism of the left, and fascism the radicalism of the right. I will be using the word in its more classical sense, meaning change that broadens and strengthens democracy. Individual radicals, radical caucuses within established institutions, and radical parties, however small, have frequently acted to democratize the ballot, popularize reforms, clarify issues, and convert some people to their programs.

Once a radical demand has succeeded, it may become so accepted that it seems liberal or even conservative. Mark Twain once observed that "the radical invents the views. When he has worn them out the conservative adopts them." Walt Whitman had a similar idea when he said that "the future belongs to the radical." Examples of this truism are found throughout our history. The goal of reducing the workday to eight hours was once regarded as impossibly utopian. Women's suffrage and independent careers for women were thought to be biologically unnatural. Labor unions were denounced by most people as alien and communistic efforts to bully and blackmail employers. Much of what we now regard as normal was proposed first by radical minorities. As Anatole France commented, "Without dreamers, we would still live in caves."

It would be easy to laugh at early prejudices. Instead, we should consider the possibility that one hundred years from now people may look back on many of the commonly accepted truths of our time and label them barbaric (assuming, of course, that our civilization lasts another one hundred years without being incinerated in a nuclear war).

This book explores some of the essential changes in the accepted truths of our society. You may find it useful for one or more of the following reasons.

First, each essay discusses when and how a particular movement began and gives its basic chronology to the present. Other texts are not as focused but have bits of information scattered throughout a general survey. Women's rights may be mentioned only in 1848 (with the Seneca Falls Convention), during the Civil War (in the controversy over female inclusion in the new constitutional amendments for black rights), in 1920 with the nationwide winning of the vote, and with the recent revival of feminism. A single essay on this subject, as on other subjects, can provide a concentrated and coherent review. It is clearer how the present fits into the flow of change.

Second, I have attempted to let people speak for themselves. When the first black newspaper, *Freedom's Journal*, was begun in 1827, it announced: "We wish to plead our own cause. Too long have others spoken for us." It is vital that we hear what others have to say, so that we can think for ourselves and decide for ourselves. Most of us now rely on the mass media, which is controlled primarily by wealthy elites. Freedom of the press belongs mainly to those who own a press.

Third, each chapter summarizes the sustaining ideals and programs of a particular movement. In most books on U.S. reformers, the reader learns little about their characteristic social and political thought, although the world has a very different appearance when seen through the prism of any of their interpretations.

You may find such ideas inspiring or spiteful, humanitarian or obnoxiously self-righteous, illuminating concepts or shouted slogans. Many reformers are like an antislavery leader of the mid-1800s who said that he needed to be all fire because he was surrounded by mountains of ice. Leo Tolstoy agreed when he said, "Why talk in subtleties when there are so many flagrant truths to be told?" You may not agree.

Fourth, each chapter focuses on issues and personalities that have living significance for our own time, rather than on colorful trivia from the past. Thus, the reader of the section on the women's movement will learn not only the primary leaders, ideas, and events, but something of the continuing themes found in the struggles for equal pay for equal work, control over one's own body (reproductive rights), and sexual identity that is self-defined rather than socially imposed. This is a book on the larger questions of a "usable past," not a warehouse of details.

Fifth, the text is illustrated with black-and-white line drawings that encapsulate the appeals of each group. Such art is often missing from surveys of social and political controversies.

Finally, each chapter concludes with a basic list of further readings, almost all published in the 1980s, along with addresses for contemporary sources of information such as organizations and periodicals. Each chapter could be considered a preface to action.

My goals may seem ambitious, but this book is a modest introduction to a few contemporary issues. It does not cover many important subjects that have no comprehensive and long-term related movements such as farm problems, prison reform, left-wing parties, the rights of people in the U.S. military, and truly democratic foreign policies. Also, about forty pages of footnotes that were in the original manuscript were deleted in this printed version. Despite such limitations, this book does provide historical background for some important issues in today's newspapers.

What were my values in writing this survey? The reader deserves to be informed, since these essays were not written by a machine. Although intellectuals like Leopold von Ranke once believed that the historian could extinguish his or her individuality, many academics now realize that there is no neutral ground from which we can observe our own culture with an innocent eye. As E. H. Carr concluded, "The historian is part of history." Values are necessary to determine what is important. An author should be conscious of his or her values, but cannot avoid using them. Even a computer has to be instructed about what data are relevant for a particular task.

Throughout this work, I am in sympathy with John Stuart Mill's belief that anything that crushes individuality is tyranny, whatever its name. Rigidly centralized systems are not treated favorably, whether they are conservative orthodoxies or "scientific" revolutionary systems, dogmatic religions or secular cults, manipulative corporate capitalism or what Allen Ginsberg called "dinosaur socialism." They all encourage the anesthesia of conformity. The machinery of civilization should be used to free people from the violence of poverty, cultural chauvinism, racism, and sexism. Many of us have benefited from earlier achievements in tearing down the walls of racial segregation and sexual discrimination, and in promoting more opportunities for the full development of all. Our society is healthier because of such changes.

This book was completed with generous assistance from Howard University, through several grants from the History Department and a university-sponsored Faculty Research Fellowship, along with an award from the National Endowment for the Humanities.

EVERYTHING IS CHANGING

Part I
"IN THE BEGINNING": THE LAND

What is the use of a house if you don't have a tolerable planet to put it on?

HENRY DAVID THOREAU

Thoreau's cabin, from the 1854 edition of *Walden; or, Life in the Woods*.

We probably assume that the immediate world around us is safe and secure. We take for granted the air that we breathe, the water that we drink, the food that we eat, and the safety of our homes and offices.

These basic facts of life have been questioned in recent years by movements for conservation, public health, and ecology. We are more conscious of pollutants in the air, chemicals in the water, pesticides and additives in food, and asbestos and other dangers in buildings.

These problems cannot be overcome by moralizing or by individual actions. We will not solve them if we eat health foods, recycle our newspapers, and put water filters on our faucets. We will not escape them if we move to some leafy suburb. Since we are a part of nature, environmental pollution will affect the quality and health of our lives and that of our children.

Legislation now restricts the use of rivers, lakes, and oceans as garbage dumps. Cars must have some emission controls. The contents of food products are more clearly labeled. There is widespread agreement that the short-term profits of a few people cannot be allowed to damage the futures of the vast majority.

Chapter 1 is a summary of the growing consciousness of these issues, the establishment of organizations, and proposed solutions. There are few easy answers. Chapter 2 illustrates that technological solutions to one problem may create other problems; our early hopes for nuclear power have been replaced by complex realities. How safe is this energy? Are we more secure because of the increasing number of atomic weapons scattered throughout the world?

None of these are solely American problems. The above-ground testing of nuclear bombs by the People's Republic of China can produce fallout in the United States. Sulfur pollution of the air from coal-burning plants in the United States can become acid rain in Canada. The massive destruction of forests in South America, Africa, Malaysia, and Indonesia could have a world-wide impact on climates. While modern reformers have expanded our understanding that there is no place to hide from such ecological consequences, few of their alternatives are simple or readily achieved.

1

Life Preservers: The Birth and Growth of U.S. Movements for Conservation and Ecology

In twentieth-century urban America, nature has been thoroughly civilized, both for better and for worse. In the morning, the city dweller turns on a faucet and gets a stream of chlorinated water. Breakfast comes from boxes, cans, and plastic packages. The streets on the way to school or to work may be lined with orderly rows of trees, some clipped grass, and a park or two. The air is likely to contain some auto and industrial pollutants. The individual who wants to escape from it all may join the millions who converge on the major seashores and "wilderness" areas.

As life became urbanized, increasing numbers of Americans were troubled about the abuse of nature. For most of the nation's history, its vast forests, pure rivers and lakes, and rich mineral resources seemed inexhaustible. The stumps of trees, the heaped rubble of mines, the smokestacks, and a hazy sky were interpreted as signs of progress. Today, however, people are often worried about the quality of drinking water, paved-over croplands, air pollution, food additives, toxic waste dumps, and the growing list of rivers, lakes, and beaches that are closed to swimming and fishing. Such concerns have been expressed through many overlapping movements, variously called conservation, ecology, public health, and environmentalism.

These movements, to which many people are now accustomed, are startlingly new. Some writers believe that humanity has been fundamentally hostile toward undeveloped nature throughout history. Sociobiologists and some psychohistorians have asserted that when the first human beings emerged perhaps 15 million years ago in Central Africa, they were less able than many other animals to succeed in dense foliage because their senses of smell and hearing were not as keen. Instead, they relied upon sight and intelligence. Both abilities worked more readily in cleared land where it was easier to see things and there was more time to react to dangers.

Beneath our modern civilized consciousness may be primitive fears of the dark felt by the precocious primates who were our ancestors. This thesis has a surface reasonableness, since recorded history covers only about five thousand years, compared to the millions of years of evolution. Probably most people have argued something on the basis of "that's human nature." This explains some of the best-selling appeal of Loren Eiseley's *Immense Journey* (1957), Robert Ardrey's *African Genesis: A Personal Inquiry into the Animal Origins of Property and Nations* (1966), Konrad Lorenz's *On Aggression* (1966), and Desmond Morris's two books, *The Naked Ape: A Zoologist's Study of the Human Animal* (1967) and *The Human Zoo* (1969).

Even if human beings are glorified animals, however, they are infinitely diverse compared to other animals. Biology is not necessarily human destiny. Cultural anthropology illustrates the complicated range of human values in the past and the present, throughout the globe. While biological reductionism can make fatalistic conclusions from heredity, it cannot explain why some cultures have venerated the spiritual powers of wilderness, or why others, such as the Arctic peoples, have lived far from the supposed ideal of green and plowed fields.

It remains true, of course, that human beings have had pervasive effects on the environment in a brief period. If one compares the history of the earth to one hour, the life of human beings on the earth would be two seconds of that hour. Humans are only 1 of the over 1,700,000 kinds of known life on the planet today, along with millions of still-unexplored forms of life. Humans became ecological dominants when they turned from being food gatherers and hunters to being farmers and shepherds about 12,000 years ago in the Middle East and 8,000 years ago in China. It was this change in human society that began to transform the earth.

The cutting of trees in mountains and the grazing of hillsides by sheep and goats quickly produced soil erosion and the siltation of rivers. Some of the results can be seen now in the denuded mountains of Lebanon, where the Phoenicians cut the timber for their famous navies, and in the scattered ruins of the Near East. The eventual eclipse of many states in this region came not only because of changes in the climate and political organization but because of early lumbering and cultivation practices.

On the positive side, some early peoples learned to manage the land for continuous productivity. The Phoenicians developed terraced farming to limit mountain erosion. The Greeks—guilty of overgrazing the land—first used manuring and crop rotation. The Romans constructed enormous irrigation systems. These experiences became part of the heritage of European agriculture, along with Greco-Roman ideals of a well-ordered nature overcoming the feared and unproductive wilderness.

Later European attitudes toward nature were shaped by human needs and ancient practices, along with the religious power of Judeo-Christian beliefs. For both Jews and Christians, humans are not an integral part of nature but separate from nature and superior to it, just as the soul is separate from the body and superior to it. Although there is the concept of human stewardship of God's creation, the environment consists of objects to be used. This theme begins in the book of Genesis, where God informs man:

The fear of you and the dread of you shall be upon every beast of the earth, and upon every bird of the air, upon all that moveth upon the earth, and upon all the fishes of the sea; unto your hand are they delivered. Every moving thing that liveth shall be meat for you; . . . have dominion over the fish of the sea and over the fowl of the air, and over every living being that moveth over the earth.

By contrast, many animistic and polytheistic religions believe that animals, plants, and inanimate objects have their own spirits, to be treated respectfully. Humanity is more integrated into nature in such religions as Buddhism, Hinduism, Shintoism, and Taoism. Christianity, however, de-animated nature. This instrumentalism may have been necessary for the emergence of rationalistic science and technology in the West. While we do not have communion with nature, we imagine that we have control over it.

Another factor in Western attitudes about nature, other than the experiences of previous societies and the teachings of Christianity, was the development of capitalist ideals and practices within the last 600 years. This new system, based upon private ownership of the means of production (such as land, minerals, and tools), manufacture for profit rather than for use, and the sale of labor as a commodity, has increased colossally what is produced and consumed. Non-Western countries have been reduced to two choices. They can become sources of raw materials, cash crops, and cheap labor for the capitalist nations, or they can economically develop themselves, by whatever means. In either case, there are tendencies to abuse the land, air, and water.

These were essential elements of the long history that preceded the Europeans' discovery of the New World and their conquest of the native peoples who already lived there. The Europeans knew something about wilderness areas, which still existed in Europe, but their colonizing struggles highlighted their negative feelings about uncivilized nature. It was not surprising that William Bradford, on leaving the *Mayflower*, described a "hideous and desolate wilderness." The Europeans struggled for food and shelter. They often fought with the so-called Indians, whom they sometimes regarded as agents of Satan and "tawney serpents." Dangerous animals were present in the woods. And people's imaginations created additional terrors. For one Puritan author, the forest was the "Devil's den of eternal night."

But the wilderness could be a place of opportunity. The faithful heard a divine call to bring "the cleare sunshine of the Gospel" into a dark and heathen land. They would be like the Jews of the Old Testament. They would wander in the wilderness, purify their faith, form an army of saints, conquer a promised land, and build a New Jerusalem. In 1629 John

Winthrop asserted, "the whole earth is the lords Garden and he hath given it to the sonnes of men, and with a general condition, Gen. 1:28: Increase and multiply, replenish the earth and subdue it."

They were sometimes restrained by ideals of common welfare and stewardship, and a few laws were passed. In 1629 Plymouth sought to regulate cutting and selling timber on colony land. In 1639 Newport, Rhode Island, prohibited deer hunting for six months of the year. Such local efforts were neither widespread nor effective, however. Even when the Crown reserved larger trees for its own use as ship masts in the late 1600s and early 1700s, such regulations were usually thwarted. Nonetheless, many early communities in New England did establish village greens or "commons" (some later evolving into parks), access to rivers was usually not shut off by private property, and seashores remained open in most places. But the majority of people did not believe in limiting the freedom of property owners, even when their actions were shortsighted.

Frontier settlers often viewed the trees on their property as little better than weeds. They might kill trees by stripping off a circle of bark around the base. Farmers could then plant among the dead trees or stumps, often exhausting the soil's nitrogen, potassium, and other minerals by an annual growth of crops like tobacco. The land could be worn out within a few years. Some farmers moved on to other cheap land. The animal life, in a similar way, could be "harvested" by killing until the beavers, otters, raccoons, bears, and other wildlife were driven toward extinction.

A NEW CONSCIOUSNESS

These long traditions of antagonism toward the wilderness were first challenged by some urban European intellectuals far from the harsh realities of frontier life. A few American city dwellers, who were physically closer to nature, contributed to this reevaluation of the countryside.

Their first appeal was religious: God was found in spontaneous nature, not in classical gardens that were precisely disciplined. By the early 1800s Deists, Romantics, and Transcendentalists asserted that the contemplation of nature would uplift humanity by inspiring a sense of the divine. For the poet William Cullen Bryant, "The groves were god's first temples."

A second rationale emerged in the early 1800s in the form of cultural nationalism. Some Americans asserted that while the young country was less cultured and sophisticated than European societies, it was superior because it was closer to the invigorating and honest soil, and because it was filled with majestic natural monuments rather than artificial creations. Philip Freneau spoke of the Mississippi as "this prince of rivers in comparison of which the *Nile* is but a small rivulet, and the *Danube* a ditch." Abigail Adams, in London in 1786, claimed that "European birds have half the melody of ours. Nor is their fruit half so sweet, nor their flowers half so fragrant." James

Fenimore Cooper talked about "the honesty of the woods" compared to the abused and exhausted Old World. The painter Asher Durand hoped that we would avoid "the pollutions of civilization" found in Europe.

A painter made the first practical suggestion. George Catlin was sketching some Indians at the headwaters of the Missouri River in 1832 when he observed some of them trading about 1,400 buffalo hides for whiskey. Foreseeing the corruption of the people and the land, he sent a letter to a New York newspaper urging the formation of a "nation's park" in the West, "containing man and beast, in the wild and freshness of nature's beauty." Catlin's ideal was not a formal garden or a park for aristocrats but a primitive region that would be open to all who would come. This probably seemed like a silly idea to most of those who heard of it. In an undeveloped country, why have an undeveloped park? The painter Thomas Cole was a more accurate prophet than Catlin when he complained of "the meagre utilitarianism" of his time, where all of nature was to be offered on the altars of mammon.

A third justification for the preservation and appreciation of nature was that broad contact with nature brought emotional renewal. While few people dismissed the progress created by farming and machines, many worried about the death of nature and suspected that the new order was not without flaws. If commercial civilization became oppressively dominant, we might become overcivilized, weak, and dull. Henry David Thoreau militantly expressed this in his writings against the land being "pockmarked with the works of man," and in his calls for "little oases of wilderness in the desert of our civilization."

Although Thoreau was unusual in his belief that wilderness was necessary to "keep the New World new," many people felt a sense of awe toward nature. This was expressed by some painters and poets. "Practical" men like the architect Frederick Law Olmsted later used this public sentiment to promote social reform. Olmsted attracted wide support for his vision of a Central Park in New York City that would be "a specimen of God's handiwork" and a public place that would soften the unnatural lives of the urban masses.

Finally, there was an appeal to business sense: planned development would serve the needs of both the present and the future. George Perkins Marsh eloquently defended this view in his 1864 book, *Man and Nature: or, Physical Geography as Modified by Human Action*. Marsh looked back to the farming and hunting practices of past civilizations and asked whether we had learned anything from their failures. He outlined a destructive sequence: trees were cut; plants and animals declined; water evaporated from the soil; erosion increased; and streams and rivers filled with silt. When there were times of drought, there were few plants to hold what water did fall. When rains came, there was flooding. The climate of an entire region might finally change for the worse. While some people had become rich, entire societies suffered decline or collapse. While Marsh advocated no

From Obscure Eccentric to Icon

An engraving from F. B. Sanborn, *Henry D. Thoreau* 1884.

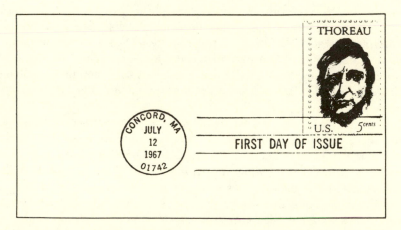

The U.S. Post Office issued this stamp in 1967 in honor of the 150th anniversary of Thoreau's birth.

TABLE OF CONTENTS.

CHAPTER I.

INTRODUCTORY.

From Marsh's *Man and Nature.*

federal laws, despite his awareness that many European forests were protected and regulated, he hoped that businessmen would become conscious of their future self-interest.

This argument was taken up by Romantics and nationalists like William Cullen Bryant. He entitled one of his essays in 1865 "The Utility of Trees," declaring that "forests protect a country against drought, and keep its streams constantly flowing and its wells constantly full." Another forceful advocate of "national forests" was Carl Schurz, the secretary of the interior from 1877 to 1888. He was convinced that we needed them as resources for the future.

By the mid-1800s, there were four rationales for the preservation of nature: spiritual benefits, nationalistic pride, usefulness, and emotional renewal (partly tied to rationales 1 and 3). But only a few visionaries championed these beliefs. City governments focused narrowly on local issues; states were eager to promote business expansion. The exceptions were limited. Some people wanted local parks, and the first state park was created in 1776 when Virginia set aside fifty acres and one spring at what is now Berkeley Springs, West Virginia, "for the poor and infirm people and suffering humanity." The federal government acted once before the Civil War when it protected the Arkansas Hot Springs in 1832 as a "National Reservation."

ORGANIZING CONSERVATION

Although it now seems reasonable that the federal government would encourage overall national interests, this view was only slowly applied to the area of American resources. In 1864 the U.S. Congress gave about ten square miles of the Yosemite Valley to the state of California—rather than establishing a federal park—as a place "for public use, resort and recreation." This episode stimulated some people to advocate that other "wonderous sites" should be protected, such as Niagara Falls, parts of the Maine woods, and the Adirondacks.

The federal government was more concerned about practical matters, such as irrigation, fishing, and the role of forests in water control. In 1871 Congress funded a U.S. commissioner of fish and fisheries and instructed the Department of Agriculture to investigate the need for forest reserves. In 1872 President Ulysses S. Grant signed a bill setting aside 2 million acres of Wyoming as "a public park or pleasuring ground," with instructions that all the timber and mineral resources be kept untapped. This later became Yellowstone National Park. Without this action, today we might see motels, amusement parks, a spa near the hot springs, private homes throughout the area, and billboards along the six-lane highway to the wonders. Why didn't this happen?

Whites had first explored this region in 1869 and 1870. Some had wanted to stake claims to the geysers and everything else, and make money. Others concluded that this land should belong to all. One, Nathaniel P. Langford, wrote two articles for *Scribner's* in 1871 that included engravings of the curiosities of this area.

Some readers suspected that the articles were more fiction than fact, but Langford was vindicated in 1871 by the director of the Geological and Geographical Survey of the Territories. He traveled to the region, accompanied by a photographer and a landscape artist, and verified Langford's descriptions.

Big money interests began to take notice, especially Jay Cooke and Company, which had financed the extension of the Northern Pacific Railroad into Montana. If Yellowstone was a park, tourists might take the train there. The railroad would make the most money if individual speculators were kept from dividing and exploiting the land.

The railroad argued in public that such "beautiful decorations" of nature should not be despoiled for the profit of a few. Surely Yellowstone deserved as much protection as Yosemite's trees. It was added that this was an important watershed and that it was too remote to be valuable for anything other than a park. The short-term interests of big business and the long-term interests of the public were compatible.

Jay Cooke and Company provided the cash and the influence to pass a bill protecting the region. The press responded with enthusiasm, praising the park as a "museum" and a "marvelous valley" full of "freaks and phenomena of nature," while agreeing that it provided a source of water downstream. Virtually everyone assumed that it would become a tourist mecca. As one article said, "Yankee enterprise will dot the new Park with hostelries and

The "Brains."

Thomas Nast on the limited vision of many "money-bags" of post–Civil War America.

furrow it with lines of commerce." Some people noted that the law could be repealed if the park got in anybody's way.

The primary concerns of the U.S. government remained pragmatic. This was reflected in the 1879 mandate of the U.S. Geological Survey to outline the mineral resources and irrigation needs of the country. Many people in the government and in the general public felt that parks should be surveyed and eventually sold like other public lands. Why should government be in the business of owning "scenery" or attempting to protect a few buffalo? When $40,000 was requested for Yellowstone in 1883, one senator responded to such criticisms with both a romantic and a practical defense. He asserted that as the country's population grew, it needed the park "as a great breathing-place for the national lungs." Despite this appeal, the appropriation was defeated and the park was taken over by the U.S. Army for thirty years.

Once Yellowstone was established, defenders rapidly developed. This included the army, which raised its status and helped to reduce poaching. Commercial interests could not do as they wished. In 1886, for example, a bill to allow a railroad through the park to promote nearby mining was defeated. Senator McAdoo of New Jersey avowed that the glory of the park was its solitude: "In the great West are inspiring sights and mysteries of nature that elevate mankind and bring it closer communion with omniscience."

A second landmark event for conservation in the late 1800s was the protection of the Adirondack Mountains in New York State. Painters and poets had spoken for this protection before the Civil War, but greater attention followed an admired book by the Rev. William H. H. Murray of Boston, *Adventures in the Wilderness; or, Camp-Life in the Adirondacks*, published in 1869. For Murray, the wilderness provided "the perfect relaxation which all jaded minds require." Some middle- and upper-class readers were impressed; modern transporation allowed them to travel to distant parts of the country, and they wished to protect camping, fishing, and hunting areas. Other classes probably did not read the book, and, at any rate, "jaded minds" among the common people were unlikely to find solace in the wilderness. The average worker put in ten hours a day for six days a week and had little money for recreation.

Influential minorities combined the romantic and practical appeals of conservation into public policy. The first report of the New York Park Commission in 1872 envisioned a park in the Adirondacks that transcended "mere purposes of recreation." It would be an instrument of "political economy" that regulated lumber production while protecting the watershed so that there was "a *steady, constant supply* of water." This report, and the first issues of *Forest and Stream* in 1873, glorified forests not only for their beauty and as havens for sportsmen, but as sturdy bulwarks against flooding, siltation, and disruptions of the Erie Canal, the Hudson River, and the port of New York City. Special interest groups could claim that they were agents of the public good. They convinced other powerful elites and some of the electorate to endorse their plans by using both idealistic and utilitarian arguments.

The weightiest ally in this struggle was the New York Chamber of Commerce, which lobbied steadily for protection of the Adirondacks because of possible damage to the harbor of New York City. In 1885 Governor David B. Hill signed an act creating a forest preserve of 715,000 acres. This was reorganized as a park in 1891. It would be "a place where rest, recuperation and vigor may be gained by our highly nervous and overworked people." In 1892 the park was expanded to 3 million acres and designated as a "ground open for the free use of all people for their health and pleasure and as forest land necessary to the preservation of the headwaters of the chief rivers of the state, and as a future supply of timber." To insure the maximum protection of this park, its status was written into the New York constitution in 1894. Today, it is the largest wilderness area east of the Mississippi, covering 8,900 square miles, an area larger than all of Massachusetts.

The Yellowstone and Adirondack parks were giant steps forward. Ur-

banization and industrialization quickened nostalgia for nature. Whereas
Thoreau's writings had been read by few, works by John Muir (1838–1914)
and other authors were admired by many. Muir had grown up in Wisconsin,
early felt a love of nature, and, after an accident that temporarily blinded
him, devoted his life to writing and speaking for nature. He was profoundly
attracted to the Transcendentalist ideals of Thoreau and Ralph Waldo Emerson, giving homage to forests as "God's first temples" and proclaiming that
"the clearest way to the Universe is through a forest wilderness." His message thrilled many who felt burdened with the noise, filth, and crowding of
city life. The remote wilderness was idealized. Muir's readers began to enlist
in his crusades against the overcutting of trees, against the plowing, plant-
ing, and exhausting of less fertile soils, and against flocks of omnivorous
sheep, which he depicted as "hoofed locusts." Muir and his followers concluded by the late 1870s that some political intervention was necessary to
protect nature from being desecrated.

The U.S. Census Bureau awakened the general public to changing realities in 1890 when it announced that the United States no longer had a
continuous frontier. Our society had expanded geographically for over two
and a half centuries. What would happen now? Would we run out of resources? Would people pile up in the cities, as in Europe? Would the small
farmer decline? Were opportunities in the United States shrinking?

More people understood that if our resources were limited, we had to
practice frugal management. Some of these people joined organizations for
nature-lovers and sportsmen, which further expanded public knowledge and
calls for legislation. The Audubon Society began its work in New York City
in 1888. The Sierra Club started with twenty-seven members in San Francisco in 1892 (one was John Muir, who would be its president for twenty-two
years). The American Scenic and Historic Preservation Society was formed
in 1895. These groups were armed with the money and political influence of
middle- and upper-class reformers. In addition, the federal government
passed the Forest Reserve Act in 1891. A professionally staffed Forest Service quickly grew, and lands were added. President Grover Cleveland used
this act in 1897 to protect 25 million acres of California. Many Westerners
were enraged, shouting that eastern bird-watchers and "imperial" outsiders
who wanted the West to be a "colony" were stunting their social and economic development. The Sierra Club, they said, was really the Sahara Club.
Defenders of the president depicted Uncle Sam as a balding man in a barber
chair, with the barber skillfully combing his scattered hair, drawn as trees.

When William McKinley took office in 1897, many Westerners and advocates of unregulated business hoped to throw off Cleveland's restraints.
Although they were not successful, they did secure passage of the Forest
Management Act of 1897. This endorsed the eventual use of reserves for
timber, minerals, and grazing land. Most conservationists agreed with this

goal. Men like Gifford Pinchot, appointed chief of the Federal Forestry Division in 1895, interpreted forests as factories that produced trees. Forests should be organized efficiently, rather than stripped or entirely closed.

It was commonly said that uniquely beautiful locations also deserved federal protection. Mount Rainier was preserved in 1899, and politicians began to nominate their favorite sites for national recognition. One predicted that these would become "the Nation's gallery of the finest works of Nature."

Before the new century began, another combination of economic self-interest and public interest produced a law that would be enormously expanded by the courts in the 1960s. Merchants in New York City were disturbed that "effluents" into their harbor could damage trade. They wanted the Corps of Engineers to regulate or eliminate the dumping of refuse into waterways. The Rivers and Harbors Act of 1899 made it a felony to dump "any refuse matter of any kind or description" into a waterway. This was interpreted, at first, to mean only obstructions to navigation, but the broadly elastic language of the original bill contained great potential for federal regulation of waterways.

After the moderate and unenergetic President McKinley was assassinated in 1901, his successor, the activist Theodore Roosevelt, more vigorously enforced old conservationist laws and proposed new regulations. President Roosevelt, an Easterner who had lived in the West, once declared that the wondrous scenery of Colorado "bankrupted the English language." He also had practical concerns, characterizing rivers and forests as public utilities.

TR was the first U.S. president to use his office as a pulpit to raise the consciousness of the public on conservation, to urge passage of stronger legislation, and to apply previous laws enthusiastically and imaginatively. Pinchot's authority was so expanded that his critics mocked him as the Czar of the Forestry Empire. Conservationists denied such fanciful claims. They countered that forest reserves were both recreation areas that prevented flabby citizens and investments in future resources.

During TR's seven years of presidential power, from 1901 to 1908, conservation was lauded as both practical and idealistic. His first legislative success was the Newlands Reclamation Act of 1902. The federal government promised to give to the states any money from the sale of U.S. lands in those states if the states would use the money for reclamation projects, such as irrigation, and if they were willing to sell the reclaimed land cheaply to settlers on long-term installments. The Newlands Act was a triumph. A Bureau of Reclamation was established by 1905, and there were twenty-four projects by 1910. Millions of acres of land, formerly worth a few cents for grazing might now be worth hundreds of dollars an acre.

Besides such legislation, TR used his office to publicize conservationist ideals. In 1908, Roosevelt invited 1,000 national leaders to a White House conference, including thirty-four state governors, delegates from sixty-eight

One popular cartoonist's description of U.S. history and his fears for the future.

conservation groups, and members of the Congress and the Supreme Court. Public awareness was expanded, state organizations were created in forty-one states, and conservation-minded individuals began to coalesce into a powerful interest group.

TR frequently acted by executive order, which did not require the approval of Congress. By such means, he removed 148 million acres of forest lands from sale, along with 80 million acres of mineral lands and 1.5 million acres of waterpower sites. This allowed the creation of fifty-one wildlife areas, five new national parks, and thirteen national monuments (established under the Antiquities Act of 1905). Such actions were often contested by business and local groups, but he successfully enlarged the territories of the Division of Forestry.

All these reforms were part of a general movement called Progressivism, in which government at many levels intervened in society and the economy to insure the stability of the system. Business practices that discredited business and public trust in government were at least moderated. When tubercular and diseased meat was reported ending up on the consumer's table as "Grade A beef," the Meat Inspection Act of 1906 restored public confidence. When opium and other narcotics were perceived as dangerously common in cough syrups and other drugstore remedies, they were controlled by the Narcotics Drug Act of 1909.

The next administration, that of William Howard Taft (1908–1912), defended TR's gains and removed more public lands from private sale. However, Taft stumbled in public relations. He fired the aggressive chief forester, Gifford Pinchot. He took most of the blame for a controversial dam in Yosemite Park that would provide water for distant San Francisco. This growing city needed water for drinking and for fire control. The latter had been vividly demonstrated in an earthquake and fire in 1906.

It was not Taft but TR who had originally approved the dam following this devastation. He was not happy with this decision. Pinchot, his friend, was a utilitarian who described the Hetch Hetchy Canyon as a swampy valley that would be improved by the dam, while satisfying the needs of San Francisco.

Muir, also TR's friend, was a preservationist. He jeered at the defenders of the dam as "temple destroyers, devotees of ravishing commercialism," and servants of mammon. In cooler moments, Muir added that San Francisco could find other sites outside this national park, which should remain unviolated. If the door were opened for commercial use of a park, all parks might be in danger.

In a revealing change from earlier American history most advocates of the dam calmly agreed with the ideal of preservation, but insisted that only "misty aesthetes," along with short-haired women, put nature first. Many conservationists, however, wanted to restrict the principle of utility, which might convert any tree or waterfall into dollars and cents. They asked, "Is there nothing more to life than a race to the trough? Does good mean only good to eat?"

The preservationists lost in 1914, but the defeat did not silence them. They had become politically insistent. They had activated a vocal segment of public opinion. They were encouraged by the establishment of the National Park Service in 1917. They urged such government agencies to increase their budgets, staff, and properties. These bureaucracies, both public and private, nurtured professional conservationists for future struggles and con-

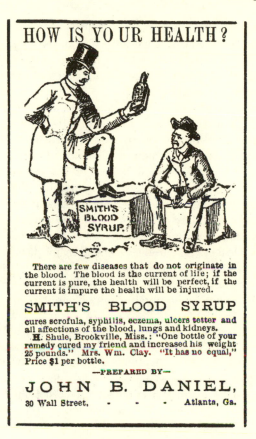

vinced much of the public that they were altruistic champions of the public's best interests. Conservationist momentum came to seem like an inexorable force of nature; it could be slowed during some periods, but it could not be entirely stopped or rolled back.

The 1920s, trumpeted as an age of permanent Republican prosperity, did blight the growth of conservation. Presidents Warren G. Harding (1920–1923) and Calvin Coolidge (1923–1928) allowed extensive leasing of public lands for grazing, timber cutting, water diversion, and mining. They relied on two laws passed in 1920, the General Leasing Act and the Water Power Act. Both authorized controlled leasing of public lands to private business. Scandals followed, including one that led to the imprisonment of Secretary of the Interior Albert Fall for taking $300,000 in bribes to lease government oil reserves at Teapot Dome, Wyoming.

Despite such problems, conservation agencies grew. The Department of Agriculture, the Forest Service, the Bureau of Fisheries, the Bureau of Mines, the Geological Survey, and the National Park Service managed natural resources. Although these agencies were often servants to business, they benefited many citizens. Farmers got advice from the Department of Agriculture. Timber workers got help fighting forest fires from the Forest Service. And tourists were more enthusiastic about the national parks when the automobile made them accessible.

President Hoover, who is generally regarded as an extreme conservative, was a sincere conservationist who believed that this policy was good business. He encouraged full professionalization of agencies such as the Forest Service, and advocated the construction of Boulder Dam, the St. Lawrence Seaway, flood-control projects, and fisheries. Hoover believed that the states, in partnership with business, should carry out these projects. Decentralization and voluntary cooperation were crucially inadequate, however, since individual states often did not have the resources or the inclination, and business was skeptical about the value of conservation.

While the New Deal era included the second major period of conservation in U.S. history, it failed to produce any comprehensive plans. Government programs were piecemeal, responding to particular and urgent problems. Nevertheless, there were some notable achievements:

—The Civilian Conservation Corps, or CCC (1933–1942) alleviated some unemployment by using the labor of 2,750,000 men in 1,500 camps to plant 1 billion trees, build roads, dig drainage canals, fight fires, and erect park buildings.

—The ravages of the Dust Bowl were reduced by the U.S. Soil Conservation Service (begun in 1935) and the use of cut-over regions and tax-defaulted lands for shelterbelts. About 18,000 miles of trees were planted on the Great Plains.

The 1920s public takes an interest in its properties.

—The U.S. Army Corps of Engineers presided over one of the New Deal's most imaginative programs, the Tennessee Valley Authority (TVA). This created more than twenty new dams, controlled rivers, improved navigation, generated cheap electricity, and formed recreational areas.

One of the casualties of World War II was the conservation movement. Young people who might have worked in the CCC camps were now in the military. Concern about resources was replaced by the need for rapid production. Following the war, which devastated most of the industrial world, Americans generally experienced great prosperity and found it difficult to imagine any future of severe limits. Even those afraid of a revival of the Great Depression often wished to enjoy the good life of the moment.

But the conservation movement was so institutionalized that setbacks were temporary. Government agencies continued to manage resources, although usually in the interests of business. Conservation societies remained small (the Sierra Club had only 7,000 members in 1950), but they continued their efforts. They had regular staffs and paid lobbyists; they enjoyed tax and mail privileges; and they had the interest of some legislators. These organizations, despite their size, educated the public with detailed information, attracted media attention, and influenced action.

The public was not entirely indifferent to such issues in the 1950s. If someone got into his private car and used some of the cheap gas of that day on the new, extensive highways, that person might go to a park, which he wanted to be as pleasant as possible. Business interests were restrained by this concern. A 1950s proposal for a dam inside one park was defeated, not only because of regard for that park, but because this dam might have opened the way to other commercial invasions. One conservationist predicted that "in our mad rush to dam every river, chop down every tree, utilize all resources to the ultimate limit . . . we might . . . destroy the very things that have made life in America worth cherishing and defending." This writer's anxiety was extreme, since no one proposed to chop down every tree. Still, many people reasonably feared that a few businesses within the parks would lead to many more.

Some of these people advocated that lands be designated permanent wilderness. A campaign for this, begun in 1956, created the National Wilderness Preservation System, which had 9 million acres in 1964.

In 1966 President Lyndon B. Johnson praised the "new conservation movement" even as the Internal Revenue Service tried to bludgeon the Sierra Club by denying it tax-exempt status. There was a proposal to build a massive dam in the Grand Canyon. Powerful economic interests favored the dam, the U.S. Army Corps of Engineers supported it—and it was rejected. The outcry against the dam was a clear signal of public support for the parks. One champion of the dam observed that "Hell hath no fury like a conservationist aroused." Critics of the dam may have agreed with the author Wallace

Stegner that there should be other ideals than "technological termite-life," "the Brave New World of a completely man-controlled environment." Sentiments like these added the Wild and Scenic Rivers Act of 1968 to the conservationist momentum.

Until this time, government agencies and conservation groups rested upon two foundation stones. First, many argued that conservation was useful. It was a prudent accounting of resources in the present, invested for the future. This philosophy dominated such agencies as the Bureau of Reclamation, the Forest Service, TVA, and the U.S. Army Corps of Engineers. A second view was popularized by a smaller group who claimed that the highest benefits from protecting nature were to be found in its psychological and social solace. This psycho-aesthetic appeal had been voiced by Thoreau, Muir, and some in the National Park Service.

FROM CONSERVATION TO ECOLOGY

A third dimension of humanity's relationship to nature was not commonly discussed before the 1960s. This was called ecology, which stressed neither money nor charm, but the broader connections between human beings and other life forms. Ecologists believed that humanity's actions were disrupting the vast web of life, of which all are a part.

The term *ecology* was first used primarily by scientists who held a holistic view of the natural world. The German zoologist who coined the word *oecology* in 1866 from the Greek *oikos*, meaning "house" or "habitat," defined it as the study of the relations between organisms and their environment. The term much later came to include subjects like human ecology (relating to such biological issues as the linkage of diet to health) and social ecology (including the study of housing and social relations among people).

Some government employees, some independent scientists, and some members of conservation groups developed this theme before the 1960s. In 1915 the Ecological Society of America was founded. This group was later chaired by Aldo Leopold, an employee of the U.S. Forest Service. Leopold touched the lives of many conservationists with his vision of ethical evolution. He believed that humanity had first behaved little better than egoistic children. People had slowly developed respect for others. First, there was respect for individuals; then, for the family, the tribe, and the nation; and, finally, for humanity as a whole. A stage was reached in which people cast off some forms of barbarism, such as open slavery and overt subjection of women, and most felt that it was wrong to kill some other creatures, such as dogs and cats. Leopold encouraged people to become more sensitive to the rest of nature.

Leopold's *Sand County Almanac*, published posthumously in 1949, brought his views to a larger section of the public. Similar principles appeared in Fairfield Osborne's *Our Plundered Planet* (1948), William Vogt's

Road to Survival (1948), Rachel Carson's *The Sea Around Us* (1951), and Osborn's *The Limits of the Earth* (1953).

Rachel Carson, who had been a marine biologist in the Fish and Wildlife Service, reached the largest audience. In 1960 she published a series of articles on poisons in the environment for *The New Yorker*. She equated herbicides and pesticides with something that already disturbed the public, the dangers of radioactive fallout.

These articles were the basis of her best-selling book in 1962, *The Silent Spring*. Life was being so stifled and killed by some of humanity's actions that winter might someday be followed by a silent spring. She cautioned that 500 new chemicals were tried in the environment each year. They were carried from soil and plants into animals and human beings. The effects of a chemical or combination of chemicals on present and future generations could not be predicted.

Although Carson did not advocate the total abandonment of spraying, the chemical industry called her book a "hoax" and Carson a "mystic." A significant part of the public, however, was apprehensive. During the next three years, forty states limited pesticides. President John F. Kennedy summoned a White House conference on conservation, and the Science Advisory Committee recommended the elimination of toxic pesticides such as dichloro-diphenyl-trichloro-ethane (DDT), which persisted in soil, plants, flesh, and bones.

There was a rising tide of ecological activism throughout the 1960s. The first wave included earlier concerns about "killer smog" in the cities (the Clean Air Act of 1963), detergent foam in groundwater, nuclear fallout (the Test Ban Treaty of 1963), and public health issues such as the use of tobacco (criticized in a surgeon general's report in 1963). Many of these problems were summarized in a 1965 presidential report entitled *Restoring the Quality of Our Environment*.

The social and cultural agitation brought on by the Vietnam War intensified previous debates and brought a youthful influx into the ecological movements. Popular skepticism about the government's role in the war was reflected in best-sellers on the "corporate state" pillaging the environment (by Charles Reich) and Theodore Roszak's fear of "technocratic totalitarianism." Public interest groups multiplied, especially after Ralph Nader's successful lawsuit against the safety standards at General Motors in 1966. Activists could use the Freedom of Information Act (1967) to gain access to some formerly secret information within the government. Further events such as a massive oil spill near Santa Barbara, California, contributed to a burst of public activity and the passage of many laws during the late 1960s and the early 1970s.

At the center of these environmental laws was the National Environmental Policy Act of 1969 (NEPA). This set up the Council on Environmental Quality to advise the president, although it did not mandate any nationwide

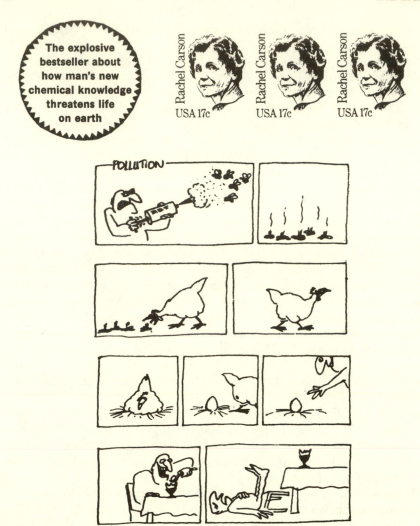

The Silent Spring was controversial at first, but its message was adopted by many, and its author became widely respected. Bottom: an ecological theme like Carson's was expressed in a counterculture journal of the late 1960s.

standards for air, water, noise, solid wastes, or hazardous substances. NEPA also failed to give any government agency a veto over governmental projects on environmental grounds. Its main power consisted of the requirement that all federal agencies must document that potential effects on environment had been considered before any major federal project began. Congress, through NEPA, directed that all laws, policies, and regulations of the U.S. government should be consistent with certain environmental goals, such as the recycling of depletable resources.

Specifically, every federal proposal for legislation or regulation change must be accompanied by an Environmental Impact Statement (EIS) discussing the need for a project, alternatives, the environment to be affected, and probable effects. This cost-benefit equation would sound an early alert if there were dangers with a project. Under NEPA, environmental protection became a part of the organization of every federal agency and department.

That's the theory. In practice, an agency can claim that a statement is unnecessary because a particular plan would have no impact on the environment. Moreover, the Council on Environmental Quality can decide that any possible impact would not be harmful. NEPA does give the public one powerful weapon: citizens and affected groups have the right to sue the responsible agency on environmental grounds to force it to change its actions.

Another basic change occurred in 1970 when many federal environmental activities were consolidated into one agency, the Environmental Protection Agency (EPA). EPA was given two main tasks: to create national pollution standards and to enforce those standards, usually in conjunction with the states. These were complicated and controversial jobs. For example, emission controls on cars raised prices, irking some consumers and automakers. Similarly, removing solid and chemical wastes from some forms of industrial production then created the problem of disposing of those wastes, such as condensed materials from smokestacks.

Despite such complaints, EPA and other federal agencies now monitor or regulate various hazards in the environment around us. The air that we breathe is analyzed for such pollutants as carbon monoxide. The Clean Air Act, passed in 1970 and amended in 1977, has been polluted, however, by numerous deals. When it became obvious that about fifty states would not meet EPA standards by a deadline of December 31, 1987, they were given an eight year extension. The water that we drink is supposedly protected by legislation such as the Clean Water Act. Nonetheless, it was estimated in 1986 that the water supply of one of every five Americans had lead concentrations above U.S. limits and that other potentially damaging substances were becoming common in drinking water because of runoff from city streets and fertilized agricultural fields. Although President Ronald Reagan denounced the amended Clean Water Act in 1986 as a "budget buster" that was larded with pork-barrel giveaways, others in the Congress maintained that clean water was an investment in America's future and could not be protected at bargain-basement prices. When Reagan vetoed this act, it was passed over his veto in 1987 by a vote of 401 to 26 in the House and 86 to 14 in the Senate. That same year EPA reported that one-fourth of U.S. lakes, rivers, and estuaries were too polluted for swimming and fishing, and that samples of groundwater taken from two dozen states contained twenty types of pesticide residue.

The food that we eat is also subject to at least minimal inspection. For example, the Federal Insecticide, Fungicide and Rodenticide Act was passed in 1961 because of worries that people were absorbing pesticides through milk, cereals, meats, and other food, producing disease and genetic mutations. This act required registration of pesticides with EPA, labeling them, and restricting their application. Its objective was to prevent unreasonable risk to human life and to the environment. To enforce this act, EPA could seize wrongfully used pesticides and impose fines and even prison terms through Department of Justice prosecution. Those affected could appeal within the judicial system.

This law is still needed since the use of pesticides exceeded 2.5 billion pounds a year by the late 1980s, more than twice that in use in 1962 when *The Silent Spring* was published. Residues of pesticides are in common foods, such as beef, chicken, lettuce, potatoes, and tomatoes. Because of this, pesticides can be found in the body tissues of 99 percent of Americans. In 1987 EPA nonetheless stopped monitoring toxic residues in body fat and blood because its staff and budget had not grown in more than a decade.

A further area of government regulation may be the place where we work. When the Occupational Safety and Health Administration (OSHA) was created in 1970, it was expected to set mandatory standards for safe and healthful working conditions in all businesses in or affecting interstate commerce. It became a lightning rod for criticisms from businesses that government was limiting their freedom, while burdening them with excessive costs and cumbersome record keeping. The number of inspectors declined, fines were sometimes avoided, unannounced inspections were not made, variances to the standards were frequently granted, and some OSHA rulings were successfully counterattacked in the courts. While OSHA established goals of preventable hazards in many businesses and raised vital issues of health and safety in the workplace, 7,500 people died each year from job-related causes, and the average fine for an accident involving a death or the hospitalization of more than four workers has been $284.

There are animals and plants that have been overwhelmed by the unsolved problems of the environment. The federal government attempted to protect these through laws such as the Endangered Species Act of 1973. This legislation authorized the secretary of the interior to declare that a species of

plant, animal, or fish was endangered—that is, threatened with extinction—and to identify its critical habitat. The federal government was then forbidden to do anything that might harm a protected life form.

The general public became aware of this law with a dramatic case in 1978. In that year, a citizens' group in Tennessee blocked the completion of a TVA dam that had been begun in 1967. The dam would create a thirty-mile reservoir and had already cost $102 million. Local farmers had sued under NEPA in 1969, arguing that valuable croplands would be lost in the project, but they were defeated. Then, when the Endangered Species Act was passed, they sued under that. A biologist from the University of Tennessee had discovered in the affected area what he claimed to be a rare species of perch, the snail darter. It then seemed that there were only about 10,000 to 15,000 in the entire world. This three-inch, tannish-colored fish became the legal basis for halting the dam because it was apparently an endangered species, and its critical habitat would be destroyed by the dam. A tangle of lawsuits involved farmers, environmentalists, the TVA, the Department of the Interior, the Congress of the United States, and the federal courts. Congress intervened and removed the jurisdiction of a federal committee over the site, while the snail darters were trapped and shipped to another home.

Why protect a few "useless" fish, or any form of life? Some, of course, are symbolic, such as the bald eagle, our national symbol. Some are beautiful, such as the willow warbler and the mission blue butterfly. Some may be discovered to have a practical value for medicine—consider the 1987 case of a powerful antibiotic found in the skin of a certain frog. Other kinds of life may be edible or helpful in genetic engineering. Some may be important for the survival of other forms of life. When one part of nature dies, other parts may suffer. In the 1960s the Chinese government conducted a massive campaign to kill birds that were eating valuable grain. The death of most birds produced an unexpected horde of insects. By the late 1980s, these issues became acute. Some biologists warned that as many as 1 million species of life would be extinct by the end of the 1990s. Each year, as tropical rain forests larger than the state of Maine are cut down and pollution intensifies throughout the world, biodiversity declines. In 1986 Dr. Edward O. Wilson of Harvard called this the most extreme reduction of life in the past 65 million years. Despite this, the Office of Endangered Species became extinct in 1987, with its duties and staff dispersed to other agencies.

Throughout the 1970s and the 1980s popular awareness grew that the environment is part of our common future and must be protected or improved. The burgeoning field of ecology law, which fully emerged in the 1970s, included many laws that still influence the quality of life for millions. Although President Richard Nixon had proclaimed the 1970s "the environmental decade," he and many others did not anticipate how far-ranging and broadly based this movement would become. Even the oldest conservation groups experienced a sudden burst of growth: the Audubon Society grew from 45,000 members in 1966 to 321,000 in 1975, and the Sierra Club swelled from 35,000 to 147,000 in the same period. Conservation, public health, and ecology were becoming part of the expectations of the general public.

The economic costs and administrative burdens did cause more resistance by the late 1970s. This was part of a common outcry against too much government and excessive federal spending. It merged with the argument that it was more important to create jobs than to conserve resources. Some of the conservative critics even described ecologists as fanatics, "modern Druids worshipping trees," obnoxious elitists who denied jobs to workers, and "woodsy witchdoctors of a revived ancient nature cult." Business interests and average citizens sometimes agreed with their complaints as they did in 1980 when the government proposed to create a new 2.4 million-acre wilderness area in the West. Critics included not only the American Pulpwood Association and the Industrial Forestry Association but numerous local people who needed work. As one local bumper sticker read, "Sierra Club— Kiss My Axe." Similarly, in states like Alaska (where the federal government owns 75 percent of the land), there is hostility between the "boomers" and the "pansy-sniffers."

After the triumphant election of Ronald Reagan in 1980, some people in his administration tried to characterize ecologists as shouting extremists who represented a minority in U.S. society. But ecology laws have not been fads. Polls throughout the 1980s demonstrated that about 65 percent wanted to keep or expand protections of the environment.

This has meant, first of all, that the public wants parks. As more Americans live in cities, more look wistfully toward open spaces. Ranch houses or ranchettes in suburbia are not enough. This popularity has threatened to flood the existing parks with too many people, too many cars, too many roads, and too many facilities. Park visits grew almost 30 percent from 1980 to 1986, from 220 million to 281 million. In 1987 President Reagan agreed that more parks were needed when he signed the legislation to create our forty-ninth federal park, the Great Basin National Park in Nevada. Other possible areas include tall grass prairie in Kansas and the Rogue River in Oregon.

Park officials also have attempted to limit the "invasion by the Winnebago tribe" by subjecting visitors to more regulations. Thus, there is now a ten-year waiting list to take a private raft down the Colorado River. The public, despite inconveniences, has never been convinced that the parks would be better operated by private companies. Nor has the majority of the public supported efforts to make strip-mining easier, to lessen the requirements for environmental impact statements, or to grant more business leases to exploit oil, gas, mineral, and timber resources on the public lands.

The federal government owns one-third of the United States, including 86 percent of Nevada, 81 percent of Alaska, 64 percent of Idaho and Utah, and over 40 percent of Arizona, California, Oregon, and Wyoming. Most Americans show little sign of wanting to divide up these lands for profit by some cost-benefit analysis. Instead, there is wide agreement with the goal of an earlier Republican, Gifford Pinchot, that natural resources should be managed so that the greatest number of people derive the greatest good over the longest period of time. This leaves unanswered many aesthetic and tactical questions. What is the practical value of saving whooping cranes, bald eagles, redwoods, and snail darters? Should the public's access to its own lands be limited? Are parks mainly stockpiles of resources for the future? Should natural forest fires be allowed to burn? How closely should we manage nature?

A second area of public ecological concern, besides the management of the parklands, is the safety of water, air, food, and consumer products. People are aware that they are living in a polluted world where their jobs, their food, and the houses in which they live can be dangerous to them. Even their garbage may come back to haunt them. At one time, it was thrown into rivers and landfills. Today, we realize that trash can be toxic to us. Bleaches, weed killers, corrosive elements of rusting machines, paint thinner, bug killers, detergents, highway de-icing salts, and fertilizers ooze into our water supplies. In modern society, how do you throw something away when there is no "away"? Even when garbage is burned, there will be air pollution and the disposal of ashes. In 1987 one entrepreneur thought that he had a solution for some of the 25,000 tons of trash that New York City generates every day: put 3,000 tons of it on a barge and ship it to a landfill in Louisiana. Louisiana, however, rejected it. It was later rejected by five other states and three foreign countries. After traveling more than 6,000 miles during two months, the rotting materials returned to New York. As our national population grows, so will such problems.

In some cases, legal action has forced safer standards. Some landfills have been closed or restricted, sometimes by actions under the Resource Conservation and Recovery Act (1976; renewed in 1984). Some chemical companies have been held liable for damages, such as the 1987 indictment of the Grace Company for pouring solvents on the ground in Woburn, Massachusetts, over a period of twenty years. Some companies, such as Johns-Manville, the manufacturer of asbestos, have attempted to escape responsibility by prematurely filing for bankruptcy.

The federal government helps to pay for cleanup through the Superfund toxic waste bill, passed in 1980 and continued in 1986. Progress has been slow, and the task is enormous. In some industrial zones, entire cities have become so contaminated by chemical wastes that they are toxic towns. Love Canal, in Niagara Falls, New York, was declared a disaster area in the late 1970s. Times Beach, near St. Louis, Missouri, was bought by the federal government in the early 1980s: its 2,400 inhabitants were removed; tons of soil were trucked away; and in 1986 several pharmaceutical and chemical companies agreed to pay $19 million as a settlement. People ask what is happening to the local industrial garbage buried in now-rusting barrels or stored in open pools. Will life-threatening chemicals seep into our drinking water or enter our food supply?

Pollution is an issue even in high tech areas with supposedly clean industries. In 1986 newspapers reported that an underground aquifer in the Silicon Valley of northern California was tainted by a highly poisonous solvent. The EPA has added sites in this region to its list of hazardous waste dumps. Another high tech pollutant is covered by the Nuclear Waste Act of 1982. Even those who support nuclear power do not want a dump site in their back yard. Most recently, biotechnology expanded this list of ecological perils by creating forms of man-made life that should be carefully tested and monitored to avoid disaster.

Most of these problems have to be solved nationally or internationally, rather than locally. Today, smog from Los Angeles is in the Grand Canyon. The Everglades National Park in Florida could die because of water pumped out far away for people and agriculture. Yellowstone's geysers like Old Faithful may shrink or even cease because of geothermal, gas, and oil drilling. Water in the Great Lakes and in major coastal areas such as the Chesapeake Bay can be slowly poisoned, both for human use and for aquatic life, by industrial, household, and human wastes, along with chlorine, fertilizers, pesticides, and herbicides. Distant smoke may fall on plant life as acid rain. And worldwide logging of rain forests, combined with industrial pollution of the air, may produce global disruptions in rainfall and temperature.

While some predictions such as Paul Ehrlich's prophecy that the oceans would be dead by 1976, have been exaggerated, many people sense that our problems are adding up, and that private enterprise and small government are not enough to provide solutions. One author summarized this with an itemized list of minor issues that led to a major conclusion:

Each small action, each shovel of dirt, each ounce of pesticide, each car exhaust, each jet plane, each backyard incinerator, each cow in the feedlot, each year of asphalt or concrete covering the water-absorbing earth, each beer can in the barrow pit, each mile of interstate, each acre of block-filled land, each building on a flood plain, each pound of garbage, each acre of overgrazed land, each factory or refinery, and, yes, each rocket shot into space has little effect. But cumulatively the effect is staggering and catastrophic. (William F. Clark, *Energy for Survival: The Alternative to Extinction* [Garden City, N.Y.: Anchor Press, 1974])

A third area of concern is shared by a smaller group. This is the conservation of nonrenewable resources, whether by reducing consumption, resource recovery from garbage, recycling cans and papers, or rebuilding the soil through crop rotation. Despite some programs, this is a consumer soci-

ety characterized by throwaways and waste, not a conserver society. The average American uses thirteen times as much energy as someone in Latin America, twenty times as much as an Asian, and thirty times as much as an African. Most of the things that are produced by this energy, from aluminum cans to cars, end their days in garbage dumps and junkyards rather than recycling plants. How long can this continue?

Finally, there are a small number of people who advocate a system of ecological consciousness, which ranges from those who focus primarily on their compost heap and self-sufficiency to those with a planetary program. Such perspectives include rural retreats, limited technology ("small is beautiful"), restraints within the existing system (such as "zero population growth"), United Nations (UN) regulation and control, and replacement of the present system with eco-socialism. All of these programs have the value of asking basic questions: What kind of world will future generations inherit? How many resources will have been squandered? Will the environment be poisoned? Will the quality of life be diminished?

SOURCES OF FURTHER INFORMATION

Books and Articles

Allen, Thomas B. *Guardians of the Wild: The Story of the National Wildlife Federation.* Bloomington: Indiana University Press, 1988.

Anderson, Walter Truett. *To Govern Evolution: Further Adventures of the Political Animal.* New York: Harcourt Brace Jovanovich, 1987.

Bailes, Kendall E., ed. *Environmental History: Critical Issues in Comparative Perspective.* Lanham, Md.: University Press of America, copublished by arrangement with the American Society for Environmental History, 1985.

Belanger, Dian Olson. *Managing American Wildlife: A History of the International Association of Fish and Wildlife Agencies.* Amherst: University of Massachusetts Press, 1988.

Berger, John J. *Restoring the Earth: How Americans Are Working to Renew Our Damaged Environment.* New York: Doubleday/Anchor, 1987.

Bookchin, Murray. *The Modern Crisis.* Montreal: Black Rose Books, 1986.

Brand, Stewart, ed. *The Essential Whole Earth Catalog.* Garden City, N.Y.: Doubleday, 1986.

Brickman, Ronald, Sheila Jasanoff, and Thomas Ilgen. *Controlling Chemicals: The Politics of Regulation in Europe and the United States.* Ithaca, N.Y.: Cornell University Press, 1985.

Brodeur, Paul. *Outrageous Conduct: The Asbestos Industry on Trial.* New York: Pantheon Books, 1986.

Brown, Lester, et al. *State of the World, 1987.* New York: Norton, 1987.

Brown, Michael H. *The Toxic Cloud: The Poisoning of America's Air.* New York: Harper & Row, 1987.

Chavkin, Wendy, ed. *Double Exposure: Women's Health Hazards on the Job and at Home.* New York: Monthly Review Press, 1984.

Clawson, Marion. *The Federal Lands Revisited.* Washington, D.C.: Resources for the Future, 1983.

Cox, Thomas R., et al. *This Well-Wooded Land: Americans and Their Forests from Colonial Times to the Present.* Lincoln: University of Nebraska Press, 1985.

Davis, Richard C., ed. *Encyclopedia of American Forest and Conservation History.* 2 vols. New York: Macmillan, 1983.

Deudney, Daniel, and Christopher Flavin. *Renewable Energy: The Power to Choose.* New York: Norton, 1986.

Durrell, Lee. *State of the Ark: An Atlas of Conservation in Action.* New York: Doubleday, 1986.

Eckholm, Erik. *Down to Earth: Environment and Human Needs.* New York: Norton, 1986.

Ehrlich, Paul R. *The Machinery of Nature: The Living World Around Us—And How It Works.* New York: Simon & Schuster, 1986.

Fenton, Thomas P., and Mary J. Heffron, eds. *Food, Hunger, Agribusiness: A Directory of Resources.* Maryknoll, N.Y.: Orbis Books, 1987.

Fox, Michael. *Agricide: The Hidden Crisis That Affects Us All.* New York: Schocken Books, 1986.

Fox, Stephen. *The American Conservation Movement: John Muir and His Legacy.* Madison: University of Wisconsin Press, 1986.

Freudenberg, Nicholas. *Not in Our Backyards! Community Action for Health and the Environment.* New York: Monthly Review Press, 1984.

Gaia Ltd. Staff and Norman Myers. *Gaia: An Atlas of Planet Management.* New York: Anchor/Doubleday, 1984.

Harf, James E., and B. Thomas Trout, eds. *The Politics of Global Resources.* Durham, N.C.: Duke University Press, 1986.

Hays, Samuel P. *Beauty, Health, and Permanence: Environmental Politics in the United States, 1955–1985.* New York: Cambridge University Press, 1987.

————. *Conservation and the Gospel of Efficiency: The Progressive Conservation Movement, 1890–1920.* Cambridge: Harvard University Press, 1986 [1959].

Hendricks, Rickey L. "The Conservation Movement: A Critique of Historical Sources," *The History Teacher* 16 (November 1982): 77–104.

Hobban, Thomas M., and Richard D. Green. *Green Justice: The Environment and the Courts.* Boulder, Colo.: Westview Press, 1987.

International Institute for Environment and Development, and the World Resources Institute. *World Resources 1987.* New York: Basic Books, 1987.

Judkins, Bennett M. *We Offer Ourselves as Evidence: Toward Workers' Control of Occupational Health.* Westport, Conn.: Greenwood Press, 1986.

Koppes, Clayton R. "Efficiency/Equity/Esthetics: Towards a Reinterpretation of American Conservation," *Environmental Review* 11 (Summer 1987): 127–46.

Legator, Marvin S., Barbara L. Harper, and Michael J. Scott, eds. *The Health Detective's Handbook: A Guide to the Investigation of Environmental Hazards by Nonprofessionals.* Baltimore: Johns Hopkins University Press, 1985.

Melosi, Martin V. *Coping with Abundance: Energy and Environment in Industrial America, 1820–1980.* New York: Alfred A. Knopf, 1985.

Milbrath, Lester W. *Environmentalists: Vanguard for a New Society.* Albany: State University of New York Press, 1984.

Miller, Sally M., ed., for *The Pacific Historical Review. John Muir: Life and Legacy.* New York: Holt-Atherton, 1986.

Nash, Roderick. *Wilderness and the American Mind,* 3d ed. New Haven, Conn.: Yale University Press, 1982.

Noble, Charles. *Liberalism at Work: The Rise and Fall of OSHA.* Philadelphia: Temple University Press, 1986.

Norton, Bryan G., ed. *The Preservation of the Species: The Value of Biological Diversity.* Princeton, N.J.: Princeton University Press, 1986.

Palmer, Tim. *Endangered Rivers and the Conservation Movement.* Berkeley and Los Angeles: University of California Press, 1986.

Pertschuk, Michael. *Revolt against Regulation: The Rise and Fall of the Consumer Movement.* Berkeley and Los Angeles: University of California Press, 1982.

Petulla, Joseph M. *American Environmentalism: Values, Tactics, Priorities.* College Station: Texas A & M Press, 1980.

Regan, Tom. *All That Dwell Therein: Animal Rights and Environmental Ethics.* Berkeley and Los Angeles: University of California Press, 1982.

Repetto, Robert, ed. *Global Possible: Resources, Development and the New Century.* New Haven, Conn.: Yale University Press, 1985.

Rosner, David, and Gerald Markowitz, eds. *Dying for Work: Workers' Safety and Health in Twentieth-Century America.* Bloomington: Indiana University Press, 1987.

Runte, Alfred. *National Parks: The American Experience,* 2d ed. Lincoln: University of Nebraska Press, 1987.

Schene, Michael G., ed. "The National Park Service and Historic Preservation" (entire issue), *Public Historian* 9 (Spring 1987).

Schuck, Peter H. *Agent Orange on Trial: Mass Toxic Disasters in the Courts.* Cambridge: Belknap/Harvard University Press, 1986.

Silber, Norman. *Test and Protest: The Influence of the Consumers Union.* New York: Holmes & Meier, 1983.

Singer, Peter, ed. *In Defense of Animals.* New York: Harper & Row, 1985.

Taylor, Paul W. *Respect for Nature: A Theory of Environmental Ethics.* Princeton, N.J.: Princeton University Press, 1986.

Thomas, Keith. *Man and the Natural World: A History of the Modern Sensibility.* New York: Pantheon Books, 1983.

Vietor, Richard H. K. *Energy Policy in America since 1945: A Study of Business-Government Relations.* New York: Cambridge University Press, 1984.

Ward, Barbara, and Rene Dubos. *Only One Earth: The Care and Maintenance of a Small Planet.* New York: Norton, 1983.

White, Richard. "Historiographical Essay on American Environmental History: The

Development of a New Historical Field," *Pacific Historical Review* 54 (August 1985): 297–335.

Whole Earth Access Mail Order Catalog, rev. ed. Berkeley, Calif.: Ten Speed Press, 1985.

Whorton, James C. *Crusaders for Fitness: The History of American Health Reformers.* Princeton, N.J.: Princeton University Press, 1982.

Winner, Langdon. *The Whale and the Reactor: A Search for Limits in an Age of High Technology.* Chicago: University of Chicago Press, 1986.

"Women and Environmental History" (entire issue), *Environmental Review* 8 (Spring 1984).

World Commission on Environment and Development. *Our Common Future.* New York: Oxford University Press, 1987.

Worster, Donald. *The Ends of the Earth: Environmental Perspectives on Modern History.* New York: Cambridge University Press, forthcoming.

————. *Nature's Economy: A History of Ecological Ideas.* New York: Cambridge University Press, 1985.

————. *Rivers of Empire: Water, Aridity, and the Growth of the American West.* New York: Pantheon Books, 1986.

Wyant, William K. *Westward in Eden: The Public Lands and the Conservation Movement.* Berkeley and Los Angeles: University of California Press, 1982.

Organizations and Publications

Requests for information should be accompanied by a stamped, self-addressed envelope.

Agricultural History, Agricultural History Center, University of California, Davis, Calif. 95616

American Farmland Trust, 1920 N St., N.W., Suite 400, Washington, D.C. 20036.

Amicus, Natural Resources Defense Council, 122 E. 42nd St., Rm. 4500, New York, N.Y. 10168

Animals' Agenda: The Animal Rights Magazine, P.O. Box 5234, Westport, Conn. 06881

Appropriate Technology, IT Publications Ltd., 9 King St., London WC2E 8HW, United Kingdom.

Audubon, Subscriptions, P.O. Box 5100, Boulder, Colo. 80321-1000

Center for Science in the Public Interest, 1501 16th St., N.W., Washington, D.C. 20036 (Publisher of *Nutrition Action*)

Citizen-Labor Energy Coalition, 1300 Connecticut Ave., Rm. 401, Washington, D.C. 20036

Common Cause, 2030 M St., N.W., Washington, D.C. 20036

Conservation Foundation, 1250 24th St., N.W., Washington, D.C. 20037

Consumer Federation of America, 1424 16th St., N.W., Washington, D.C. 20036

Consumers Union of the United States, 256 Washington St., Mt. Vernon, N.Y. 10553

Defenders of Wildlife, 1244 19th St., N.W., Washington, D.C. 20036

Department of Labor, Occupational Safety and Health Administration, 200 Constitution Ave., N.W., Washington, D.C. 20210

Earth First! The Radical Environmental Journal, P.O. Box 5871, Tucson, Ariz. 85703

Environment, 4000 Albemarle St., N.W., Washington, D.C. 20016

Environmental Action, 1525 New Hampshire Ave., N.W., Washington, D.C. 20036

Environmental Comment, The Urban Land Institute, 1090 Vermont Ave., N.W., Washington, D.C. 20005

Environmental Defense Fund, 1616 P St., N.W., Washington, D.C. 20036

Environmental Ethics, Department of Philosophy, University of Georgia, Athens, Ga. 30602

Environmental Law Reporter, Environmental Law Institute, 1616 P St., N.W., Washington, D.C. 20036

Environmental Protection Agency, 401 M St., S.W., Washington, D.C. 20460

Environmental Review, American Society for Environmental History, History Dept., Oregon State University, Corvallis, Ore. 97331

EPA Journal, Superintendant of Documents, U.S. Government Printing Office, Washington, D.C. 20402

Fund for Renewable Energy and the Environment (formerly the Solar Lobby), 1001 Connecticut Ave., N.W., Suite 638, Washington, D.C. 20036

Greenpeace USA, 1611 Connecticut Ave., N.W., Washington, D.C. 20009

Health/PAC, 17 Murray St., New York, N.Y. 10007

Humane Society of the United States, 2100 L St., N.W., Washington, D.C. 20037

International Wildlife, National Wildlife Federation, 1412 16th St., N.W., Washington, D.C. 20036

Izaac Walton League of America, 1701 Ft. Meyer Drive, Suite 1100, Arlington, Va. 22209

Journal of Forest History, Forest History Society, 701 Vickers Ave., Durham, N.C. 27701

Living Wilderness, Wilderness Society, 1400 I St., N.W., Washington, D.C. 20006

Mother Earth News, P.O. Box 3122, Harlan, Iowa 51593-2188

Multinational Monitor, P.O. Box 19405, Washington, D.C. 20036

National Parks, National Parks and Conservation Association, 1015 31st St., N.W., Washington, D.C. 20007

National Wildlife, National Wildlife Federation, 1412 16th St., N.W., Washington, D.C. 20036

Not Man Apart, Friends of the Earth, 530 7th St., S.E., Washington, D.C. 20003

People for the Ethical Treatment of Animals, Box 42516, Washington, D.C. 20015

Public Citizen, 2000 P St., N.W., Washington, D.C. 20009

Rain, 1135 S.E. Salmon, Portland, Ore. 97214

Resources, Environmental Task Force, 1012 14th St., N.W., Washington, D.C. 20005
Resources for the Future, 1616 P St., N.W., Washington, D.C. 20036
Science for the People, 897 Main St., Cambridge, Mass. 02139
Sierra, 730 Polk St., San Francisco, Calif. 94109
Sierra Club Legal Defense Fund, 2044 Fillmore St., San Francisco, Calif. 94115
Union of Concerned Scientists, 26 Church St., Cambridge, Mass. 02238
Whole Earth Review, 27 Gate Five Road, Sausalito, Calif. 94965
World Wildlife Fund, 1250 24th St., N.W., Washington, D.C. 20037

2

Nuclear Power, Ltd.

Most people once believed that nuclear power created more solutions than problems. It seemed cleaner than the soot, ashes, and smoke of coal-generated power. Uranium appeared to be a cheap and abundant fuel. The new technology was supposed to be the scientific solution to many of our energy and defense needs.

Although some people still believe this, many more are disturbed about the failed promises of nuclear power. The worst fear is that nuclear wastes will contaminate parts of our earth for thousands of years, either because of rapidly accumulating by-products from nuclear generators or because of its use in an apocalyptic war.

Such concerns are new, but the knowledge of radioactivity is not. Uranium, under the name of pitchblende, was mined by the late 1500s in areas that are now in Germany, Austria, and Czechoslovakia. The radium in pitchblende glowed. It was not known that unstable elements gave off atomic particles, or that such particles caused positive and negative mutations in plants and animals. It was known quite early, however, that the miners of pitchblende had lung problems.

The first experiment with radioactivity was conducted in 1895. Professor Wilhelm Roentgen of Bavaria, the experimenter, did not use uranium. Rather, he passed an electric current through a glass tube to produce a different form of energy. Roentgen could not identify this, so he labeled it an X ray.

Thomas Edison quickly used this knowledge to build a fluoroscope, which he demonstrated in 1896 at an electric fair in New York City. Fairgoers had a chance to see their own bones and organs! Similar X-ray machines were used sometimes by dentists and salespeople in shoe stores as late as the 1950s. Despite a few practical applications, X rays were a novelty, and they were the research interest of a small number of scientists. There were growing worries about tissue damage, especially after the deaths from cancer of several early radiologists and researchers.

These researchers were the first to conclude that the atom was not the final and undividable unit of matter. In the 1930s Enrico Fermi wrote that the bombardment of uranium with neutrons might produce new "trans-uranic" elements. Neutrons would split an atom, producing two new atoms and other neutrons, which could in turn split other atoms. This process, called fission, might begin a chain reaction that would release a tremendous burst of energy.

FROM THEORY TO WEAPON

Albert Einstein wrote a decisive letter to President Franklin Roosevelt in 1939. He feared that Nazi Germany might have the ability to use atomic theory to create weapons. FDR responded by authorizing a Uranium Committee. The first nuclear reactor was soon built under Stagg Stadium of the University of Chicago. Enrico Fermi, the leader of the project, successfully produced a sustained nuclear reaction by 1942. At this point, the U.S. government committed vast resources. General Leslie Groves was appointed head of the Manhattan Project, which from 1942 through 1945 spent $2 billion for materials, payroll, and facilities at such sites as Hanford, Washington, and Oak Ridge, Tennessee. Oak Ridge, for example, consisted of 54,000 acres about eighteen miles from Knoxville. It employed 20,000 people and spent $300 million to create a U-shaped building, one-half mile long on each branch. This facility produced uranium for a proposed bomb. The uranium was transferred to Los Alamos, New Mexico, a site about twenty miles from Santa Fe where a private boys' school had been taken over by the military.

A small city of 6,000 was created. The facilities were spartan, with muddy streets, occasional worms coming out of the water faucets, and parties that resorted to the use of 200-proof lab alcohol. Nonetheless, both the scientists and the staff apparently felt a sense of camaraderie. Such men as J. Robert Oppenheimer, the director of Rapid Rupture, were caught up in the fascination of scientific and technical discovery. Few people worried about undisposable wastes or the long-term effects of their work. Instead, this project was seen as a potentially vital contribution to the war effort and a basic investigation into the nature of matter.

Ironically the war with Germany ended several months before the bomb was tested on July 16, 1945. Einstein later claimed, "If I had known that the Germans would not succeed in constructing the atom bomb, I never would have moved a finger." But the momentum of the experiment continued after Germany's surrender, both because the war with Japan continued and because it now had a life of its own.

A test site had been readied about twenty miles from Los Alamos, at Alamogordo (which is Spanish for "journey of death"), New Mexico. No one knew whether the bomb would work. Plans on paper sometimes do not. It was equally unclear what would happen if the bomb did explode. A few scientists took bets on whether the atmosphere over New Mexico would be detonated, and the governor had evacuation plans. When the explosion came, the watching scientists had varied responses. One concluded, "Don't expect to die a natural death." Oppenheimer said that he remembered a Hindu text that began, "Now I am become Death, the destroyer of worlds." Some used images of Faust's bargain with Satan for power, or the fall of man from grace. Other scientists were more narrowly pragmatic. When Enrico Fermi was questioned about the ethics of this weapon, he replied, "Don't bother me with your conscientious scruples. After all, the thing's superb physics."

To this point, the efforts of about 600,000 people had produced four bombs. The United States was insisting upon the unconditional surrender of Japan. The Japanese government balked, hoping for a settlement that would guarantee the continuance of the emperor. President Truman, who had not been aware of the nuclear project until the sudden death of FDR, then made the decision to use the bomb.

On August 6, 1945, a single plane flew about six miles over Hiroshima, Japan, a city about the size of Houston. The Japanese air force had been destroyed, and the plane was too high for anti-aircraft fire. It met no opposition. The town had been spared from earlier bombing, and the people may have thought that this was a reconnaissance plane. A single bomb, nicknamed Little Boy, was dropped about 8:15 A.M., as people were in the streets going to work and children were in school. After a fall of no more than ten to fifteen seconds, it exploded about 1,900 feet above the ground. The temperature at the center of the blast was 7,000°C, producing hurricane winds and shock waves faster than the speed of sound. About 70,000 to 80,000 men, women, and children were killed within nine seconds. Among the survivors were many who would die slowly of wounds from flying splinters and objects, along with bleeding, pus-filled sores that would not heal.

Several days later, a second bomb, called Fat Man, was dropped on

Nagasaki. Another 70,000 military and civilian people died instantly. Some of these people left only vaporized shadows on streets and walls. In addition to these victims, another 80,000 or more died later in both cities.

Since these bombs prompted the final Japanese surrender, most of the U.S. public was grateful. Truman spoke of the alternative possibility of a costly American invasion to compel the Japanese to end the war, although the Japanese navy and air force had been wrecked, starvation was imminent, and American terms could have been more flexible. In the years that followed, some critics argued that the bomb was really aimed at the Soviet Union as a demonstration of U.S. power. Others asserted that the United States would not have used such a cruel weapon on a white people, but did not feel so restrained in using it on the "colored Japs." The latter argument is diminished by the reality that equally devastating firestorms were created by conventional Allied weapons in such German cities as Dresden. Modern warfare has not made polite distinctions between races and ethnic groups and between military and civilian life.

The reverberations from these two bombs have continued to the present. Among the survivors, there have been higher than average rates of psychological problems, cancers, and deformed children. It has been difficult for nuclear survivors, or even children of nuclear survivors, to find marriage partners. Because of all of these memories, the Japanese have refused to allow their postwar governments to develop nuclear weapons, despite the capacity to do so.

The Soviet Union proved that other nations could acquire this terrible new weapon when it exploded its first A-bomb in September 1949. This device was six times more powerful than Little Boy. The U.S. nuclear monopoly ended, and many Americans, startled, began a search for the spies who must have given the presumably backward Russians the scientific secrets that were needed. The same sequence occurred with the hydrogen bomb, which was detonated by the Americans in November 1952. This used fusion, where energy is released by *combining* atoms, not by splitting them. A Russian H-bomb followed in August 1953. Each of these last two explosions was 500 times greater than the one at Hiroshima.

The U.S. government during the late 1940s and 1950s began to develop nuclear policies that would be consistent with its national and international interests. The government encouraged private American utilities to switch from coal and oil power to nuclear power, which the government praised as the energy of the future. Nuclear wastes from these new plants could also be used to create nuclear weapons.

Various national and international agencies were created to regulate nuclear energy, such as the Atomic Energy Commission, or AEC (1946), the UN Atomic Energy Commission (1946), and the International Atomic Energy Commission (1956). The U.S. government was actively involved in promoting and regulating the new industry, both at home and abroad.

Throughout the 1950s the federal government asserted that nuclear energy would be used mainly for peaceful purposes. Under Eisenhower's Atoms for Peace program, begun in 1953, the United States offered foreign countries enriched uranium, technology, and capital. The Atomic Energy Act of 1954 further allowed private U.S. companies to own reactors and to control fissionable material.

Public fear of the military use of nuclear weapons was partially calmed by the establishment of the Federal Civil Defense Administration in 1951. This agency began programs for urban sirens in case of nuclear attack, radio alerts, and fallout shelters. It was commonly argued that nuclear war would be survivable with such programs.

CRITICS OF THE NUCLEAR ARSENAL

The first dissenters did not focus on the abolition of all uses of nuclear energy, but on the need for reasonable safeguards and limits on nuclear weapons. The largest such group was the National Committee for a Sane Nuclear Policy (SANE), founded in 1957. By 1958 it had 130 chapters and 25,000 members. Smaller and more militant elements included the Committee on Nonviolent Action, which engaged in such activities as sailing a boat, the *Golden Rule*, into one of the South Pacific test sites in 1958.

Many more people were disturbed by nuclear fallout. This was material thrown into the atmosphere by above-ground tests in both the Soviet Union and the United States. It drifted above the earth, scattered, and fell with the rain or air currents. In 1954 there were reports of illness among some Japanese fishermen who had accidently entered a test area. In 1955 there was proof of radioactive rain in Chicago. By 1959 there was documentation of strontium 90 in milk, caused by cows eating grass that had been contaminated by nuclear fallout. Many were worried by what the poet Lawrence Ferlinghetti called this "strange rain" of "perverted pollen," noting that "it has become obvious that the law of gravity was still in effect and that what blows up must come down on everyone including white citizens."

Public concern sometimes limited what the government or business could do. In 1959 the AEC indicated that it would allow the disposal of radioactive wastes in the Atlantic Ocean about twelve miles from Boston, but this plan was halted by local protest. In 1962 a plan to build a reactor in Queens was scrapped because of the dangers that it might pose to the huge population of New York City.

A few conservationists had more basic criticisms of all nuclear energy. In the early 1960s David Brower, the president of the Sierra Club, resigned when it refused to reject nuclear power (a position that it later adopted in the 1970s). Brower went on to form the Friends of the Earth.

Beyond such activists, there was broad public suspicion that nuclear energy posed various threats. This was expressed in films that featured "The

Blob," "The H-Man," and "the attack of the Crab Monsters," or the death of humanity as in "On the Beach" (1959). Such doubts were heightened when there was a face-to-face confrontation between the United States and the Soviet Union with the spectre of a shooting war or a nuclear holocaust, as in the Cuban Missile Crisis of 1962.

This was the background for the first significant success in limiting nuclear weapons, the 1963 Test Ban Treaty. All major nations except France and the People's Republic of China agreed to cease testing nuclear weapons above ground. This apparently controlled the problem of fallout, and many hoped that it would lead to further arms reduction agreements. After 1963, the first antinuclear movement declined for five reasons.

First, the federal government appeared to be acting to solve various difficulties. Besides the Test Ban Treaty, there was a Nuclear Nonproliferation Treaty in 1968 that had the support of forty nations by 1970. The National Environmental Policy Act of 1969 and the Environmental Protection Agency, created in 1970, promised protection of the environment. The Strategic Arms Limitations Talk (SALT) treaty in 1972 also seemed to be a step toward arms reduction. Even criticism of the Atomic Energy Commission as too tied to business interests stimulated greater care: In 1967 it had taken a utility company an average of ten months to get a license for a nuclear reactor; by 1971, it took twenty months. The AEC itself was abolished by the 1974 Energy Reorganization Act and replaced by the Nuclear Regulatory Agency, which acted slowly through its Atomic Safety and Licensing Board. Some people still had doubts, but it was easier to conclude that the government should be trusted.

Second, the government and the military vigorously promoted nuclear weapons as inevitable, scientific, and patriotic. Missiles were given names like Davy Crockett, Minuteman, Honest John, Hound Dog, Nike-Zeus, and Poseidon. Prophecies were made like President Johnson's 1968 speech "Nuclear Power: Key to a Golden Age for Mankind." It was difficult to counter such powerful optimism.

Third, the problems of controlling nuclear weapons seemed bewilderingly complex, involving technologies, defense issues, and foreign relations. The average person was likely to throw up his hands in despair and say, "I'll have to trust the experts." Common sense and morality seemed to be banished by statistics, technicalities, and the acronyms for our weapons systems, such as ABM, AWACS, MIRV, and MX.

Fourth, many people felt powerless against the established views. To the threat of nuclear war they said, "I don't want to think about it." To the dangers of all kinds they concluded, "I can't do anything about it." The psychiatrist Robert Lifton described this as a kind of "psychic numbing." People want to live as though they are safe, even though they know otherwise.

Fifth, many activists of the 1960s and 1970s were diverted to other issues, such as civil rights, Vietnam, and ecology. However, these movements also

convinced significant numbers of people that the government did not necessarily act in their behalf, that much of what it said was propaganda for special
interests, that the experts were often wrong (especially when their basic
assumptions were wrong), and that people who were organized and militant
did have power.

AGAINST ALL NUCLEAR POWER

In the 1970s these old and new activists coalesced into the second historic
movement against nuclear power, a movement that was more socially and
intellectually comprehensive than the first, which had narrowly focused on
"reasonable" policies for nuclear weapons. This new movement drew upon
such diverse groups of people as conservationists, pacifists, antiwar militants
from the Vietnam period, public health critics, ecologists, consumer advocates, and independent scientists. By the late 1970s, many national organizations were centered on nuclear issues, along with local coalitions like the
Prairie Alliance (Illinois), the Paddlewheel Alliance (Indiana-Kentucky),
Northern Thunder (Wisconsin), and the Northern Sun Alliance (Minnesota-
Wisconsin). While not all those opposed to nuclear weapons were also opposed to nuclear power plants, many activists tended to favor banning all
nuclear materials, with the possible exception of those used in medicine.

Those who were utterly opposed to all uses of nuclear energy, whether for

peaceful or military purposes, had a number of basic reasons for their protest.

First, they stated that the mining and processing of radioactive substances is dangerous to the people involved. Miners inhale dust and radon gas. They are four times more likely to get lung cancer than the general public. Even if mine ventilation were improved, this risk could not be eliminated.

The processing of what has been mined results in piles of waste from several dozen mills. These dumps will continue to give off radon gas and other substances for thousands of years, and some of it could enter water supplies in surrounding areas. There are now about 90 million tons of such mill tailings, concentrated in New Mexico (which produces 42 percent of U.S. uranium), Arizona, Colorado, Utah, Oregon, Washington, South Dakota, Texas, and Wyoming. In some cases, this waste has been used for dangerous purposes, such as landfill. In Grand Junction, Colorado, it was discovered that 5,000 homes had been built on contaminated ground. The occupants were receiving the radioactive equivalent of 553 chest X rays a year. One can easily imagine that this revelation made it difficult to sell such houses.

Second, there are potential dangers in moving these materials. There could be accidents with trucks, tractor trailers, trains, and planes, perhaps in a heavily populated area. Many motorists have seen a truck marked with a sign for radioactive materials barreling down an interstate or a major highway at speeds well over the legal limit of fifty-five-miles per hour.

Third, there are significant risks for those who work with nuclear substances. One famous example was the case of Karen Silkwood, who was employed in an Oklahoma plant that made fuel rods for generators. At the time of her controversial death in an auto accident in 1974, she was accusing her employer, Kerr-McGee, of gross negligence in allowing its employees to be contaminated with radioactivity. Years of litigation followed, with a seesaw of victories and defeats. Finally, in the summer of 1986, Kerr-McGee settled with the Silkwood estate by paying $1,380,000. While it admitted to no guilt in Silkwood's case, the trials contributed to raising safety standards in the industry, either voluntarily or through such promptings as court orders.

Fourth, sites for reactors are likely to have flaws. While it may be convenient to build along the coasts, near water for a coolant source, there could be fault lines at such locations. Urban sites would be disastrous if there were an accident and the reactor's safety mechanisms failed. Such an episode nearly happened in 1966 when the Enrico Fermi breeder reactor near Detroit suffered a partial meltdown, which could have devastated much of the region.

Fifth, no form of technology is perfect, and the repercussions of a major accident at a nuclear plant are too great to risk. In the United States, this fact became more widely evident in 1979 when the Three Mile Island facility in

Pennsylvania suffered a near meltdown. Some radiation was released, one plant was thoroughly contaminated, and there was several billion dollars worth of damage at the site. Cleanup took years, and the long-term health and genetic effects cannot be fully predicted. This last fact was expressed in a T-shirt motto: "I survived Three Mile Island—I think."

Is nuclear power safe? Congress may have thought differently when it passed the Price-Anderson Indemnity Act in 1957. This act, renewed in 1987, limits claims against the federal government and commercial companies if there is an accident that destroys vast amounts of property, kills many people, and renders any land unlivable. The Price-Anderson Act provides a shield for both the state and business against paying the full costs of any catastrophic failure, even if an industry was guilty of "gross negligence and willful misconduct." If there were no threat, there would be no need for this financial security blanket.

The American public was reminded of the perils of nuclear power in the spring of 1986. An explosion occurred at a plant in Chernobyl, eighty miles north of Kiev, the third largest city in the USSR. Radioactive smoke billowed from the broken reactor, and a nuclear cloud drifted over many of the countries of Europe. Near the plant 135,000 people were evacuated, and surface water, air, crops, and soil were contaminated. While the Chernobyl accident was not the worst that could have happened, it did kill about three dozen people within several weeks; it rendered several square miles of land unfit for habitation and crops; and it will affect the lives of thousands eventually through cancers, lowered immune systems, and birth defects. The immediate cost was approximately $3 billion.

James K. Asseltine, a Nuclear Regulatory Commission (NRC) member, later warned that one-half of the nuclear reactors of the United States also had an unacceptably high probability of failure in case of a nuclear accident. While others assert that American systems are much safer, there is no guarantee that such an event can never happen here. Complex high technology can fail calamitously, as the public learned throughout 1986 when the *Challenger* space shuttle exploded in January, a Titan 34-D was destroyed after launch in April, and a Delta space flight was aborted in May. The investigations following these failures extensively documented that both people and the machines that they build are subject to errors. One basic mistake at a nuclear plant might produce results that generations of people would have to suffer.

Sixth, critics of nuclear power believe that even without such disasters, there can be negative impacts on the environment. These include thermal pollution (when millions of gallons of heated water are returned to their source, disrupting the natural environment); air particles (inhaled plutonium the size of a grain of pollen can cause cancer); and electrical fields created by power poles that are used to transmit output, which may have harmful effects on animals and people.

Seventh, where can the nuclear ashes, garbage, or waste be stored? After several decades, this problem has not been solved. By 1986 there were over 10 million cubic feet of radioactive wastes in the United States, including strontium 90, cesium 137, and plutonium 239. Just one commercial reactor will generate about 500 pounds of such waste a year (by comparison, the Nagasaki bomb had ten pounds in it). There are hundreds of such commercial reactors throughout the world, in addition to military nuclear facilities and the reactors that power nuclear submarines. What will be done with the mushrooming heaps of nuclear garbage? How can wastes be safely stored for several thousand years or, in some cases, longer?

At first, nuclear wastes were likely to be put in metal drums and dumped in trenches or in the ocean. It soon became obvious that rust, moisture, and chemical reactions would release some wastes into the soil and the water. Since even stainless steel, glass, and ceramic containers will disintegrate, and since ocean dumping may threaten life in the seas and our own lives, it has been suggested that radioactive elements be deposited in salt domes and other "stable" geological formations. Potential sites have been located in the Finger Lakes region of New York State, the Gulf Coast, Utah, and New Mexico. Even this solution contains flaws. Seepage into any surrounding areas, any earthquakes, or later efforts to mine other minerals nearby would have to be monitored for thousands of years. What is there in the unstable and brief history of human civilization that gives us confidence that this can be done successfully?

Some people have turned to exotic solutions, like shooting this nuclear trash into space, although this might be astronomically expensive. Other people have retreated to old ideas, such as dumping it in the oceans. As late as 1982, Congress unanimously voted to forbid a navy plan to sink old nuclear submarines off the coasts of California and North Carolina. The submarines had become radioactive after their years of use and would have to be destroyed at a rate of three or four a year for thirty years. How does one dispose of a dangerous submarine? Shoot it into space?

The Nuclear Waste Act of 1982 mandated a vigorous search for regional burial sites, but when the preliminary list was announced in 1986, the governors of almost all the states that were mentioned made official protests. The Department of Energy first retreated to a short list that covered only western states where a smaller population could mean less political fallout and then, in 1987, was forced to resume its search for an eastern dump.

An eighth problem is that after about thirty years nuclear reactors become radioactive junk. Will they be dismantled? Will they be entombed in concrete? Who will do this work? Who will pay?

Ninth, there are few limits on the spread of nuclear weapons. This spread is politely called *proliferation*. Nations that have nuclear power plants have the potential to use wastes from these plants for bombs. Small nations can now have big weapons. Anyone who reads the newspapers knows that the

How Long Will Various Nuclear Wastes Be Dangerous to Life?

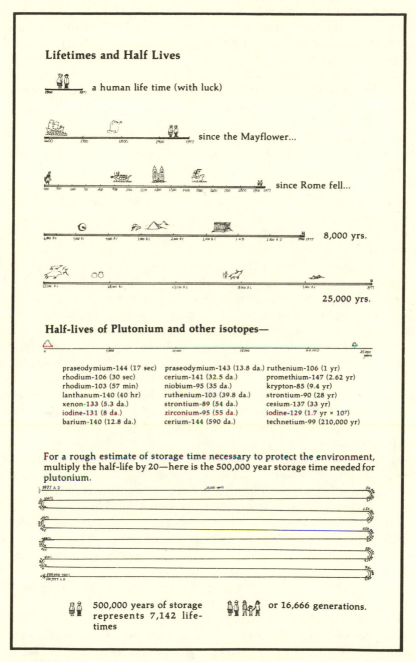

Lifetimes and Half Lives

a human life time (with luck)

since the Mayflower...

since Rome fell...

8,000 yrs.

25,000 yrs.

Half-lives of Plutonium and other isotopes—

praseodymium-144 (17 sec)	praseodymium-143 (13.8 da.)	ruthenium-106 (1 yr)
rhodium-106 (30 sec)	cerium-141 (32.5 da.)	promethium-147 (2.62 yr)
rhodium-103 (57 min)	niobium-95 (35 da.)	krypton-85 (9.4 yr)
lanthanum-140 (40 hr)	ruthenium-103 (39.8 da.)	strontium-90 (28 yr)
xenon-133 (5.3 da.)	strontium-89 (54 da.)	cesium-137 (33 yr)
iodine-131 (8 da.)	zirconium-95 (55 da.)	iodine-129 (1.7 yr × 10⁷)
barium-140 (12.8 da.)	cerium-144 (590 da.)	technetium-99 (210,000 yr)

For a rough estimate of storage time necessary to protect the environment, multiply the half-life by 20—here is the 500,000 year storage time needed for plutonium.

500,000 years of storage represents 7,142 life-times

or 16,666 generations.

A "half-life" is the time it takes for a radioactive substance to reduce its level of radioactivity by one-half. For example, this takes 57 seconds for rhodium and 210,000 years for technetium.

world is not populated solely by well-fed, comfortable, and rational people. Atomic ayatollahs and dictators are a genuine possibility, if not a probability. Few Americans would like to see the Union of South Africa with nuclear weapons. Few would be enthusiastic about such weapons in Libya, Syria, Israel, Iran, Iraq, Argentina, Brazil, Pakistan, India, North Korea, and South Korea. But what is going to stop them? It is possible that several of these countries already have atomic bombs.

In 1979 the U.S. government attempted to forbid *Progressive* magazine from publishing "The H-Bomb Secret—How We Got It, Why We're Telling It." The main secret was that it is no longer very difficult for a nation, or even a sophisticated group of terrorists, to acquire nuclear weapons. The United States has spread atomic power throughout the world. The great majority of the 600 reactors in fifty-two countries were built by General Electric and Westinghouse. These peaceful atoms can become bombs. There may soon be bombs everywhere. Who is naive enough to assume that none will ever be used?

One response to many of these arguments has been that nuclear power is necessary, whatever its flaws, as a source of cheap electricity. Yet nuclear power only appears to be cheap because of massive government subsidies. The United States underwrites such energy by producing the enriched uranium itself and selling it to commercial businesses at a favorable rate, by huge grants for research and development, by tax write-offs, and by protecting the nuclear industry from many lawsuits if a catastrophe should happen at a plant. Every taxpayer has helped to build this industry and to pay for its profits. Even so, the actual record of most of the plants is one of severe cost overruns and limited production. By the late 1980s, as the *Washington Post* reported, there was a significant possibility that the private building of nuclear power stations might cease. Some experts, however, predict a "second coming" of nuclear power in the 1990s. The research needs of the so-called Star Wars project, when combined with profit demands of existing nuclear interest groups and the failure to develop other sources of energy, may create a crisis that would stampede or overwhelm public opinion.

A second justification for nuclear power is that it is essential for national defense. By the late 1980s the United States had over 23,000 atomic warheads and the Soviet Union a similar number. The 1987 agreement between the USSR and the United States to eliminate intermediate-range nuclear forces (the INF Treaty), along with the proposed START talks in 1988, offered some hope for fewer threatening weapons.

Has this stockpile made Americans stronger and safer? The president of the California Institute of Technology, Dr. Marvin Goldberger, has estimated that one Poseidon submarine has the capacity to destroy the Soviet Union as an operating country. He added that the United States has thirty-two such vessels. Even if the Soviet Union destroyed the United States and most of its missiles in a surprise attack, there would be enough left to

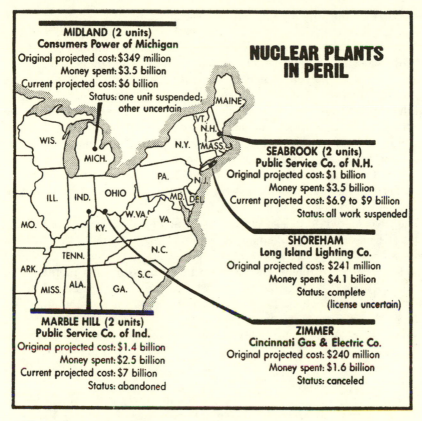

NUCLEAR PLANTS IN PERIL

MIDLAND (2 units)
Consumers Power of Michigan
Original projected cost: $349 million
Money spent: $3.5 billion
Current projected cost: $6 billion
Status: one unit suspended; other uncertain

SEABROOK (2 units)
Public Service Co. of N.H.
Original projected cost: $1 billion
Money spent: $3.5 billion
Current projected cost: $6.9 to $9 billion
Status: all work suspended

SHOREHAM
Long Island Lighting Co.
Original projected cost: $241 million
Money spent: $4.1 billion
Status: complete (license uncertain)

MARBLE HILL (2 units)
Public Service Co. of Ind.
Original projected cost: $1.4 billion
Money spent: $2.5 billion
Current projected cost: $7 billion
Status: abandoned

ZIMMER
Cincinnati Gas & Electric Co.
Original projected cost: $240 million
Money spent: $1.6 billion
Status: canceled

© The Washington Post 1984

obliterate Soviet society many times over. Despite this, the number of such weapons has grown steadily. This is ominous because some military officers and some government officials speak of a "winnable" nuclear war, because humanity has a history of violence and instability, and because the chances for malfunction and error will not always be in America's favor. The authorities say that every precaution has been taken and that nothing can go wrong, but neither people nor systems are perfect.

Let us say that these weapons are used. The reason for their use will not be important, whether it is because a computer chip failed, flying geese are interpreted as missiles on a radar screen, a lunatic presses the right buttons, or there is a "rational" decision to use them.

Physicians for Social Responsibility has outlined what would happen if even one tiny, one-megaton bomb exploded in the middle of New York, Chicago, Los Angeles, San Francisco, Atlanta, or Houston. There would be a temperature of about 7,000°C at the center, shock waves, 500-mile-per-hour winds, and 98 percent of the people killed within a mile and a half of

Ground Zero (the spot directly under the explosion). The bomb would not make any distinctions between men or women, military or civilian, the elderly or babies, army buildings or hospitals—no distinctions of any kind.

Within a circle about three miles from the explosion 50 percent would die instantly, and 30 percent would be seriously hurt from flying debris and burns. Probably one-half of these would die later. Only reinforced concrete buildings would survive. At four miles out, one of every two people would be killed or injured, brick and frame houses would be destroyed, there would be radiation sickness, many areas would be uninhabitable for years, and most urban hospitals and services would be gone. There will be no defenses. If a major war begins, some of those thousands of bombs could not be deflected. Just one would crush a city. Instead of Greater Washington, D.C., we would have Crater Washington, D.C.

The government does have survival plans that have been prepared by the Federal Emergency Management Agency (FEMA). In the early 1980s it proposed a series of evacuation routes from the cities, as a modern version of "run for the hills." Although a nuclear war might be over thirty minutes after it began, it could be possible to join a hysterical mob clogging all of the highways out of the cities. For those who did escape, it was not altogether clear how they were going to survive in the countryside. In 1986, FEMA announced a revised plan to build 600 bunkers for government officials and property documents. The rest of the population was urged to resort to "self-help," since "the program recognizes the need of citizens to assume greater responsibility for their survival protection."

Meanwhile, the government has plans for the hasty removal of 4,000 to 5,000 top officials to Mount Weather, a huge series of reinforced shelters near Berryville, Virginia. Here, there is a stockpile of money, draft cards, change of address cards, and other essentials for the continuance of American civilization. Critics have disparaged these plans as escapist fantasies out of *Alice in Wonderland,* pathetic childish delusions, and masterful examples of what the sociologist C. Wright Mills once called "crackpot realism" (where details make no sense if one doesn't accept the basic assumptions). The government asserts that such complaints are cynical defeatism.

Perhaps you are not a cynical defeatist, and you have put your trust in a home bomb shelter, or a public bomb shelter. If you are near a blast site, however, you are most likely to be cremated, baked, or suffocated by the fire storms above or around your shelter. If you survive, you will need supplies to stay there for days or weeks. Don't forget plastic jugs of water, canned foods, some containers for human wastes, a source of electricity, and, probably, tranquilizers. Some people may find such prospects disheartening and succumb to the fatalism of one Washington official: "My plan is to go down to the parking level two floors down and pray for a few moments before the bombs hit."

Let us hope that you are not among the 80 to 160 million dead that have

been estimated by both the Congressional Office of Technology and the Arms Control and Disarmament Agency. What would your life be like?

If you are in an urban area, you would have to contend with many unburied corpses. You may hesitate to cremate them, which would generate radioactive ashes. Perhaps they could be disposed of by bulldozing them into pits. Such a solution may hinder you in discovering later what happened to your grandfather, sister, or friends.

Many survivors will have their eyes blinded and bloody from the nuclear flash, which can cause blindness from as far away as thirty-five miles. Many will be deafened by the blast. Many will be burned. Many will have puncture wounds from flying debris. It is easy to forget how fragile people are.

Even if you appeared to be physically sound, you might have psychological damage and/or radiation sickness. The latter could involve the rupture of lungs and organs, skin cancers, vomiting, and a slow death. Disease would reach plague dimensions because of the dead bodies of people and animals and because of the reduced resistance caused by radiation.

And who would take care of these people? Most doctors and nurses would be dead. Most hospitals would be destroyed. There would not be enough plasma, antibiotics, anesthetics, and laboratories. You might derive solace from the National Defense Stockpile of Strategic and Critical Materials,

which includes something to alleviate this chaos of pain: tons of opium and morphine.

Very well, you have survived. What are you going to eat? The local supermarket is unlikely to be in full service. Do you imagine that you will jump into your car and drive somewhere? Do you think that water will continue to come out of the faucet when you turn it? Will the lights come on at night when you flip a switch? Have you thought of your neighbors becoming violent looters? Are you well stocked with weapons? How long would civilization last under these circumstances? How long would it take for humans to revert to their animal origins?

But this is not the worst. The explosions and fires would fill the atmosphere with particulate smoke, soot, earth, and chemicals such as PCBs, dioxin, vinyl chloride, cyanide, and carbon monoxide. This would poison the air, generate nitrogen oxides that would eat up part of the ozone layer that protects life from much of the ultraviolet rays from the sun, turn the rain into acid, and prevent the sun from shining through for months. The temperature might fall abruptly inland, though less by the coasts, where ocean waters would hold some heat. Whether this would produce a sudden "nuclear winter" or a "nuclear fall," the trauma and interruption of photosynthesis would kill many plants and animals. When the sun reappeared, the bombardment of ultraviolet rays might kill some people and animals that remained while causing cancers and the destruction of some of the plant life that had persisted. Portions of the planet that had not been directly bombed would suffer fundamental disruptions in their weather patterns. Although the war might last only minutes, the consequences would last for centuries. Perhaps archaeologists from some distant planet will someday visit Earth and speculate on how primitive bands of apes had once built large cities and what had caused their ruin.

ENERGY ALTERNATIVES

If Americans finally decide that nuclear power is too dangerous to use and urge its worldwide abandonment, what will be the alternative sources of energy? About 16 percent of all U.S. electricity in 1986 came from nuclear plants compared to 31 percent in West Germany and 65 percent in France. If atomic energy is shut off, will the lights go out?

Some individuals, organizations, and local governments are already conscious of the importance of conservation and recycling, in order to limit the energy needed for new production. The United States, with 7 percent of the world's people, consumes 35 percent of the world's resources and creates more than 50 percent of the world's annual garbage (about 3.2 pounds per American per day). A recycled aluminum can saves 95 percent of the energy needed to make a new one. Trash can be burned for energy. Waste heat from present generating plants can be recaptured.

To encourage such an energy diet, the federal government should provide tax incentives for projects such as weatherization of homes and offices, insist upon returnable bottles, and allocate more money to nonnuclear research. Approximately a billion dollars a year is now spent from the taxpayers' money to promote nuclear development, whereas tiny sums have been expended for other possibilities. By comparison, the Swedish government appropriated $200 million in 1978 for a three-year project to consider other sources of energy than oil, gas, and atomic.

There are many alternatives on any list. While no single one is sufficient and many have their own problems, they may satisfy our energy needs if used in some combination.

For example, the United States is the Saudi Arabia of coal, with enormous reserves, and coal is presently the basis for one-half of U.S. electricity. There are dangers, however, with surface and underground mining, black lung for miners who inhale particles, radioactivity in coal, thermal and air pollution from coal stations, and smoke mixing with moisture in the air to form acid rain. Coal would not be an easy solution.

Another alternative that is often forgotten is the potential from small dams. New England alone has as many as 9,000 low-level dams not presently used for small-scale hydroelectric power. The U.S. Army Corps of Engineers has estimated that there are 49,500 such dams throughout the United States.

Another simple and renewable energy source is wood. A 1970s study in New England indicated that forest management could produce, by the year 2000, the energy equivalent of 2.3 billion barrels of oil, while creating numerous jobs and leaving valuable ash. But this source of energy also may produce, unless strictly regulated, significant air pollution.

"Biomass" energy—derived from organic matter—does not have such a negative possibility. Many forms of surplus crops could be fermented to create a clean-burning fuel alcohol. Thus, cornstalks can be converted into ethyl alcohol; other farm substances can yield methane and methyl alcohol.

Windpower might also be considered. Despite our conventional image of windmills in Holland, aerospace technology has been applied to these ancient sources of energy. Light metals, new designs, and storage systems for calm days (involving flywheels, compressed air, or the production and storage of hydrogen gas) mean that this can be a constant source of energy. In 1987 there were about 7,000 "wind turbines" at Altamont Pass, forty-five miles from San Francisco, making this a kind of wind farm. Many places in the Great Plains, Great Lakes, and Alaska have dependable air currents. Such regions would never have to worry about increases in the cost of wind.

Geothermal sources are equally predictable. For example, the Salton Sea area in California has 4,000 square miles that could be tapped with wells only 5,000 feet deep. Although wells might produce land collapse and earthquakes, they could be located far away from populated areas. If so, the interior heat of the planet would be "mined" without a threat to the public.

Tides are an additional form of earth power. In some restricted estuaries, such as in the Bay of Fundy, which has thirty- to thirty-five-foot tides, tides could be used to turn huge turbines.

More novel is the possibility of using ocean thermal energy conversion. In the Gulf of Mexico, the surface water may be 70° and the near subsurface only 40°. A floating tube might circulate an easily vaporized liquid, like ammonia. This would vaporize at the top of the tube, be recirculated to the bottom, liquify, and return to the top, while moving a generating turbine.

Finally, the greatest energy source is the sun. Photovoltaic cells are consistently productive in places like Florida, California, and Arizona. Even in New England, which uses 40 percent of all oil imported into the United States, solar cells could fill 40 to 60 percent of energy needs. Additional energy can be derived from winds, tides, timber, and small hydro plants. The Massachusetts Energy Policy Office has estimated that $480 million would put solar hot water systems into half of the buildings in the state, creating, in the process, 32,000 jobs and saving 9.5 million megawatts of electricity a year.

Solar energy could be tapped on an even grander scale. Huge "power towers" with many solar cells would generate electricity for a city like Barstow, California. A chain of solar satellites 22,000 miles up, strung around the world, would be able to provide continuous energy, transmitted to earth by microwave beams.

Such beams might cause, however, nervous and physical disorders, along with genetic damage. Beyond such medical doubts, solar satellites pose the danger of centralized control of big business. General Electric, Westinghouse, Grumman, and Martin Marietta have expressed an interest in these satellites. A change in energy sources, even to solar power, would not necessarily be more democratic. Any change might be dominated by all-energy conglomerates. As one writer put it, "The United States may run out of oil someday, but there will always be an Exxon."

One other objection to abandoning nuclear power has been that the Third World supposedly needs cheap and vast nuclear energy, along with conven-

tional gas and oil sources, in order to develop. In fact, it is the Third World
that has been the most harmed by high petroleum prices: it cannot depend
upon this energy source in what will soon be a post-petroleum world, and it
will not find its solutions in atomic power. Nuclear plants usually cost $1
billion to build, money that these countries often borrow from the Export-
Import Bank. This leaves them burdened by debt. The plants depend upon
foreign fuel and, often, foreign technicians. They provide few jobs. They
require expensive transmission lines for a distribution grid. They divert
money and effort from basic roads, schools, health care, agriculture, and
housing. And they create nuclear waste. Nuclear power, rather than being
an instrument of national growth, helps keep Third World countries dependent on industrialized nations. Western companies that can no longer sell
reactors in their own countries have been trying to market them in the Third
World.

Alternative forms of energy, by contrast, may be most appropriate for
modern economic development. Agricultural societies have better opportunities for biomass energy, solar power, windpower, waterpower, and geothermal power. These may be scorned as "primitive," but they offer genuine
freedom and progress.

Despite rising concerns about nuclear power throughout the world, it
remains to be seen if enough people will organize to pressure businesses and
governments to adopt safer technologies. Given the feelings of power-
lessness among many people, the dominant influence of corporations, the
complacency of governments, the central role of military spending in many
economies, and the fact that over one-half of all scientists are now employed

by the military-industrial complexes, it may be that the world is accelerating toward the apocalypse. It would be comforting if there was more evidence that human civilization will not end in an atomic sunset, but it is more likely that such optimism is no longer realistic.

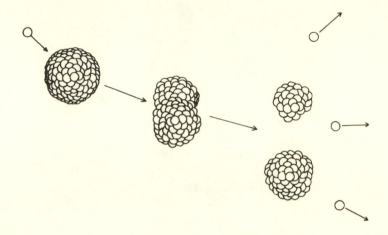

SOURCES OF FURTHER INFORMATION

Books

Ackland, Len, and Steven McGuire, eds. *Assessing the Nuclear Age*. Chicago: Bulletin of the Atomic Scientists; distributed by the University of Chicago Press, 1986.

Albert, Michael, and David Dellinger, eds. *Beyond Survival: New Directions for the Disarmament Movement*. Boston: South End Press, 1983.

Alperovitz, Gar. *Atomic Diplomacy: Hiroshima and Potsdam*, rev. ed. New York: Penguin, 1985.

Ball, Howard. *Justice Downwind: America's Nuclear Testing Program in the 1950s*. New York: Oxford University Press, 1986.

Bartlett, Donald L., and Jane B. Steele. *Forevermore: Nuclear Waste in America*. New York: Norton, 1985.

Blackburn, John O. *The Renewable Energy Alternative: How the United States and the World Can Prosper without Nuclear Energy or Coal*. Durham, N.C.: Duke University Press, 1987.

Bottome, Edgar. *The Balance of Terror: Nuclear Weapons and the Illusion of Security in a Nuclear Age, 1945–1985*. Boston: Beacon Press, 1986.

Boyer, Paul. *By the Bomb's Early Light: American Thought and Culture at the Dawn of the Atomic Age*. New York: Pantheon Books, 1985.

Bulletin of the Atomic Scientists. *The Final Epidemic: Physicians and Scientists on Nuclear War*. Chicago: University of Chicago Press, 1982.

Caldicott, Helen. *Nuclear Madness—What You Can Do*. New York: Bantam Books, 1981.

Carter, Luther J. *Nuclear Imperatives and Public Trust: Dealing with Radioactive Waste.* Baltimore: Resources for the Future; distributed by the Johns Hopkins University Press, 1987.

Charlton, Michael. *From Deterrence to Defense: The Inside Story of Strategic Policy.* Cambridge: Harvard University Press, 1987.

Child, James W. *Nuclear War: The Moral Dimension.* New Brunswick, N.J.: Transaction Books, 1986.

Clarfield, Gerald H., and William M. Wiecek. *Nuclear America: Military and Civilian Power in the United States, 1940–1980.* New York: Harper & Row, 1984.

Crabb, Cecil V., Jr. *American Foreign Policy in the Nuclear Age,* 4th ed. New York: Harper & Row, 1983.

Ehrlich, Paul R. *The Cold and the Dark: The World after Nuclear War: The Report of the Conference on the Longterm Worldwide Consequences of Nuclear War.* New York: Norton, 1984.

Evan, William H., and Stephen Hilgartner, eds. *The Arms Race and Nuclear War.* Englewood Cliffs, N.J.: Prentice-Hall, 1987.

Greene, Owen, Ian Percival, and Irene Ridge. *Nuclear Winter: The Evidence and the Risks.* New York: Basil Blackwell, 1985.

Greenwald, David S., and Steven J. Zeitlin. *No Reason to Talk about It: Families Confront the Nuclear Taboo.* New York: Norton, 1987.

Gyorgy, Anna, and friends. *No Nukes: Everyone's Guide to Nuclear Power.* Boston: South End Press, 1979.

Halperin, Morton. *Nuclear Fallacy: Dispelling the Myth of Nuclear Strategy.* New York: Ballinger Publications, 1986.

Howlett, Charles F., and Glen Zeitzer. *The American Peace Movement: History and Historiography.* Washington, D.C.: American Historical Association, 1985.

Institute for Defense and Disarmament Studies. *Peace Resources Book 1986.* Cambridge, Mass.: Ballinger Publications, 1986.

Katz, Milton S. *Ban the Bomb: A History of SANE, The Committee for a Sane Nuclear Policy, 1957–1985.* Westport, Conn.: Greenwood Press, 1986.

Kennan, George F. *Nuclear Delusion: Soviet-American Relations in the Atomic Age.* New York: Pantheon Books, 1982.

Khan, Sadruddin Aga, ed. *Nuclear War, Nuclear Proliferation, and Their Consequences*. New York: Oxford University Press, 1986.

League of Women Voters Education Fund. *The Nuclear Waste Primer: A Handbook for Citizens*. New York: Schocken Books, 1986.

Lebow, Richard Ned. *Nuclear Crisis Management: A Dangerous Illusion*. Ithaca, N.Y.: Cornell University Press, 1987.

Levine, H. M., and D. Carlton. *The Nuclear Arms Race Debated*. New York: McGraw-Hill, 1986.

Lifton, Robert J., and Richard Falk. *Indefensible Weapons: The Political and Psychological Case against Nuclearism*. New York: Basic Books, 1982.

Lovins, Amory, and L. Hunter Lovins. *Brittle Power: Energy Strategy for National Security*. Andover, Mass.: Brick House Publishing, 1982.

McNamara, Robert S. *Blundering into Disaster: Surviving the First Century of the Nuclear Age*. New York: Pantheon Books, 1986.

Mazuzan, George T., and J. Samuel Walker. *Controlling the Atom: The Beginnings of Nuclear Regulation, 1946–1962*. Berkeley and Los Angeles: University of California Press, 1984.

Miller, Richard L. *Under the Cloud: The Decades of Nuclear Testing*. New York: Free Press, 1986.

Nuclear Free America Staff. *Consumer's Guide to Boycotting the Nuclear Industry*. Philadelphia: New Society Press, 1987.

Perrow, Charles. *Normal Accidents: Living with High-Risk Technologies*. New York: Basic Books, 1985.

Powaski, Ronald E. *March to Armageddon: The United States and the Nuclear Arms Race, 1939 to the Present*. New York: Oxford University Press, 1987.

Price, Jerome B. *The Antinuclear Movement*. Boston: Twayne/G. K. Hall, 1987.

Rhodes, Richard. *The Making of the Atomic Bomb*. New York: Simon & Schuster, 1987.

Rose, John P. *The Evolution of U.S. Army Nuclear Doctrine, 1945–1980*. Boulder, Colo.: Westview Press, 1982.

Roussopoulos, Dimitrios I. *The Coming of World War Three: A New Agenda: From Resistance to Social Change*. Toronto: Black Rose Books, 1987.

Seaborg, Glen, and Benjamin Loeb. *Kennedy, Krushchev, and the Test Ban*. Berkeley and Los Angeles: University of California Press, 1983.

———. *Stemming the Tide: Arms Control in the Johnson Years*. Lexington, Mass.: Lexington Books, 1987.

Schell, Jonathan. *Abolition*. New York: Avon Books, 1986.

———. *The Fate of the Earth*. New York: Avon Books, 1982.

Sherwin, Martin J. *A World Destroyed: Hiroshima and the Origins of the Arms Race*, with a new introduction. New York: Vintage, 1987.

Spector, Leonard S. *Going Nuclear*. Cambridge, Mass.: Ballinger Publications, 1987.

Szilard, Leo. *Toward a Livable World: Leo Szilard and the Crusade for Nuclear Arms Control*. Cambridge, Mass.: MIT Press, 1987.

Taylor, Theodore B. *A World without Nuclear Weapons*. Cambridge, Mass.: Ballinger Publications, 1987.

Tomain, Joseph P. *Nuclear Power Transformation*. Bloomington: Indiana University Press, 1987.

Union of Concerned Scientists Staff, ed. *Safety Second: The NRC and America's Nuclear Power Plants*. Bloomington: Indiana University Press, 1987.

Wade, Nicholas. *A World beyond Healing: The Prologue and Aftermath of Nuclear War*. New York: Norton, 1987.

Waller, Douglas C. *Congress and the Nuclear Freeze: An Inside Look at the Politics of a Mass Movement*. Amherst: University of Massachusetts Press, 1987.

Wallis, Jim. *Peacemakers: Christian Voices from the New Abolitionist Movement*. New York: Harper & Row, 1983.

———, ed. *Waging Peace: A Handbook for the Struggle against Nuclear Arms*. New York: Harper & Row, 1982.

Williams, Robert C., and Philip C. Cantelon, eds. *The American Atom: A Documentary History of Nuclear Policies from the Discovery of Fission to the Present, 1939–1984*. Philadelphia: University of Pennsylvania Press, 1984.

Wittner, Lawrence. *Rebels against War: The American Peace Movement, 1933–1983*, rev. ed. Philadelphia: Temple University Press, 1984.

Zuckerman, Edward. *The Day after World War III*. New York: Avon, 1987.

Organizations and Publications

Requests for information should be accompanied by a stamped, self-addressed envelope.

Atomic Industrial Forum (pro-nuclear), 7101 Wisconsin Ave., Bethesda, Md. 20814-4891

Bulletin of the Atomic Scientists, 5801 S. Kenwood Ave., Chicago, Ill. 60637

Center for Defense Information, 1500 Massachusetts Ave., N.W., Washington, D.C. 20005

Coalition for a New Foreign and Military Policy, 712 G St., S.E., Washington, D.C. 20003

Council for a Livable World, 110 Maryland Ave., N.E., Washington, D.C. 20002

Critical Mass Energy Project, c/o Public Citizen, 215 Pennsylvania Ave., S.E., Washington, D.C. 20003

Federal Emergency Management Agency, Federal Center Plaza, 500 C St., S.W., Washington, D.C. 20472

Jobs With Peace, 76 Summer St., Boston, Mass. 02110

Mobilization for Survival, 853 Broadway, Rm. 418, New York, N.Y. 10003 ("Better active today than radioactive tomorrow.")

National Association of Atomic Veterans, 702 Hwy. 54 E, Eldon, Mo. 65026

National Association of Radiation Survivors, 78 El Camino Real, Berkeley, Calif. 94705

Nuclear Free America, 325 E. 25th St., Baltimore, Md. 21218

Nuclear Times, 1601 Connecticut Ave., N.W., Washington, D.C. 20009

Physicians for Social Responsibility, 1601 Connecticut Ave., N.W., Washington, D.C. 20009

SANE, 711 G St., S.E., Washington, D.C. 20003

Union of Concerned Scientists, 26 Church St., Cambridge, Mass. 02238

U.S. Atomic Energy Commission, P.O. Box 62, Oak Ridge, Tenn. 37830

Women's International League for Peace and Freedom, 1213 Race St., Philadelphia, Penna. 19107

Women Strike for Peace, 145 S. 13th St., Rm. 706, Philadelphia, Penna. 19107

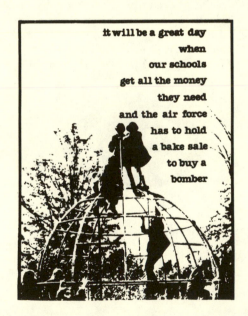

Part II

"AM I MY BROTHER'S KEEPER?" RACIAL AND ETHNIC PLURALISM

> Cain said to Abel his brother, "Let us go out to the field." And when
> they were in the field, Cain rose up against his brother, Abel, and
> killed him. Then the LORD said to Cain, "Where is Abel your broth-
> er?" He said, "I do not know; am I my brother's keeper?" And the
> LORD said, "What have you done? The voice of your brother's blood
> is crying to me from the ground."
>
> Genesis 4:8–10

The United States was founded by violence against the native peoples (whose
lands were stolen), violence against millions of African slaves, and violence
against its neighbors, the Mexicans. Like the bloody sin of Cain, this history
has stained American society.

Members of these groups still are likely to begin their lives stunted by
malnutrition in their mother's womb, then to be "educated" in the poverty,
crime, and despair of a subculture, and warehoused in inferior schools. IQ and
vocational testing later proves that they are backward. Their futures will probably include long periods of unemployment, second-rate jobs, and ill health,
concluding with retirement on minimal pensions. Their problems are attributed frequently to inherent characteristics of "the Indian," "the black,"
and "the Mexican." Such stereotypes are descended from earlier cartoonish
ones of drunken Indians, grinning blacks eating watermelons, and torpid Mexicans dozing under their sombreros.

These groups have not "melted" into the supposed melting pot of America.
Individuals have succeeded, but the masses of these people are no longer
needed as cheap manual labor and they have few possessions that the dominant
whites require. Will they be consigned to the status of useless people?

Efforts to provide systematic reparations for past losses, whether in the form
of affirmative action, minority recruitment, quotas, or money, generally have
been stymied by cries of reverse discrimination. White workers, competing for
limited jobs within the existing system, resent and fear special privileges for

others. As this moral and economic impasse continues, the gap between the haves (usually white) and the have-nots (usually nonwhite) grows ever greater.

Let us attempt to see American history through the eyes of the dispossessed natives, enslaved blacks, landless Mexicans, and colonized Puerto Ricans and speculate on what the future may hold for our brothers and sisters.

3

The Original Americans:
The So-called Indians

We in the United States are all the children of immigrants. No form of humanity evolved spontaneously in North and South America. Some of our ancestors came here voluntarily; others, like the Africans, involuntarily.

The first immigrants, and the first "Americans," were Asiatic peoples who traveled from what is now Siberia to Alaska 20,000 to 40,000 years ago. At that time, during the last Ice Age, huge quantities of water were frozen in the glaciers, and the ocean levels had fallen more than 400 feet. It was possible to walk from Asia to North American on a vast land bridge. Even today, only sixty miles of water separate the Soviet Union from Alaska.

For thousands of years, there were waves of Asian migration. Although these people had similarities, such as black hair, brown eyes, and brown skin, there were considerable variations in average height and appearance. This migration may have ended 3,000 years ago, after the glaciers began to melt and the land bridge was covered by what is now the Bering Sea.

Meanwhile, the new arrivals spread throughout the land. Pushed by other tribes or by the search for food, they were scattered finally from Alaska to Newfoundland (a distance of 6,000 miles) and south to the tip of South America (15,000 miles). Different cultures developed to suit different climates, terrains, plants, and animals. Even these factors changed as temperatures rose, some land became dry, other areas were covered with water, and types of vegetation altered. Some formerly common species became extinct, such as the wooly mammoths, American camels, and giant mastodons. In these varying environments, a wide range of native cultures flourished.

An Aleut drawing from the Alaskan region and a pictograph carved into a southwestern rock wall.

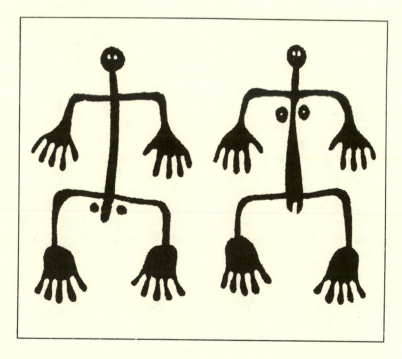

EUROPEAN CONQUERORS

Christopher Columbus, then, did not discover these lands in A.D. 1492. Nor did any of the explorers, such a Leif Ericson, who may have been here earlier. Some modern scholars have concluded that by the time Columbus arrived, there were as many as 75 million people in North, Central, and South America, divided into perhaps 2,000 separate cultures.

Although the native peoples had their own names for themselves, Columbus called them "Indians" because of his mistaken assumption that he was near the East Indies. He was actually more than 9,300 miles off. Later, the natives were labeled "American Indians," after Amerigo Vespucci, an explorer who was wrongly given the credit for discovering the New World. An American Indian like Vine Deloria, Jr., can complain legitimately, "Even the name Indian is not ours. It was given to us by some dumb honky who got lost and thought he landed in Asia."

For many white Americans, the word "Indian" conjures up simple images: an impassive man grunting "ugh"; someone on a horse hunting a buffalo; a red man in a teepee with his squaw; or a bloodthirsty, painted savage ambushing a wagon train and tomahawking a screaming woman. These are racist cartoons, just like many images of The Black, The Jew, and The Chicano. In fact, tribal Americans spoke as many as four hundred languages, some as divergent as French from Arabic, or English from Mandarin Chinese. They lived in many types of houses, using such materials as wood, earth, baked mud bricks, bark, and animal skins. Some people were settled in agricultural villages; others were nomadic. Some were peaceable and some were warlike. Given this social and cultural diversity, any one image of "the Indian" cannot be true.

Most of the native Americans gave the native Europeans a friendly reception. When Columbus arrived in what is now called the Caribbean, there were probably several million people in the area. The first people that he met were the Arawak, who were startled by these strange white beings, wearing so many odd clothes and coming in what seemed to them enormous boats. Columbus observed:

They believe very firmly that I, with these ships and people, come from the sky, and in this belief, they everywhere received us, after they had overcome their fear. And this does not result from their being ignorant (for they are of a keen intelligence and men who navigate all these seas . . .), but they have never seen people clothed or ships like ours.

Did the Arawaks see the Europeans as "people from the sky"? It is difficult to say; only the word of Columbus has survived. The Arawaks had no written language, only oral tradition. When the people later died out, their history died with them. But Columbus did admit that these fishing and farming people were generous with all that they had. Columbus described an unspoiled earthly paradise that he believed might be near the original Garden of Eden.

This sort of generosity was common. When the English attempted to settle Roanoke Island in 1587, a colonist, Arthur Barlow, praised the local people: "We were entertained with all love, and kindness, and with as much bountie, after their own manner, as they could possibly devise. We found

An example of Pueblo-style living from the Southwest.

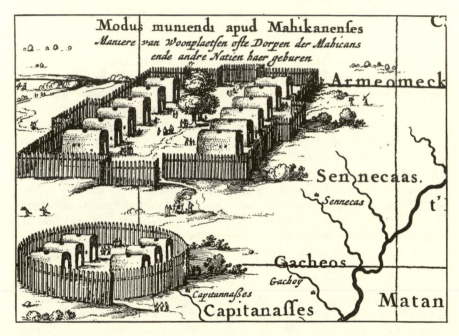

An Iroquois village in the East, as depicted on a 1655 map that was circulated in Europe.

the people most gentle, loving and faithful, void of all guile and treason." Similarly, the first English at Jamestown in 1607 depended upon chief Powhatan for food, the Pilgrims at Plymouth in 1620 needed the aid of Squanto and food from the natives, and the Puritans in Massachusetts Bay in 1630 conceded that, although they had "scarcely houses to shelter ourselves, and no doors to hinder the Indians access to all we had—where our whole belongings, weake wives and little ones lay open to their plunder . . . yet they took none of our food, nor hurt our Children or wives in the least measure."

The native nations often saw the Europeans as another tribe with which they could share the land, as potential allies against other tribes, and as useful trading partners with whom they could exchange food and other goods for kettles, metal fishhooks, guns, and pots. The initial responses of the natives were seldom hostile.

If this was a new Eden, it was the Europeans who played the role of serpent. Two entries in the diary of Columbus glimpse the future: "It appeared to me that the people are ingenious and would make good servants" (October 12, 1492); and, "The people are very unskilled in arms . . . [W]ith 50 men they could be subjected and made to do all one wishes" (October 14, 1492).

Textbooks always include the heroic first voyage of the *Niña*, the *Pinta*, and the *Santa Maria*, but they are often silent about the second voyage. Columbus returned to the Caribbean with seventeen ships, 1,500 men, bloodhounds, and horses. A system of forced labor was begun, along with a compulsory tax on each inhabitant under Spanish control, to be paid in gold. Native leaders were threatened with torture, mutilation, and death if they did not pay. The violence of the Spanish and the new diseases that they brought with them cruelly reduced the native population. The island now shared by the countries of Haiti and the Dominican Republic once had more than 1 million indigenous people. This number fell by one-third from 1494 to 1496. By the 1508 census, there were 60,000 natives; by 1512, 20,000; by 1548, perhaps 500. On the other side of the ledger, the island was producing $1 million a year in gold by 1513. To replace the dead natives, the Spanish turned to the importation of African slaves.

The story elsewhere moves toward the same tragic conclusions. At Roanoke, Arthur Barlow conceded that the natives were "much grieved" when their hospitality was scorned by the suspicious English. Perhaps the English thought that respect would only come from force. When a silver cup was missing, the English sent armed men to a village and burned it. Relations deteriorated. As one colonist wrote, "Some of our companie towardes the ende of the yeare, shewed themselves too fierce, in slaying some of the people, in some towns, upon causes that on our part might easily have been accepted." When the supply ship failed to arrive in 1588 because of the invasion of England by the Spanish Armada, the Roanoke settlers were isolated. When aid came in 1589, they had vanished. Most of them may have died because of starvation or warfare. Some could have been absorbed into the tribes, since Elizabethan words were later reported in the local dialects, along with blond, blue-eyed Indian children.

Powhatan also hoped to starve the Jamestown colonists after they abused his support. Since most of the corn that sustained the colony in its first years was forcibly obtained from the native people, war was probably inevitable. While the colonists did suffer—in 1622, almost one-third of the whites were killed—new colonists continued to arrive. The Indians were displaced or destroyed. By 1667 only eleven of the twenty-eight tribes that Captain John Smith had described in 1608 still existed. The rest were dead or dispersed.

Of perhaps 30,000 natives in 1608, there were only 2,000 in 1669. This could be called genocide, the murder of whole nations or peoples.

Why were the natives so thoroughly defeated? Even when European invaders found large empires in South America, they easily won. Hernán Cortés between 1519 and 1521 conquered the Aztec empire of 10 million with fewer than 600 Spanish troops, sixteen horses, fourteen cannon, a few bloodhounds, and native allies. Francisco Pizarro likewise subdued the Incan forces, representing a land of over 6 million, with fewer than 200 troops. Although warfare went on for centuries and the Indians did win a few battles, such as the extermination of Gen. George Custer's soldiers in 1876, the final result was always the same: defeat.

As a parallel to the present, it might be useful to imagine a flying saucer landing in Washington, D.C. Strange-looking beings emerge from it, along with powerful animals upon which they ride. They have weapons and armor against which Americans are almost helpless. They begin to kill people. Others collapse from diseases that the strangers have brought, just as Europeans brought smallpox, diphtheria, tuberculosis, typhoid fever, and measles. If the population had no immunity to these new infections, many would sicken and die. The invaders might also destroy the churches and most public buildings, force many survivors to work for them, and kill or imprison the old leaders. Some Americans would go over to the side of the invaders, and some believe that they are actually gods or supernatural beings. Under these circumstances, American society could collapse rapidly. That process happened throughout the new world: disease, destruction, despair. The white invasion began a holocaust for the native peoples.

The Europeans used four basic rationalizations for conquering the Indians, and these remained strong throughout the next three centuries. First, the Europeans regarded their success as a sign of divine approval. Since the natives were not Christians, they supposedly needed the civilizing discipline of European religions. In North America, some of the Puritans believed the Indians to be descendants of the lost tribes of Israel and sought to translate the Bible into native tongues in order to form villages of "praying Indians." Many other Puritans, however, denounced the more independent natives as "tawney serpents" who were agents of the devil. In 1637 when the English and their native allies killed or enslaved the entire Pequot tribe, the Rev. Increase Mather was confident that "on this day we have sent six hundred heathen souls to hell." Less brutal were those people who hoped that "the light of Christian civilization" would part the "clouds of ignorance and superstition" of the pagans. Many years would pass before the Euro-Americans allowed the native people full freedom to practice their own religions through such legislation as the American Indian Religious Freedom Act in 1978.

The second justification for the Europeans' behavior is no longer acceptable in polite society. It was assumed that the Indians were racially inferior.

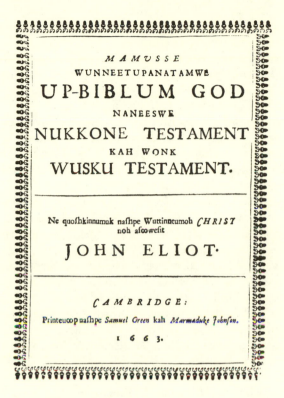

William Bradford, in 1620, depicted an America that was "unpeopled," except for "savage and brutish men, which range up and down, little otherwise than the wild beasts." Some of the English loathing derived from the supposed laziness and lower-class habits of the natives (as the English perceived such things). But the natives were also dismissed as less than human. They were bucks, squaws, vermin, serpents, and dogs. The wars with the Indians were, in part, race wars. When Col. John Chivington ordered the massacre of a group of Cheyenne that were attempting to surrender at Sand Creek, Colorado, in 1864, he spoke for many whites: "Kill and scalp all, big and little; nits make lice." Even a well-educated man like Theodore Roosevelt said in 1889 that the only good Indian, in nine out of ten cases, was a dead Indian. He added that he wouldn't inquire too closely into the case of the tenth.

Although racist images of Indians remain common, they are less pervasive than in the days of my North Dakota childhood, when my grandfather ranked the Sioux as the lowest of the low, referring even to the despised blacks as "Mississippi Indians." It is difficult to pull out all of the roots of such prejudice. Several years ago, I saw a news report on a Minneapolis television station about a mother and two children who had burned to death in a fire on the Indian skid row. My first spontaneous thought: "Oh well, they were only Indians."

Indian hostility, the third excuse for white behavior, was usually prompted by the actions of the whites. It has always been convenient to see the enemy, whether they be the Raritans or the Russians, as hostile and malevolent beings, while we are noble humanitarians.

Fourth, it was said that the natives were primitive creatures who had done little to develop the land. Progress meant dividing up the earth into private farms, cutting trees, making money, and building cities. If entire peoples were evicted or killed as a result, this might be regrettable, but necessary.

In fact, the natives varied considerably in culture, housing, and agriculture. Some of the Spanish thought that they were dreaming when they first saw Tenochtitlán, the capital city of the Aztec empire. It was the home of 200,000 to 300,000 people. Some of the Spanish compared it to Venice because it was on an island in a lake, contained many stone temples and other buildings, and had vast marketplaces. Similarly, the communistic regime of the Incas was impressive. It stretched 2,500 miles, from modern Ecuador to central Chile, with elaborate road and irrigation systems.

None of the 600 Indian societies in North America, totaling more than several million people, were so advanced. Still, they had their own distinctive values, some of which the Europeans admired, such as the Iroquois federation system of politics that linked the Mohawk, Oneida, Onondaga, Cayuga, and Seneca peoples.

Most of the tribes rapidly adopted European objects and practices that they found useful. Horses, which had not existed in the Americas before the coming of the Spanish, were acquired following the Pueblo revolt of 1680. They so quickly became a part of the life of the Plains Indians that it is now difficult for the popular mind to imagine them without the horse. Natives quickly appreciated and used guns, traps, metal fishhooks, needles, knives, axes, hoes, mirrors, blankets, tools, and metal cooking utensils.

But the Europeans benefited most from this interchange. Imagine what would have happened if Columbus and other Europeans had found no people living in the Americas:

—Labor would not have been as available.

—Fishing and hunting sites would not have been identified already, along with appropriate local methods of fishing and hunting.

—Furs would not have been obtained from established hunters.

—Trails and village locations would not have been used immediately by the Europeans.

—Travel would not have been as easy without native ways of manufacturing bark canoes, snowshoes, and toboggans.

—Indian use of local medicinal plants would not have been a source of knowledge.

—Native foods would not have nourished the Europeans. Indians have contributed one-half of the world's present agricultural plants. They originally domesticated potatoes, maize (corn), peanuts, tomatoes, squash, sweet potatoes, avocados, lima beans, and cucumbers. Some crops, like the potato, had already become a major part of the diet of the Irish poor by 1630. The population of Europe was able to grow faster because of such plants.

—Customers for European products would not have been present in large numbers.

—Mineral deposits would have to be searched for. The discovery of such wealth by some of the native peoples had been a powerful magnet for European settlers. An Aztec writer said that when the Spanish were presented with welcoming gifts of gold, their faces "burst into smiles; their eyes shone with pleasure. . . . They picked up the gold and fingered it like monkeys; they seemed to be transported with joy; their hearts were illumined and made new." Some of the earliest English settlers hoped to repeat the Spanish success. Captain John Smith complained that at Jamestown, "there was no talke, no hope, but dig gold, wash gold, refine gold, load gold [in a ship] with so much gilded durt."

European power was built on the ruins of other civilizations, in the New World and elsewhere. The pillaging of the Aztecs and the Incas brought a flood of gold into Europe, which doubled the supply in circulation by 1600. In North America, mineral discoveries in California, in Nevada (the Comstock Lode), in the southern Dakotas (the Black Hills), in Colorado (Pike's Peak), and other locations meant hundreds of millions of dollars. From the European point of view, these discoveries stimulated their economies and laid the basis for much of their global influence. From the native point of view, Indians might be living more comfortably if any of that money had been held in trust for them. The development of Europe was substantially based upon the exploitation of most of the rest of the world.

The fourth reason for this exploitation, that the natives were obstacles to progress, is not accurate since they were initially vital for European success.

WHAT TO DO WITH DEFEATED PEOPLE

Not all European powers treated the indigenous peoples in the same way.

The Spanish needed Indian labor since only a few Spanish emigrated to the new world. The natives were converted to, and partly protected by, the Catholic church, while being used as long-term workers in the fields and in the mines. Once this mission system was in practice, major aspects of native culture persisted, while sexual contact created a substantial mestizo (mixed race) class, with a status between that of the Spanish and the natives. Nonetheless, the universities were open only to whites, there were few Indian priests, and guns and horses were restricted.

The French trading post model was different. The French came primarily as fishermen, trappers, and traders. They had few large settlements. They tried to maintain friendly relations with the natives as trading partners. This included significant racial intermixture between the French and the tribal peoples.

For the English, the Indians were fundamentally useless. In North America, it was difficult to turn them into farm laborers. Their fur trade was often dominated by other Europeans. Their lands on the East Coast had few precious minerals. There was little sexual contact, since the first English colonists tended to come in family units, rather than as single men. The Indians had one thing that the English wanted: land. This would be permanently occupied by farms, villages, and towns.

Our history is, from the native point of view, the story of land-grabbing and money-hungry whites dispossessing and disinheriting the original Americans until they became exiles in their own country. Treaties guaranteeing their territories were bent if not broken when the whites discovered something that they wanted, whether it was gold in the Black Hills of the Dakotas in 1875, uranium on western lands in the 1950s, or coal on the Cheyenne reservation in Colorado today. In 1796 George Washington acknowledged that it would take "a Chinese Wall" or a line of troops between the whites and the Indians to prevent "the encroachment of settlers."

When there are basic confrontations between different cultures, four outcomes are possible: extermination, assimilation, separatism, or pluralism.

The first option, extermination, was never an official policy, and only certifiable maniacs would have endorsed it. As President Ulysses S. Grant warned in his first address to Congress in 1869, "A system which looks to the extinction of a race is too horrible for a nation to adopt without entailing upon itself the wrath of all Christendom and engendering in the citizen a disregard for human life and the rights of others, dangerous to society." Still, it was fashionable to say that the only good Indian was a dead Indian.

The official ideal was generally the second option: assimilation. The natives would vanish by becoming "like us," in other words, culturally exterminated. Some of the natives took the whites at their word and adopted much of the civilization of the conquerors as a way of protecting themselves and of preserving some of their values. The classic examples were the Five Civilized Tribes: the Cherokee, Choctaw, Chickasaw, Creek, and Seminole. Many of them lived on settled farms and in villages, wore white styles of clothing, established schools, and wrote governing documents. The Cherokees invented their own alphabet so that their language could be written down, set up a printing press, and published a newspaper, *The Cherokee Phoenix*. On a less positive note, they became so civilized that some of them owned slaves.

But all of this, along with their treaties ratified by the U.S. Senate, did not protect them. The whites wanted their land. In 1830 Congress passed the Indian Removal Act to transport all native peoples in the East to a location west of the Mississippi River.

ᏣᏩᏯ · CHEROKEE   Ꮷ·ᎠᎤᎤ·Ꮒ. · PHŒNIX.

VOL. I.   NEW ECHOTA, WEDNESDAY JUNE 4, 1828.   NO. 15.

New Echota, the Cherokee capital, was located in northern Georgia.

Although some of the "conservative" factions among the Indians had predicted this, the "progressives," led by such men as John Ross of the Cherokees, appealed to the U.S. Supreme Court. Despite a legal victory, President Andrew Jackson and his supporters had the power to do as they wished.
A small number of the Cherokee (500 out of 20,000) signed a treaty agreeing
to the removal of the entire tribe. They began to be rounded up in 1835.
Homes were looted and burned. Some graves were robbed. Whites divided
up the land as the natives were gathered into camps for transportation. As
one last humiliation, they were forced to pay for their own removal from
U.S. treasury funds set aside as reimbursement for their losses.

Despite this carnival of greed, which at least some whites knew about,
white opinion was congratulatory. Some said that the Indians would be
better off in the west. Others asserted that the eastern land would now be

John Ross

fully used. Most were silent about the thousands of Cherokees and others who died on the 800-mile forced march, which would later be called the Trail of Tears, from Georgia to Oklahoma.

The U.S. government talked about assimilating the Indians, but it failed to provide the necessary resources. Government programs have been ridiculously underfunded, such as George Washington's $20,000 yearly budget line to turn all Indians into animal raisers and farmers. Other programs have been grossly insensitive to the natives' own feelings and beliefs. The crudest ideal of assimilation was expressed by Captain Richard Henry Pratt, the head of the Carlisle Indian Boarding School, in 1879: "Kill the Indian and save the man." Such arrogant demands for de-Indianization naturally provoked hostility. The Dawes Act of 1887 tried to break up tribal lands into individual farms, the Indian Citizens Act of 1924 made the native Americans U.S. citizens, and the federal government tried to "terminate" the reservations in the 1950s and "relocate" the people in the mainstream of white life. Indians who assimilated, however, were often accepted neither by whites because of their race, nor by their own people.

Instead, separatism is still the way of life of many natives, from choice and necessity. There are about 450,000 people living on 270 Indian reservations in twenty-six states. Most of the 50 million acres that tribes own in the continental United States (separate from Alaskan lands) were not wanted by the whites. These often grim regions have been called rural ghettoes, slums in the wilderness, and open-air jails for America's prisoners of war. Sometimes the people on these lands were removed several times from other areas. The Winnebagos, for example, were displaced six times between 1829 and 1866, with their population declining by half. A Sioux leader asked why the Great White Father did not put wheels on his red children, the better to move them. Still, few people thought that confining the natives to reservations would be the final solution to "the Indian problem."

Efforts to exterminate, assimilate, or separate the Indians have produced the legacy with which we live, just as we live with the heritage of slavery in black-white relations. We have reservations, racist stereotypes about Indians, government agencies like the Bureau of Indian Affairs (founded in 1824), and a massive collection of laws, regulations, court rulings, and decisions of the attorney general of the United States. No other ethnic group is regulated. There is no Bureau of Jewish Affairs; there are no statutes governing Italian Americans; there are no reservations for ethnic Scandinavians.

This history has generated inferior standards of living for most of the 1.4 million Indians today. They suffer four times more deaths among their children; their housing is, in 70 percent of all cases, below federal standards; suicide rates are double the white rate; alcoholism is three times the white rate; unemployment ranges 25 to 85 percent on the reservations; 40 percent of students drop out before finishing high school; 33 percent of rural Indians' and 23 percent of urban Indians' incomes are below the poverty line (compared to a 14 percent average for the United States overall); and most of those employed have minimal incomes. These problems are rooted in the demoralization of entire peoples caused by earlier attempts to pacify or destroy them.

White America is not unique in its hostility or indifference to natives. The Australians frequently abused the Aborigines. Tribal minorities in Africa are often discriminated against by other Africans. The Japanese have not assimilated their own native tribe, the Ainu. Some Brazilians are murdering Amazonian Indians; of 1 million in 1900, only 200,000 remain, with more than eighty tribes eliminated. There are few governments that are multiethnic, multiracial, or multicultural, and which accept or support diversity among their populations. Such examples might include Switzerland, India, and the Union of Soviet Socialist Republics, although states of this kind may diverge from their ideals in practice.

Most recently, there has been a growing appreciation of the fourth option of pluralism. This requires, at a minimum, a toleration of people who differ from those in the majority, but ideally it includes a willingness to understand differences and to learn from them. The public's consciousness of this possibility was raised by the 1960s and 1970s expressions of Red Power, the Angry Indian, Native Power, the New Indian, and Pan-Indianism. This was the overall equivalent of Black Power and Black Pride and was part of the wave of radical and reform movements of that period. Various native leaders and organizations called for a renewal of their ancient cultures, for more respect from white America, and for a return of tribal lands. Popular books declared that *Custer Died for Your Sins* and *We Talk, You Listen*. Bumper stickers proclaimed that "Columbus Did Not Discover America" and "Custer Had It Coming!" Assimilationist Indians might be dismissed as Aunt and Uncle Tom-Toms and radishes (red on the outside and white on the inside).

Many Indians insisted: We have the right to decide who we are. We are the inheritors of thousands of years of art, philosophy, social beliefs, and religion. We have much to offer to the world. We are neither quaint relics nor empty-headed animals.

This pride could be expressed in romantic fantasies that tribal Americans were the first ecologists, that their religions were universally beneficent compared to the vengeful, prudish, and guilt-ridden Jehovah, and that their societies were nobler because they were closer to nature. In fact, it is improbable that modern U.S. citizens would prefer living in reconstituted native cultures, but people may be intellectually and emotionally enriched by attempting to appreciate ways of life dissimilar to their own.

Throughout these past U.S. debates on what to do with the Indians, the wishes of the natives were seldom taken seriously. Their opinions were discounted as those of savages, defeated enemies, or disorganized factions. Instead, the earliest organizations that spoke for the Indians were dominated by eastern non-Indians. By the 1880s the Indian Rights Association (IRA) and Friends of the Indians publicized injustices and proposed reforms that would assimilate the natives into the Anglo-Saxon mainstream. Herbert Welsh, an early president of the IRA, compared the Indian reservations to "islands against which the waters of a restless sea of civilized are steadily beating."

These associations did arouse sympathy for Indians, as did books like Helen Hunt Jackson's *A Century of Dishonor* (1881). In addition, they contributed to the professionalization of the Bureau of Indian Affairs. Nonetheless, they were paternalistic; the Indians were treated like children. Under their programs, the reservations were nurseries for civilization in which the natives would slowly mature into self-reliant farmers and workers. This childhood lasted, however, for decades after the Indians became citizens in 1924.

John Collier, an organizer for the Indian Defense Association, began his crusade in 1922 for sensitivity to the values and hopes of natives. Although he could be self-righteously confident, his work saved some native lands from rapacious whites, and he was an inspiration for the Indian Reorganization Act of 1934. He was then commissioner of Indian Affairs from 1933 to 1945. Collier helped to revive some native institutions on the reservations and to renew the production and appreciation of arts and crafts. Such progress during the 1930s may not have been a complete New Deal for the Indians, but many of them benefited from the legal changes, welfare programs, and illuminating debates of this decade.

World War II accelerated the emergence of Indians who spoke for themselves. About 25,000 served in the army and tens of thousands worked in the war industries and as farm laborers. It was a time of social dislocations, and some Indians organized either to promote or to oppose change. In 1944, representatives from forty-two tribes established the National Congress of American Indians (NCAI), the first successful national organization of Indians. It mobilized its tribal and individual members against such inequalities as the denial of the vote to Indians in New Mexico and Arizona.

The NCAI fostered the growth of new Indian leaders, as did the wartime acquisition of job skills in the military, college education through GI loans, and Indian experiences in the cities. Some Indians joined and supported national organizations in the 1950s when conservative whites threatened to eliminate native lands and to terminate federal benefits.

In 1961 about 500 Indians met at the American Indian Chicago Conference to discuss the challenges that they faced collectively, not just as individual members of specific tribes. The established leaders were pleased to hear that the newly elected president John F. Kennedy would not dismantle the land base of many tribes. Some younger members of the conference wanted a militant program based upon traditional values, not programs that lead toward assimilation into white society. Later a tiny group started the National Indian Youth Council (NIYC).

Although NIYC was small, it achieved the goal of one of its founders: "to raise some hell." It participated in a series of "fish-ins" in Washington State in 1964, when a local tribe was denied its treaty-protected fishing rights. The ban was broken openly, and the protesters were arrested. This confrontation, along with the physical presence of the actor Marlon Brando, brought public attention to the group.

These aggressive actions were compared to the black civil rights movement of that time. Such comparisons were not accurate, however, since natives often sought government compliance with old treaties and improvements in reservation conditions, not desegregation and final integration into white society.

Despite these differences, some Indians gained a few slogans, tactics, and ideas, along with some inspiration, from black movements. Natives got their own American Indian Civil Rights Act in 1968, and they received benefits from such War on Poverty agencies as the Office of Economic Opportunity, Head Start, the Job Corps, and the Neighborhood Youth Corps.

Although moderate Indian organizations grew during the 1960s and the 1970s, the focus of the public was frequently on radical groups like the American Indian Movement (AIM, 1968) and the startling events of this period. The latter certainly included the 1969 "invasion" of Alcatraz Island in the San Francisco Bay. The twelve-acre island, formerly the site of an infamous prison, was occupied for over a year and a half. The Indians of All Tribes offered to buy it for $24 in glass beads and red cloth so that it could become a native cultural center. Instead, they were evicted.

Also, there was the 1971 sit-in at the Washington, D.C., office of the head of the Bureau of Indian Affairs, the 1972 seizure of the entire headquarters of the Bureau of Indian Affairs, the 1973 burning of the Chamber of Commerce building in Custer, South Dakota, and, in 1973, the seventy-one day AIM occupation of the town of Wounded Knee, South Dakota, by over 200 Oglala Sioux.

The demonstrators at Wounded Knee announced that they had deposed the U.S.-approved tribal leaders and had established the Independent Oglala Sioux Nation. They chose Wounded Knee because it was the site of the last Indian massacre, on December 29, 1890. Indians had then gathered to celebrate the Ghost Dance religion, which they hoped would cause the hated whites to disappear, the dead to rise, and the buffalo to return. Instead, the Seventh Cavalry killed about 150, including 44 women and 18 children. All of them were buried, along with their horses, in a single mass grave, later billed as a tourist attraction. The "new" angry Indians wanted to symbolize old injustices, while pointing to the problems of the surrounding Pine Ridge Reservation, covering 3 million acres. The unemployment rate was almost 50 percent in the summer and over 70 percent in the winter; a third of the families were on welfare; alcoholism and drug addiction were common; and most government programs created little more than a well-paid director, a staff, several secretaries, and minimal benefits.

"I TRUST THE UNITED STATES GOVERNMENT COMPLETELY. I TRUST THEM TO LIE AND CHEAT. I TRUST THEM TO KILL ME AND MY PEOPLE AT THEIR EARLIEST OPPORTUNITY. I HAVE ABSOLUTE TRUST THAT THE GOVERNMENT IS A CRIMINAL MURDERER." — DENNIS BANKS

From the letterhead of a fundraising appeal.

The occupiers not only spotlighted their issues, but they escaped criminal convictions because of errors of the prosecution. The reaction of the local white communities was less complicated: a *New York Times* poll claimed that 95 percent wanted the Indians shot, and a National Guardsman expressed his disappointment that the government had not used its sixteen armored personnel carriers, helicopters, and arsenal that included AR-15s, M-16s, 30-, 50-, and 60-caliber machine guns, grenade launchers, and gas.

Although the public focused on such dramas, more important, in the long run, were the growth of major national organizations for Indians, the passage of such legislation as the Indian Self-Determination and Education Act in 1973, and the development of specialized new groups such as the Native American Rights Fund, which was founded in 1970 with money from the Ford Foundation. These old and new institutions acquired the organizational skills, lobbying expertise, and funds to advance native rights.

This expertise became evident in the later land cases presented to the Indian Claims Commission (1946–1978) and to other courts. The commission heard arguments during the 1970s for native control of almost the entire state of Maine and the Black Hills surrounding Mount Rushmore. In the first case, the Passamaquoddy and Penobscot won 300,000 acres and a trust fund of $37 million. In the second case, the Supreme Court did not offer the Sioux any land in 1980, but they were tempted with an award of over $100 million. Such gains could not have been made without steady and costly pressure. The future will bring further claims based upon almost-forgotten treaties.

Other predictions can be made with confidence. Indians will not vanish. Some of them compare themselves to the Jews: Although some Jews are totally assimilated and others are highly traditional, most have adjusted to different environments without losing their Jewish identity. Although some

Indians are absolute assimilationists and others are absolute traditionalists, most have been, and will continue to be, somewhere in between. There will be a wide spectrum of Indian opinion, based upon the history of each tribe, reservation needs, and local circumstances.

Some native languages, customs, and religious rituals will continue. Many will be authentic renewals and adaptations. Some will be part of tourist shows by people dressed in phony regalia that traditionalists scorn as Santa Claus costumes.

Reservations are unlikely to become industrial parks, although many are developing businesses, accounting systems, purchasing programs, and investment policies. One door was opened into the world of high finance by the Indian Tribal Government Tax Status Act of 1982. This gives the tribes the right to issue tax-exempt revenue bonds.

Some reservations may prosper, especially those with the lands that include one-half of all U.S. uranium deposits, one-third of low-sulfur coal, one-fifth of oil and natural gas reserves, bauxite, water, and other resources. The great white taxman may then attempt to assert IRS jurisdiction. Also, if coal and other resources are needed from reservation land, there may be deals with tribal elites and the relocation of Indians. In one case in the late 1980s, the government attempted to remove 5,000 to 10,000 Dineh (Navajo) from Hopi lands in Arizona, while constructing a five-strand barbed-wire fence across 340 miles.

One final prediction is that the federal government will continue to be an Indian giver, periodically taking back its previous dole. Both the Carter and the Reagan administrations cut programs that provided job training, education, housing, health care, welfare, and employment. Some of this Indian assistance was premised on the assumption that it was payment for the lands that were taken from them. Nevertheless, programs have been reduced. Indians are still likely to begin their lives with inadequate diets, to be minimally educated, to find few jobs on the reservation, and to be unprepared for jobs in the cities.

The private sector has been urged to overcome the burden of this history. If it cannot, and if the government does not help, we can expect Indian protests. Although some Americans may resent these complaints, it would be ironic to shout at the original Americans, "If you don't like it here, why don't you go back to where you came from!"

SOURCES OF FURTHER INFORMATION

Books and Articles

"The American Indian" (articles by Patricia Nelson Limerick, Stephen Cornell, and David Edmunds), *Wilson Quarterly* 10:1 (1986): 99–145.

"American Indians, Blacks, Chicanos, and Puerto Ricans" (entire issue), *Daedalus* 110 (Spring 1981).

Axtell, James. "Colonial America without the Indians: Counterfactual Reflections," *Journal of American History* 73 (March 1987): 981–96.

———. "Europeans, Indians, and the Age of Discovery in American History Textbooks," *American Historical Review* 92 (June 1987): 621–32.

———. *The Invasion Within: The Contest of Cultures in Colonial North America*. New York: Oxford University Press, 1985.

———. "A Moral History of Indian-White Relations Revisited," *The History Teacher* 16 (February 1983): 169–90.

Bolt, Christine. *American Indian Policy and American Reform: Case Studies of the Campaign to Assimilate the American Indians*. Winchester, Mass.: Allen & Unwin, 1987.

Cadwalader, Sandra L., and Vine Deloria, Jr., eds. *The Aggressions of Civilization: Federal Indian Policy since the 1880s*. Philadelphia: Temple University Press, 1984.

Cronon, William. *Changes in the Land: Indians, Colonists, and the Ecology of New England*. New York: Hill & Wang, 1983.

Deloria, Vine, Jr. *American Indian Policy in the Twentieth Century*. Norman: University of Oklahoma Press, 1985.

———. *Behind the Trail of Broken Treaties: An American Declaration of Independence*. Austin: University of Texas Press, 1985.

Deloria, Vine, Jr., and Clifford M. Lytle. *American Indians, American Justice*. Austin: University of Texas Press, 1983.

———. *The Nations Within: The Past and Future of American Indian Sovereignty*. New York: Pantheon Books, 1984.

Drinnon, Richard. *Facing West: The Metaphysics of Indian-Hating and Empire Building*. Minneapolis: University of Minnesota Press, 1980.

Dunbar, Leslie W., ed. *Minority Report: What Has Happened to Blacks, Hispanics, American Indians, and Other Minorities in the Eighties*. New York: Pantheon Books, 1984.

Edmunds, R. David, ed. *American Indian Leaders: Studies in Diversity*. Lincoln: University of Nebraska Press, 1980.

Green, Rayna. *Native American Women: A Contextual Bibliography*. Bloomington: Indiana University Press, 1983.

Gunn, Paula Allen. *The Sacred Hoop: Recovering the Feminine in American Indian Traditions*. Boston: Beacon Press, 1987.

Guyette, Susan. *Issues for the Future of American Indian Studies*. Los Angeles: University of California, American Indian Studies Center, 1987.

Hagan, William T. *The Indian in American History*, 3d ed. Washington, D.C.: American Historical Association, 1985.

Horsman, Reginald. "Well-Trodden Paths and Fresh Byways: Recent Writings on Native American History," in *The Promise of American History*, Stanley I. Kutler and Stanley N. Katz, eds. Baltimore: Johns Hopkins University Press, 1982, pp. 234–44.

"The Impact of Indian History on the Teaching of United States History." 5 vols. Chicago: Newberry Library, 1985–1987.

Jennings, Francis. *Ambiguous Iroquois Empire*. New York: Norton, 1984.

_____. "A Growing Partnership: Historians, Anthropologists, and American History," *The History Teacher* 14 (November 1980): 87–104.

_____. *The Invasion of America: Indians, Colonialism, and the Cant of Conquest*. New York: Norton, 1976.

_____, general editor. The Newberry Library Center for the History of the American Indian Bibliographical Series [30+ vols. to 1987]. Bloomington: Indiana University Press.

Josephy, Alvin M., Jr. *Now That the Buffalo's Gone: A Study of Today's Indians*. Norman: University of Oklahoma Press, 1984.

Kelly, Lawrence C. *The Assault on Assimilation: John Collier and the Origins of Indian Policy Reform*. Albuquerque: University of New Mexico Press, 1983.

Krech, Shepard, III, ed. *Indians, Animals, and the Fur Trade: A Critique of Keepers of the Game* (the title of a 1978 book by Calvin Martin). Athens: University of Georgia Press, 1981.

Lincoln, Kenneth, and Al Logan Slagle. *The Good Red Road: Passages into Native America*. New York: Harper & Row, 1987.

Littlefield, Daniel F., and James W. Parins, eds. *American Indian and Alaska Native Newspapers and Periodicals* [1826–1985], 3 vols. Westport, Conn.: Greenwood Press, 1984–1986.

Martin, Calvin, ed. *The American Indian and the Problem of History*. New York: Oxford University Press, 1986.

Moses, L. G., and Raymond Wilson, eds. *Indian Lives: Essays on Nineteenth- and Twentieth-Century Native American Leaders*. Albuquerque: University of New Mexico Press, 1986.

Nash, Gary B. *Red, White and Black: The People of Early America*, 2d ed. Englewood Cliffs, N.J.: Prentice-Hall, 1982.

Nichols, Roger L., ed. *The American Indian: Past and Present*, 3d ed. New York: Alfred A. Knopf, 1986.

Olson, James S., and Raymond Wilson. *Native Americans in the Twentieth Century*. Urbana: University of Illinois Press, 1986.

Pevar, Stephen L. *The Rights of Indians and Tribes*. New York: Bantam Books, 1983.

Prucha, Francis Paul. *The Great Father: The United States Government and the American Indians*, 2 vols. Lincoln: University of Nebraska Press, 1984.

_____. *The Indians in American Society: From the Revolutionary War to the Present*. Berkeley and Los Angeles: University of California Press, 1985.

Ruoff, A. LaVonne Brown. "American Indian Literatures: Introduction and Bibliography." *American Studies International* 24 (October 1986): 2–52.

Stuart, Paul. *Nations within a Nation: Historical Statistics of American Indians*. Westport, Conn.: Greenwood Press, 1987.

Sturtevant, William C., general editor. *Handbook of the North American Indians* [20 vols. projected]. Washington: Smithsonian Institution Press, 1978–.

Sutton, Imre, ed. *Irredeemable America: The Indians' Estate and Land Claims*. Albuquerque: University of New Mexico Press, 1986.

Swagerty, W. R., ed. *Scholars and the Indian Experience: Critical Reviews of Recent Writings in the Social Sciences*. Bloomington: Indiana University Press, 1979.

Tickner, J. Ann. *Self-Reliance vs. Power Politics: American and Indian Experiences in Building Nation States*. New York: Columbia University Press, 1986.

Vecsey, Christopher, and Robert W. Venables, eds. *American Indian Environments: Ecological Issues in Native American History*. Syracuse, N.Y.: Syracuse University Press, 1980.

Weeks, Philip, ed. *The American Indian Experience: A Profile, 1524 to the Present*. Arlington Heights, Ill.: Harlan Davidson, 1988.

Wilkinson, Charles F. *American Indians, Time and the Law: Historical Rights at the Bar of the Supreme Court*. New Haven, Conn.: Yale University Press, 1987.

Williams, Walter L. *The Spirit and the Flesh: Sexual Diversity in American Indian Culture*. Boston: Beacon Press, 1986.

Organizations and Publications

Requests for information should be accompanied by a stamped, self-addressed envelope.

Akwesasne Notes, P.O. Box 196, Rooseveltown, N.Y. 13683-0196

American Indian Historical Society, 1493 Masonic Ave., San Francisco, Calif. 94117

American Indian Movement, 2300 Cedar Ave. S., Minneapolis, Minn. 55404

American Indian Quarterly, Native American Studies, 3415 Dwinelle Hall, University of California, Berkeley, Calif. 94720

Americans for Indian Opportunity Assoc., 1010 Massachusetts Ave., N.W., Washington, D.C. 20001

Arrow, Inc., 1000 Connecticut Ave., N.W., Washington, D.C. 20036

Association on American Indian Affairs, 95 Madison Ave., New York, N.Y. 10016

Bureau of Indian Affairs, Department of the Interior, 18th and C Sts., N.W., Washington, D.C. 20006

Choctaw Heritage Press, Rt. 7, Box 21, Philadelphia, Miss. 39350

D'Arcy McNickle Center for the History of the American Indian, Newberry Library, 60 W. Walton St., Chicago, Ill. 60610

Indian Law Resource Center, 601 E St., S.E., Washington, D.C. 20003

International Indian Treaty Council, 444 Second Ave., #32a, New York, N.Y. 10010-2528.

National Congress of American Indians, 804 D St., N.E., Washington, D.C. 20002

National Indian Education Association, 1115 2nd Ave., S., Ivy Tower Bldg., Minneapolis, Minn. 55403

National Indian Youth Council, Inc., 318 Elm St., S.E., Albuquerque, N.M. 87102

Native American Public Broadcasting Consortium, 1800 N. 33rd St., Lincoln, Neb.
  68583
Native American Rights Fund, 1506 Broadway, Boulder, Colo. 80302-6296
Native Self-Sufficiency, Seventh Generation Fund, Box 10, Forestville, Calif. 95436

4

Contributions by Disinherited Blacks

Would America have been America without her Negro people?
W. E. B. DuBOIS, *The Souls of Black Folk* (1903)

Slave labor built many of the foundations for European societies in the New World. For several centuries, millions of people were taken from their homes in Africa, sold like hogs or cattle to make profits for a few, and compelled to work for the benefit of their white masters. The money from selling these human beings, and from their labor, helped to propel the West to its major rank in the modern world.

How did whites gain such power? In the early 1400s, they were comparatively few and lived in generally insignificant countries on the relative fringes of civilization. They began to overrun the world by the late 1400s, with the Europeanization of the New World being only one illustration of this vast expansion of influence that resulted in whole cultures being conquered, exploited, or exterminated. Even today, Western models of industrialization, Western financial controls, and many Western cultural standards are widespread. This includes such Communist countries as the People's Republic of China, which is carrying out the theories of two Germans, Dr. Karl Marx (a philosophy Ph.D.) and Friedrich Engels (a textile merchant).

Two crucial and interrelated factors in this surge of European influence were Christianity and business. From A.D. 1095 to A.D. 1275 Catholics launched nine crusades or holy wars against the Muslims in the Near East. The goal was to recapture such holy places as Jerusalem, but these crusades also stimulated the businesses necessary to clothe, feed, arm, and transport the troops, along with expanding foreign trade. Some Europeans developed a taste, for example, for spices like pepper, cloves, cinnamon, and nutmeg, none of which grow in Europe. While these spices were highly desirable as a means to preserve food in the days before refrigeration and as one way to make a bland diet more interesting, they were extremely expensive because of the cost of transporting them from such areas as modern India, Sri Lanka, and Indonesia.

Visions of profit moved some Europeans to search for an ocean route to these Spice Islands. The Portuguese reached the middle of the west coast of Africa by 1445 and sailed all the way to Calcutta, India, by 1449. News of this travel was spread by an early example of a communications revolution (like the later radio, television, and space satellite): the printing press. In contrast to rare and costly handwritten books, presses resulted in an explosion of information. Awareness of the Portuguese success prompted other nations to compete, which resulted in better ships, improved military equipment, and advances in ocean travel, such as the first compasses, which were adapted from Arab and Chinese versions.

Trade contributed to another change in European society: the creation of more powerful nation-states. Many local and regional merchants resented the petty lords who taxed them and disturbed trade with small wars. Many of them wanted a strong national monarch to bring order to the marketplace and to protect their interests. Thus, businessmen generally bankrolled the emerging kings of England, France, and Spain. Furthermore, they put up much of the money for early expeditions to new lands.

In all these roles, they were forerunners of capitalist society. Although Westerners take for granted that capitalist values are "natural" and that they have always existed, this is not the case. Throughout most of human history, and throughout most of the world, other systems prevailed. In many societies, land and raw materials have been owned communally. Under capitalism, they are private property. In many societies, things are produced for immediate consumption or small-scale bartering. Capitalism, however, produces things only if there is a market for their sale for a profit. In many societies, labor has been legally bound to the land or to some other person, or has been directly regulated in some other way. By contrast, workers in a capitalist society can sell themselves for whatever price they can get.

Religion was often used to justify Europeans' business activities. They appealed to their God, who they believed had given the earth and its peoples to true believers to dominate. Such intolerance has helped to make Christianity one of the most expansionist of world religions, so that 1 billion people (perhaps one out of every three believers) are now Christian. Western values have been spread by this faith, as would be obvious if we compared it to the values of Buddhism or Islam.

The Portuguese brought these religious and commercial values to Africa in the 1400s. They set up trading posts but did not move inland because of the power of local rulers and the fear of diseases against which they had little immunity. (Africa was not formally divided into European colonies until after 1830.) Although the Portuguese disliked the "paganism" of the inhabitants, they enjoyed the profits of the areas that were later called the Grain Coast, the Ivory Coast, the Gold Coast, and the Slave Coast.

The presence of the Portuguese and other Europeans eventually disrupted all African civilizations. The influx of European products curtailed local economic development. The old caravan routes were rendered less profitable by the new sea routes. The sale of European guns, along with the demand for slaves, stirred warfare. It should not be forgotten, of course, that some Africans benefited from these developments. The best illustration may be the slave trade. Few Africans were captured by European raiders. Instead, they were purchased from other Africans for such items as guns, liquor, textiles, and bars of iron and copper. Slavery already existed in most African societies.

African slavery, however, was a social condition, not a racial one. Slaves were captives of war, debtors, or criminals. Even as slaves, they had established rights, and their descendants were unlikely to be in bondage. The European definition of slavery seldom included the right to marry, hold property, buy one's own freedom, or have children who would be free.

Although the European slave trade began slowly in A.D. 1441, the need to replace the dying native peoples of the New World brought a rapid increase in the 1500s. The first use of African slaves in the Caribbean in 1502 marked the beginning of a forced migration of about 10 million human beings over several hundred years. This dispersion of such peoples as the Bakongo, Ewe, Hausa, Ibo, Mende, and Yoruba has become known as the African diaspora. About 350,000 of the total number were brought to North America, where they became the ancestors of today's Afro-Americans.

As this trade grew larger and more lucrative, it became convenient for the Europeans to consider Africans a subhuman or inferior species. This was a change in historical perspective. The ancient world had known Africans not only as slaves (although most of the slaves of the Greek and Roman empires had been white), but as wealthy merchants, ambassadors, and kings. Most of the gold in the West came by trading with Africa from A.D. 700 to about A.D. 1500. Still, the European depiction of Africa now became thoroughly negative: "the dark continent." Much contemporary misinformation is part of this tradition. While it can now be proven that the earliest forms of humanity evolved in Africa millions of years ago, the average person is unlikely to think of it as the "mother" continent. Rather, the name "Africa" is likely to evoke images of naked savages, steaming jungles, and malarial mosquitoes. The facts are much more complex: Africa is the second largest continent on earth (after Asia), covering one-fifth of the total land surface and having hundreds of languages and cultures. Despite being systematically robbed by outsiders for centuries, it still produces 67 percent of the world's gold, 35 percent of the platinum, 77 percent of the diamonds, and large percentages of such other minerals as copper, chromium, tin, and manganese. The profits from this are still often controlled by whites, and the Africans continue to be blamed for their own poverty.

Africans arrived in colonial North America one year before the *Mayflower*. In 1619 twenty "negars" were sold by a Dutch trader in Jamestown, Virginia. These Africans were not treated as slaves, apparently, but as indentured servants. This class of labor originally consisted of those whites who had not been able to pay their own way to America and had signed a contract to labor during a period of four to seven years in return for their passage to America, food, shelter, and clothing, but no pay. By 1776 between 60 and 77 percent of those who had migrated *freely* to America had come as indentured servants.

The English areas of the New World were vast compared to England, a country about the size of modern New York State. Some colonists looked to Africa as an alternative source of labor. While the first Africans they bought were often treated differently from white indentured servants, some later owned land, successfully sued whites, and even purchased slaves for their own use. Despite this early ambiguity, however, the status of black workers tended to be unequal to that of white workers.

Massachusetts recognized permanent servitude in 1641, but slavery did not grow rapidly anywhere during the first decades of North American colonization. The market in human beings was stimulated eventually by the growing need for labor, combined with fewer white settlers from a more prosperous England and more slave traders from more European countries. By 1776 one out of every seven Americans was an African slave.

The number of slaves grew because they were profitable. It was difficult to get dependable long-term workers for exhausting rice and tobacco farming. Indentured workers often left when their contracts expired. African slaves, on the other hand, belonged to their owners, and they were identified easily because they came from a separate race.

As a general rule, the belief in black inferiority was stronger when it was more profitable to hold such a belief. In 1793, for example, the U.S. House of Representatives considered a bill to abolish slavery throughout the United States. The old tobacco lands brought less money because they became exhausted from bad farming practices. The American Revolution broke many trade ties with England. In Virginia more than 10,000 slaves were freed between 1782 and 1790. However, 1792 was the year in which Eli Whitney invented the cotton gin. This machine allowed cotton to be cheaply separated from its seeds, a process that had been done by hand. Lush profits from this crop, combined with the opening of new lands in Alabama and Mississippi, revived slavery. By 1860 cotton comprised 50 percent of the nation's exports, reaching 2.3 billion pounds a year. In the North, however, slavery was unprofitable on small family farms in a different climate, and it was no coincidence that northern slavery withered away. Despite this, the

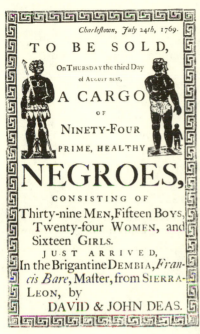

Charleſtown, July 24th, 1769.

TO BE SOLD,

On THURSDAY the third Day
of AUGUST next,

A CARGO

OF

NINETY-FOUR

PRIME, HEALTHY

NEGROES,

CONSISTING OF

Thirty-nine MEN, Fifteen Boys,
Twenty-four WOMEN, and
Sixteen GIRLS.

JUST ARRIVED,

In the Brigantine DEMBIA, *Francis Bare*, Maſter, from SIERRA-LEON, by

DAVID & JOHN DEAS.

RAFFLE

Mr. Joseph Jennings respectfully informs his friends and the public that, at the request of many acquaintances, he has been induced to purchase from Mr. Osborne, of Missouri, the celebrated

DARK BAY HORSE, "STAR,"

Aged five years, square trotter and warranted sound; with a new light Trotting Buggy and Harness; also, the dark, stout

MULATTO GIRL, "SARAH,"

Aged about twenty years, general house servant, valued at *nine hundred dollars*, and guaranteed, and

Will be Raffled for

At 4 o'clock P. M., February first, at the selection hotel of the subscribers. The above is as represented, and those persons who may wish to engage in the usual practice of raffling, will, I assure them, be perfectly satisfied with their destiny in this affair.

The whole is valued at its just worth, fifteen hundred dollars; fifteen hundred

CHANCES AT ONE DOLLAR EACH.

The Raffle will be conducted by gentlemen selected by the interested subscribers present. Five nights will be allowed to complete the Raffle. BOTH OF THE ABOVE DESCRIBED CAN BE SEEN AT MY STORE, No. 78 Common St., second door from Camp, at from 9 o'clock A. M. to 2 P. M. Highest throw to take the first choice; the lowest throw the remaining prize, and the fortunate winners will pay twenty dollars each for the refreshments furnished on the occasion.

N. B. No chances recognized unless paid for previous to the commencement.

JOSEPH JENNINGS.

NEGROES.

Juſt arrived,

In the Ship William, Captain Hill
from Dominica,
The pick of a CARGO from the
Gold Coaſt,
CONSISTING OF
Prime Young Fellows,
Wenches, and Boys.

southern demand for slaves meant that the slave trade within the United States flourished even though Congress forbade the importation of new slaves in 1808.

Imagine what it was like to be one of the first slaves. You were torn from your family and land, removed from your familiar language and religion, and shipped in chains in a boat that typically allowed you a space about 5½ feet long, 16 inches wide, and 3½ feet between the decks. People around you may have sickened and died. You arrived in a strange country and were examined like a horse, with an inspection of your teeth, eyes, and muscles. You were under the total control of someone of another race who did not look like you and who spoke a different language. You were probably housed in a log cabin with dirt floors, worked at stoop labor, and knew that you and your children were unlikely ever to escape from these conditions. For you, America was not a land of opportunity, but a prison. Even after the end of legal slavery in 1865, you probably didn't own a house, land, seeds, or farm animals. You were likely to be a sharecropper, keeping only a portion of what you produced on a white man's land and buying your supplies at a white man's store. You were now in debt slavery. Your debts were your new chains. The black writer Albion Tourgee was right when he said that freeing the slaves without providing any assistance was "cheap philanthropy."

During all of these centuries that Africans were being detribalized into Afro-Americans, with their many languages and cultural differences being replaced by a common language, common values, and a common suspicion of whites, there were persistent forms of resistance. These included escape to less repressive areas, everyday opposition to exploited labor, types of violence, agitation for the end of slavery, calls for the creation of a separate black state, formation of independent black organizations, and efforts to achieve equal opportunities and constitutional rights. These have been the main currents of black liberation struggles to the present. Although they have not been completely separate, it may be useful to view them individually before asking what gains have been made by our own time.

RESISTANCE TO INEQUALITY

While few people escaped during transport to the slave ships and the journey to the new land of their bondage, other than by suicide, more opportunities existed when they arrived. The runaway slave advertisement was a common feature in southern newspapers. Congress had responded to protect white property by the Fugitive Slave Act of 1793. Nonetheless, as slavery declined in the North, it became a promised land. By the early 1800s, there were sufficient escape routes for this method to be called the Underground Railroad. Between 1800 and 1860, perhaps 60,000 slaves gained their freedom by fleeing to the North, or to Mexico and other territories where their liberty would be relatively secure. The passage of the

Underground Railway "Routes"

CAUTION!!
COLORED PEOPLE
OF BOSTON, ONE & ALL,

You are hereby respectfully **CAUTIONED** and advised, to avoid conversing with the
Watchmen and Police Officers of Boston,

For since the recent **ORDER OF THE MAYOR &
ALDERMEN**, they are empowered to act as

KIDNAPPERS
AND
Slave Catchers,

And they have already been actually employed in
**KIDNAPPING, CATCHING, AND KEEPING
SLAVES.** Therefore, if you value your **LIBERTY**,
and the *Welfare of the Fugitives* among you, *Shun*
them in every possible manner, as so many *HOUNDS*
on the track of the most unfortunate of your race.

Keep a Sharp Look Out for
KIDNAPPERS, and have
TOP EYE open.

APRIL 24, 1851.

100 DOLLS. REWARD.
RAN AWAY

From me, on Saturday, the 19th inst.,

Negro Boy Robert Porter,
aged 19; heavy, stoutly made;
dark chesnut complexion;
rather sullen countenance,

with a down look; face large; head low on the
shoulders. I believe he entered the City of
Washington on Sunday evening, 20th inst. He
has changed his dress probably, except his
boots, which were new and heavy.

I will give $50 if taken and secured in the
District of Columbia, or $100 if taken north
of the District, and secured in each case and
delivered before the reward shall be good.

Dr. J. W. THOMAS.

Pomunky P. O., Charles Co., Md.

Fugitive Slave Act of 1850, which gave slaveholders harsher powers to recapture their "troublesome property," caused intense debate before the
Civil War.

After the war, it was difficult to leave the quasi-slavery of sharecropping,
but as many as 7,000 joined the "colored exodus" to Kansas in the 1870s;

others were part of the ranks of the Great Black March westward that established twenty-five black towns in Oklahoma in the 1890s; and many shifted to urban areas of the South where they might be more successful. Such migrations grew with the labor demands of World War I and World War II, with hundreds of thousands abandoning the South for better lives in the North. Although they encountered what William Wells Brown called in 1854 "colorphobia," or what Frederick Douglass described as the "caste freedom" of the North, there were more chances for education, political power, and social advancement. Recently, however, with the Sun Belt boom, there has been a reversal of this pattern, with greater black migration *to* the South.

Most, however, struggled where they were. Under slavery, people had little incentive to work. They played dumb, acted awkward, broke equipment, feigned illness, maimed animals, temporarily ran away, stole, and destroyed property. Some said, we had to lie to live; we had to steal to get what was rightfully ours. Such resistance was undramatic, but it might produce a beating or some other punishment. One toothless old slave reported that when he claimed to have a toothache, the master responded by pulling out twenty teeth and a piece of his jawbone.

From this everyday resistance developed a kind of underground slave culture. Although Professor Stanley Elkins once asserted that the inner mental world of the slave was "limited to catfish and watermelons," other academics such as Lawrence Levine refuted this by analyzing slave songs, stories, and sermons. If some of the slave tales are read as allegories, with Egypt as the South, the pharoah as the master, Moses as a slave leader, the Israelites as the slaves, and the Promised Land as freedom, their hidden meanings become visible.

On a less positive note, it could be argued that the long night of slavery continues to cast a shadow over much of black life. It may be difficult for many blacks to avoid internalizing the pervasive antiblack ideas of this culture. Especially in ghetto communities,

black comes to mean not only deprivation and frustration, but also membership in a community of persons who think poorly of each other, who attack and manipulate each other, who give each other small comfort in a desperate world. Black comes to stand for an identity as no better than these destructive others. The individual feels that he must embrace an unattractive self to function at all. (Lee Rainwater, *Behind Ghetto Walls* [Chicago: Aldine, 1970], p. 387)

Today, such people may not resist a slave system, but a welfare system that treats them as clients, and a society that warehouses them rather than offering full education and employment.

Besides everyday resistance to oppression and attempts to escape from its worst forms, there has been a long history of violence. When one race subordinates another, this is always a possibility. Slave revolts occurred on

some of the ships and in several regions of the country. The most serious plots in colonial America happened in New York City. One attempted rebellion in 1712 resulted in over two dozen blacks being burned, hanged, and, in one case, broken on the rack. Another plot, in 1741, was crushed with thirty-three people executed, nineteen of them being burned alive. Other prominent conspiracies included those of Gabriel Prosser in Virginia (1800), Denmark Vesey in Charleston, South Carolina (1822), and Nat Turner in Virginia (1831). The number of these revolts can be disputed. Some authors claim over 200 and some as few as 12. What is not in doubt is that many whites feared a day of retribution.

In the 1960s black militant H. Rap Brown proclaimed violence to be "as American as apple pie." What Brown meant was that the nation has had a history of violence, from its beginnings to the present. Blacks have sometimes benefited from violence, especially when it was officially sanctioned. In the American Revolution, thousands of blacks earned their freedom, some by serving on the rebel side and others by supporting the legal government through Lord Dunmore's Ethiopian Regiment. In every war since, black opportunities improved because of white America's need for black labor and troops.

These opportunities were seldom granted easily. In 1861 blacks were forbidden to join the Union army, and runaway slaves were returned to their legal owners, since the federal government claimed that this was a war to preserve the national state. As the war became more desperate, these policies changed, and Lincoln was driven to emancipation and to the use of black labor as a military necessity.

By 1865, there were approximately 185,000 black soldiers (150,000 of whom had been slaves), 200,000 black army laborers, and 30,000 black sailors. Although black soldiers were not at first paid the same as whites and few were allowed to become officers, 18 percent of the free black male adults of the North were involved in the war. About 38,000 blacks, from both the North and the South, died. Blacks were not given their freedom and oppor-

Lincoln throws in his last chance, a black ace. (*Punch*, 1862, on the preliminary Emancipation Proclamation.)

tunities; they paid dearly for whatever they got. These contributions and the dynamics of the war led to a racial revolution instead of a war merely for the preservation of the Union. The Thirteenth Amendment (1865) ended legal slavery, the Fourteenth Amendment (1868) declared blacks to be citizens, and the Fifteenth Amendment (1870) proclaimed the right of black men to vote. (Women, both black and white, remained voteless in much of the United States until 1920.) Even when the Republican party abandoned its southern black allies in 1877, and when white indifference and such terrorist groups as the Ku Klux Klan (founded in 1866) suppressed black rights, a new plateau had been reached that was higher than anything in the past.

In each war there have been black contributions and black demands for better treatment. In World War I, 13 percent of inductees were black; there were 371,000 black soldiers; and leaders like W.E.B. Du Bois urged the motto "We return from fighting; we return fighting." In World War II, there were about a million black men and women in the military, and black leaders promoted a Double V campaign, for a democratic victory abroad and at home. The Korean War and the war in Vietnam further expanded the ranks of black veterans. Some of these veterans were set on the road to militancy, such as the ex-Marine Robert F. Williams, the author of *Negroes with Guns* (1962). More often, black veterans were insistent upon fairer chances in life.

What has disturbed white America has not been official violence, but unofficial violence. When the white John Brown attempted to arm a slave insurrection at Harper's Ferry in 1859, his last words before his execution have echoed up to the present: "I, John Brown, am now quite certain that the crimes of this guilty land will never be purged away but with blood." Brown could be dismissed as a maniac or a terrorist; the well-adjusted person accepted the ancient institution of slavery. Although Brown was defeated and hanged, his extreme act compelled the nation to confront the issue of slavery. He cut through the polite hypocrisies of his day.

Such unofficial violence has a long history, including the Watts riot in Los Angeles during 1965 (which left thirty-four dead), civil disturbances in 150 cities in 1967 (with forty-three dead in Detroit), and many riots in 1968 following the killing of Dr. Martin Luther King, Jr. In the latter case, the government's commission decided that riots were produced by explosive inequalities in American society. As the Kerner Report stated in 1968: "Our nation is moving toward two societies, one black, one white—separate and unequal."

Militant black organizations grew out of this environment. Although such groups as the Black Panthers were commonly portrayed as violent because of their black leather jackets, strident language, and advocacy of firearms, they were often the victims of violence. In 1969 the leader of the Black Panthers in Chicago, Fred Hampton, was killed when over one hundred rounds of ammunition were fired into his apartment by authorities. Roy Wilkins, a moderate black spokesman, asserted, "All you had to do was to be a Panther and you became a target. I classified it as murder then and I still classify it as murder." Later revelations demonstrated illegal Federal Bureau of Investigation (FBI) plans to disrupt the Panthers and schemes by police agencies to use whatever means necessary to harass the party.

The 1980s opened with a similar fiery outburst. A thirty-three-year-old black insurance executive was stopped in Miami for a traffic violation. He was beaten to death by several policemen, supposedly for resisting arrest. Although one officer described the victim as having been "gang tackled," and another said that he had not resisted, the attackers were acquitted by an all-white jury. In the racial violence that followed both the original death and the acquittal, there were several days of rioting, eighteen people were killed, and about $100 million in damage was done. In places like Miami, society is a racial powder keg, with a new generation of unemployed black youth coming to riot age. As the mayor of Miami concluded, "There's no way those of us who live in air-conditioned comfort can live side-by-side with people who are ten to a room that's infested with rats. We've got to recognize the reality of where we live, what we are, who we are, and where we're going." The downtown renewal of many cities may be icing on a rotten cake.

In a town like Baltimore, where I lived for many years, there are glass pavilions in the Inner Harbor, but it is one of the poorest cities in the United States, with definite worries about people with rocks.

The widespread belief throughout much of U.S. history that blacks and whites would never live together in equality has provoked such black responses as violence, escape from some oppression, and negative and perhaps self-destructive forms of resistance. For those who believed that equal justice was not possible, another black tradition has been separatism. Thus, the African Methodist Episcopal Church essentially began in 1787 when Richard Allen and other black members of a white church were forced to sit in the balcony. Some other black leaders of the early 1800s, such as Henry Highland Garnet and Martin R. Delany, similarly concluded that white America would never treat blacks justly and advocated a separate black state, whether in North America, Central America, the Caribbean, or Africa.

Whites who agreed founded the American Colonization Society during 1816 and 1817 and worked for the creation of the African country of Liberia in 1822. Although 19,000 blacks were glad to leave the United States by 1865, others, such as Frederick Douglass, declared that blacks were not foreigners but citizens who should fight for equality. Many hopeful blacks were disheartened, however, by the Fugitive Slave Law of 1850 and by the Dred Scott decision of 1857, in which the Supreme Court ruled that blacks had never been citizens of the United States, were not then citizens, and would never be citizens. One solution was to leave the country, and President Abraham Lincoln got Congress to put up money for a trial colony in Haiti, which failed. This history, followed by the problems of Reconstruction and the Supreme Court ruling in *Plessy v. Ferguson* (1896) that separate facilities for whites and blacks were legal so long as they were equal, seemed to give credence to Bishop Henry McNeal Turner's charge that the Constitution was "a dirty rag, a cheat, a libel and ought to be spat upon by every negro in the land." Turner decided, "Africa is our home. Every man who has the sense of an animal must see that there is no future in this country for the Negro."

White resistance to assimilation, integration, or respectful pluralism has provided the basic impetus for political black nationalism (whether as a separate caucus within an established party or as a call for a separate state), cultural black nationalism (such as the Harlem Renaissance of the 1920s), and economic black nationalism (ranging from black capitalism to black communalism).

Marcus Garvey, a Jamaican immigrant, combined these forms of black nationalism into one movement in the early 1920s. His organization in Harlem, the Universal Negro Improvement Association, stirred the imagination of millions with its call for Negro Zionism. This would be a cultural return and, if possible, a physical return to the homeland. Garveyism sometimes had the appearance of a fraternal order, like the Elks or Masons, because of its fanciful uniforms, ceremonies, and parades, but its goals were serious.

One of Garvey's positive accomplishments was his education of people in vision. He insisted that blacks could not rely upon whites for their identity; they had to control their own ideals or they would be emotionally and intellectually defeated and enslaved. Black Americans were urged to see their lives as part of a broader history. The rising or falling star of Africa had affected, and would affect, the status of African peoples scattered throughout the world. Only the greater cultural, political, and economic unity of Africans could offer the full realization of their potential. Contemporary versions of this are U.S. black concerns about apartheid and the Rev. Jesse Jackson's trips to African countries.

A second achievement was his attempt to create organizations to foster this unity, including the Negro Political Union, the newspaper *Negro World*, the Black Star Line of ships, and the African Orthodox Church. Garvey demanded that blacks go beyond the "prayers and petitions" to white organizations that had made them little more than "seasoned beggars." Millions of poor people, acting collectively, could be powerful.

Garvey, however, did not become a black Moses. His message contained false hopes. First, the slogan "Back to Africa" was escapist and utopian. It avoided struggle in the real world, even though individual Garveyites worked in many reform and radical activities. Second, Garvey advocated the strict separation of the races, even to the extent of praising the Ku Klux Klan, the Anglo-Saxon Clubs, and the White America societies. This discouraged attempts to work together with whites for progressive change. Third, Garvey's ideas, based upon race, were insufficiently sensitive to the roles of class, region, and culture in social change movements. The black middle class, the urban masses, and rural people may have divergent interests. The educated, light-skinned W.E.B. Du Bois dismissed Garvey as "the Jamaican jackass," while Garvey characterized Du Bois as a snobbish "white man's Negro."

The contradictions in Garveyism were exemplified by a 1923 letter that was written by eight black leaders and sent to the attorney general of the United States. They urged an investigation of the funding for Garvey's projects. This resulted in Garvey's conviction for mail fraud and a five-year prison sentence. Garvey may not have been a crook, although he was an incompetent businessman, but this action splintered his movement. After his deportation to Jamaica in 1927, Garveyism declined in the United States, and Garvey himself was almost penniless and forgotten when he died in London in 1940.

Garveyism as an influence, however, lives on. Later groups such as the Nation of Islam and the Republic of New Africa claimed some of this legacy, just as did individuals like Malcolm X (1925–1965), whose father had been a Garveyite. It is true that the flaws of Garveyism live on as well and are factors in the limited influence of modern descendants.

Many Americans find it comforting to dismiss black nationalism, violence, and escapist tendencies as exotic sideshows to the main theme of steady progress toward integrated equality. On the contrary, an understanding of this history is vital to understanding contemporary black-white relations. Without this knowledge, one might be surprised that many polls in the 1980s showed that large percentages of blacks were convinced that white Americans paid major attention to racial injustice only in the face of violence. It might also be surprising to learn that many of the views of black Americans on both domestic issues and foreign policies (such as U.S. involvement in South Africa) differ substantially from those of white Americans. Many blacks have an undercurrent of skepticism, feeling that they are outsiders who have been betrayed by the dominant society.

In fact, progress toward racial equality has usually come sporadically and unevenly. The first opponents of slavery were generally ignored or despised. When Samuel Sewall wrote "The Selling of Joseph" in 1701, attempting to prevent blacks from being priced "like horses and hogs," he met with little sympathy. David Walker, a free black man who wrote the famous *Appeal* of 1829, died young and impoverished. William Lloyd Garrison, the editor of *The Liberator* (founded in 1831), was commonly considered a nuisance or a lunatic.

Nonetheless, America has come a long way. Few people would now point to the endorsements of slavery in the Bible, claim that slavery was a paternalistic system, or assert that blacks have been destined by God and nature to be menials. These were once accepted "facts of life."

The destruction of slavery, however, did not mean black equality with whites. Many of the social and political gains of the Civil War were lost by the end of the 1800s. In 1884, for example, Alabama adopted a new state constitution that reduced the number of black voters from about 140,000 to 3,742. Likewise, Louisiana had reduced the 130,000 black voters of 1896 to a

mere 5,000 by 1900. White terrorist societies such as the Ku Klux Klan prospered. Lynchings of blacks were not uncommon; there were 235 in 1892. Blacks were often driven from occupations in which they had been present (such as carpentry, baking, and tailoring), denied entrance into various unions, and screened from law schools, medical schools, and other institutions that trained for the professions. Although many white Americans saw the late 1800s as a time of progress and hope, black Americans generally led stunted lives of segregation and discrimination.

Booker T. Washington (1856–1915) was one of those blacks who struggled to advance both himself and his race. Born into slavery, he was freed at the end of the Civil War. Those were days of few opportunities. He was able, with great effort, to gain an advanced education, although only 314 American blacks had B.A.'s even by 1876. During his later years as head of the Tuskegee Institute in Alabama, he constructed a black-run school that had, by 1914, 107 buildings, 2,345 acres, 200 faculty, 1,500 students, and an endowment of $2 million. It was the largest school, white or black, in the South.

Washington sought to inculcate useful knowledge in his students, along with discipline, thrift, and productivity. He did not publicly call for eventual integration, saying that "in all things that are purely social we can be as separate as the fingers of one hand." Nonetheless, he privately financed legal challenges to the denial of black jurors, segregated facilities, peonage (exploited farm labor), and voting restrictions. His segregated institution, which promoted a kind of economic black nationalism (as Garvey described the Washington program), implicitly reached toward an integrationist goal.

Outside the South, his work was carried on by the National Negro Business League (begun in 1900) and the National League on Urban Conditions among Negroes, established in 1911 and later called simply the National Urban League. Despite such patient work for the moderate economic improvement of blacks, there were powerful whites who were fiercely hostile. Governor James Vardaman of Mississippi scoffed, "I am just as opposed to Booker T. Washington, with all of his Anglo-Saxon reinforcements, as I am to the coconut-headed, chocolate-colored typical little coon, Andy Dotson, who blacks my shoes every morning."

Washington also had his black critics. Although many black farmers and middle-class people admired his practical views and useful programs, he was also called short-sighted and timid. The northern-born W.E.B. Du Bois (1868–1963) became one of the best-known of these critics.

At first Du Bois agreed with Washington that it was unrealistic for blacks to chase after the "meteors" of immediate social and political equality. It was more reasonable to wed the race to hard work and the savings bank. Du Bois was later convinced, however, that less could be accomplished by accommodation than by agitation. Washington's school and his philosophy trained blacks to adjust to rural life, to focus on short-term aspirations, and to be servants or craftsmen in occupations that were shrinking (such as black-smithing and shoemaking). Du Bois, by contrast, emphasized the development of a "talented tenth" of black intellectuals, businessmen, and professionals who would be the vanguard of the black race.

One of the first attempts to gather such an elite was the Niagara Movement, founded by twenty-nine representatives from thirteen states in Niagara, Ontario, in 1905. These men engaged primarily in symbolic politics, such as entering the town of Harper's Ferry in 1906 with a call for continuing John Brown's fight against slavery by struggling for equal citizenship, full education, and an economic chance in life for all.

This prophetic group heralded the alliance of black and white progressives that was established in 1910, the National Association for the Advancement of Colored People (NAACP). Black protest had a national voice that would not be apologetic in response to insults. While the National Urban League helped black labor find urban housing and employment, and many southern blacks were rightly fearful of open complaints, the NAACP used the courts to attack discrimination, held demonstrations and meetings, and published in order to educate the public. *The Crisis*, a newspaper, began publication in 1910. It was edited by Dr. Du Bois for the next twenty-four years. While *The Crisis* was growing to a circulation of 100,000 by 1920, the NAACP developed legal cases against discrimination in housing, public facilities, and the military. It petitioned Congress for a federal antilynching bill, which was never passed. The arduous work of the NAACP proved what Frederick Douglass said, that progress does not come without struggle. As Langston Hughes concurred in his history of the NAACP, "Freedom isn't free."

Black migration to northern urban centers during the 1920s and 1930s expanded the influence of the NAACP, as did some of the New Deal programs of the 1930s. World War II was a more decisive event. Blacks were initially excluded from most of the defense industries or were hired as menials. A. Philip Randolph, a black labor leader and socialist, threatened a protest march on Washington in 1941. He said, "We shall not ask our white friends to march with us. There are some things that Negroes must do alone." President Roosevelt was stimulated to issue Executive Order 8802, banning racial discrimination in defense industries and the federal government, but not in the military. (The last segregated army unit was not disbanded until 1955).

The labor needs of the war, combined with a reduction in racial discrimination, allowed the number of black defense workers to rise to 8 percent of the total, black federal workers to increase by 500 percent (to 300,000), and the 700,000 blacks in the army to be more fairly treated. The federal government and the military became powerful engines for social change. Such opportunities encouraged black migration out of the South, reaching a total of 1.3 million during the decade 1940 to 1950.

Social and economic opportunities, along with more secure employment

and hopes for further progress, helped to give birth to the civil rights struggles of the 1950s and 1960s. These would grow into a second Reconstruction.

The NAACP, with a burgeoning membership and budget and a record of
thirty-four victories out of its first thirty-eight cases before the Supreme
Court, realized its greatest symbolic and practical victory in 1954. The highest court in the United States struck at the half-century-old principle of
"separate but equal" for blacks and whites. In *Brown v. Board of Education
of Topeka,* the court rejected such facilities as inherently unequal since they
inplied superior and inferior races.

At the moment of this legal success for the NAACP, other spontaneous
movements arose that were not legal and educational so much as direct
confrontations with segregation. Although the court had ruled, local customs
were resistent to change without local protests. The year 1955 saw a dramatic example of this when the arrest of a black seamstress in Montgomery,
Alabama, was met by a 382-day black boycott of the bus system of that city.
For years, blacks had gone to the back of the bus. Rosa Parks and many
others were no longer willing to do so.

Out of this conflict emerged a new leader: the Rev. Dr. Martin Luther
King, Jr. He was neither an NAACP lawyer nor an Urban League businessman; he was a visionary activist. The integrationist battles of this period
all saw him as an organizer or commentator: President Eisenhower's use of
troops to desegregate the Little Rock, Arkansas, high school in 1956; the
founding of the Southern Christian Leadership Conference in 1957; the
beginning of black "sit-ins" at segregated places in 1960; the "freedom rides"
of mixed black and white teams on the newly desegregated interstate bus
system, starting in 1960; and the March on Washington in 1963, when a
quarter of·a million Americans gathered before the Lincoln Memorial. At
this event, there were stirring speeches by black and white leaders, along
with eulogies for activists of the past, such as W.E.B. Du Bois. Even though
Dr. Du Bois had joined the Communist party and moved to Ghana, Roy
Wilkins, the leader of the NAACP, generously noted that, "Regardless of
the fact that in later years Dr. Du Bois chose another path, it is incontrover-
tible that at the dawn of the twentieth century, his was the voice calling you
here today."

These struggles led to the Civil Rights Act of 1964 and the Voting Rights
Act of 1965. Although Dr. King has since been memorialized for his contributions to this legislation, it should not be forgotten that during his last years
before his murder in 1968, he was frequently denounced for his attacks on
racism in the North, his scorn for the war in Vietnam and U.S. military
spending, and his call for a more equitable distribution of wealth in U.S.
society.

The people and groups that we remember most today have fostered integration of blacks into the mainstream of the United States. Some have
stressed vocational training; some, legal challenges to discrimination; some,

direct action. But all have sought to break down the barriers of racial inequality in this country. Those who failed to work with the white majority, or
refused to do so, declined into relative insignificance or actual collapse, such
as the Congress of Racial Equality (CORE, 1942) and the Student Nonviolent Coordinating Committee (SNCC, 1960; now defunct).

The efforts of integrationist groups, combined with changes in the economy, the need for black labor during wartime, and greater sensitivity by the
white power establishment to world opinion, have produced considerable
racial improvement in American society during this century.

WHAT HAS BEEN ACHIEVED?

To see what has changed and what has not, compare the life of a nineteenth-century black leader, Frederick Douglass, to the life of a twentieth-
century black leader, Malcolm X. Malcolm is less well known than Martin
Luther King, Jr., but as a son of the lower class his career may be more
representative of the black community of his day. After a comparison of
these two men, we will ask how a Frederick Douglass or a Malcolm X might
develop if they were born into a typical black home of the late 1980s.

Both Frederick Douglass and Malcolm X lived at a time when conditions
virtually conspired against their success. The circumstances of their births,
early family life, education, and job opportunities did little to nourish their
abilities.

Frederick Douglass did not know the name of his white Maryland father,
nor the precise date of his birth. When he was later asked about his origins,
he satirically replied that "genealogical trees did not flourish among the
slaves." He saw his mother only a few times, since she was a slave on a
plantation twelve miles away and died when he was very young. He was
raised by his grandmother, who died when he was seven. Years later, when
he escaped from slavery, three brothers and a sister remained slaves.

Malcolm's family life, nearly a century later and in the North, was not
much improved. His mother had been born as the result of her mother's
rape by a white man. His father, a Baptist minister who was an admirer of
Marcus Garvey, was killed when Malcolm was six (his skill was crushed and
the body laid across a railroad track and almost cut in half). Following this
murder, his mother suffered a mental collapse and was institutionalized for
twenty-six years. When the family disintegrated, the young Malcolm and his
siblings spent their early years in different boarding homes and state
institutions.

The educational opportunities of the two men were not encouraging. In
the case of Douglass, it was a crime to teach a slave to read and write.
Although the wife of one master taught him the alphabet and a few simple
words, his continued instruction was forbidden when the master learned of
it, since this "would spoil any nigger." Douglass's later education was self-

acquired. As he told one admirer who had requested his autograph in 1895, "Though my penmanship is not fine, it will do pretty well for one who learned to write on a board fence."

Malcolm, living in Mason, Michigan, had more formal education. He remembered, though, that his books said little or nothing about black history and that his school (in Michigan, not Alabama) was pervaded with racial bigotry. When he told his favorite white English teacher that he wanted to become a lawyer, the man's response was "That's no realistic goal for a nigger." It was understandable that Malcolm dropped out of school at the age of fifteen. Later, when he was in prison as a drug hustler and thief, he went through the dictionary from A through Z, picking up the vocabulary to read. After this, he felt that he could go through a book and know what it was saying. Eight years of schooling had not taught him this.

Given such backgrounds for Malcolm and Frederick, the jobs open to them were few. Although Douglass entered a skilled trade, that of a ship caulker in Baltimore (with the provision that his master get almost all his wages), he was later denied similar work in New Bedford, Massachusetts, by racist laborers. Instead, he was reduced to unskilled jobs just as Malcolm was a shoeshine boy, hotel bus boy, and waiter in a dining car (among his legal activities).

In the cases of both men, religion was vital in overcoming the negative self-images that dominated their earliest years. One of Douglass's few opportunities for early leadership and meaning, even during his days as a slave, had been in religious groups in Baltimore. In the Zion Methodist Church Douglass got opportunities to speak and organize. When he escaped, he joined the Methodist church in New Bedford. There, as elsewhere, blacks had their own churches because of the profound intolerance of almost all white Christians. One positive outgrowth of this, however, was an independent institution that fostered black leaders.

For Malcolm X, the Nation of Islam transformed his life. While in prison, he heard the teaching of Elijah Muhammad, who said that he spoke for "the Negroes in the mud." Malcolm was told that white society had made him a criminal by keeping him ignorant, deprived, and without a decent job. This message gave him a sense of hope for the first time in his life: "It had an electrical effect on me. But bending my knees to pray—that *act*—well, that took me a week. You know what my life had been. Picking a lock to rob someone's house was the only way my knees had ever been bent before." Before this conversion experience, he had felt lost and alone. After it, his life had meaning, dignity, and direction.

At this point in the lives of both men, another basic element of their identity changed: their names. Frederick Douglass began his life as Frederick Augustus Washington Bailey. After his escape, he changed his name to avoid recapture, first to Frederick Stanley, then to Frederick Johnson, and finally to Frederick Douglass (after a white character in Sir Walter Scott's novel *The Lady of the Lake*). He insisted upon retaining the "Frederick" as one link to his past.

Malcolm was born Malcolm Little, which he later called his slave name. When he converted to the Nation of Islam, he dropped the "Little" and replaced it with an "X," in keeping with their practice, to stand for his unknown African heritage.

Finally, both men succeeded, not only because of their own efforts, but because of the aid of institutions. Douglass was rescued from manual labor by various abolitionist societies that allowed him to become a full-time speaker and writer. Malcolm was given a platform by the Nation of Islam for his powerful messages.

Both men succeeded despite their environment rather than because of it. Black men and women of similar potential were likely to die of poverty, disease, and crime while they were young, or have their hopes and imaginations warped or killed. Racial injustice limited the creation of many strongly independent blacks in both the nineteenth and twentieth centuries.

But what about today? If Frederick Douglass and Malcolm X were born into typical black homes of the 1980s, would their lives be different?

First, the average black family is not Bill Cosby's television family. The reality is that six of every ten black babies were born out of wedlock in 1986, compared to three out of ten in 1970. One-third of these were born to teen-aged mothers who may be little more than children themselves. This contrasts with about one of every ten white children born out of wedlock.

Many simple explanations have been given for this, such as the general loosening of moral standards in recent years, the evil effects of sex education, and teen-aged promiscuity, but the problem has many origins. For some young people who have few hopes for a good education, job, or home, a child may be proof of manhood or womanhood. A baby also can be a way to spite a parent, to demonstrate independence, to have an achievement, or to own something. It may satisfy many emotional needs.

If Frederick or Malcolm were born into such a home, where over half of all black children are now in female-headed households, the cultural and economic picture would be bleak. The mother usually finds it difficult to get further job training, or to find day care for her children if she does have a job. Programs such as AFDC (Aid to Families with Dependent Children) were created intentionally by conservatives with the goal of keeping the mother in the home rather than at a job. Also, birth control and abortion services have come under increasing attack—often by the same conservatives who complain about welfare children—so that further children may follow. Despite considerable rhetoric about putting welfare mothers to work ("workfare"), the reality has been limited day care for their children and severe cuts in federal job-training programs that might allow them some opportunities in life.

This situation is not improving. In 1970 three of every four black children were in families that had two parents in the home. In 1987, more than half of black children were in families headed solely by women. There were 2.9 million such families, constituting 42 percent of all black families.

What will be the future of these children? Such a home environment perpetuates poverty, lower-class "black English," few expectations, limited discipline, and other problems that will mark the child for life. Their descendents will probably suffer the same.

Although many black families have improved economically in recent years, female-headed households depress the overall average. Families headed by black women suffer both from the lower average incomes given to women (owing to sex discrimination) and lower incomes to blacks (from race discrimination). It has been a negative factor in historical trends. In 1939, the median income of black families had been 39 percent that of white families. In 1975 it had risen to 62 percent. By 1981 it slipped back to 56 percent. In 1986, 63 percent of black families were in the lowest two-fifths of the earning scale.

The poverty, frustration, and hopelessness of such families is social dynamite. Conservatives, rather than seeking structural reforms, have preferred cosmetic changes, such as an effort to redefine poverty and thus eliminate (on paper) millions of poor. In 1982 a person was poor who belonged to an urban family of four receiving less than $9,862 a year in cash income. If the government included noncash benefits such as Medicaid, food stamps, and housing subsidies, that person could suddenly cease to be poor. For example, 3.8 million elderly poor, both black and white, might no longer be classified as poor if they were assumed to receive, as income, the full market value of the Medicaid and Medicare benefits.

Frederick or Malcolm would have more chances in life if they were born into a middle-class family—and this is now more likely. The number of black families that earned more than $25,000 a year grew from 10.4 percent of the total in 1970 to 24.5 percent in 1982 (measured in constant dollars). The gap between the median income of married blacks and married whites, for example, has narrowed to about $6,000.

Even if Frederick or Malcolm were born into a black middle-class household, he might fear that his parents would divorce, since the black divorce rate reached 178 per 1,000 by the mid-1980s, about twice that of whites.

Nonetheless, a modern black child will probably have a more positive black identity than children did in earlier periods. At one time, a white child might have said, "I'm English, German, and Irish," and a black child, "I'm nothing." Today, black history and black literature are no longer invisible. White newspapers print more than crime statistics about blacks, and black publications no longer have many ads for skin bleaches like Tan-off, or hair straighteners like Permanent Straight that were once signs that many blacks accepted white definitions of beauty. American culture has changed, even if "black is beautiful" annoys some (since white standards of beauty are assumed), "black power" sometimes startles (but white power does not), and "black studies" may be called provincial (even though education is often white studies). Cultural biases are not as crushing as in the past, though they do persist. An antiracism manual that was published by the National Education Association summarized this:

Our national heroes, holidays, symbols, and myths are culturally racist. Adam and Eve were white, Jesus was white, angels are white, Santa Claus is white, all of fairyland is white, astronauts are white, Presidents are white, Dick and Jane are white, the figure at the top of the evolution charts in biology textbooks is white. Most of our national holidays commemorate white heroes. Only in sports, and then only recently, have blacks won any real cultural acclaim. But think for a moment about the trophies we present to black athletes. Have you ever seen a trophy with other than a white figure on it? ("Education and Racism: An Action Manual" [Washington, D.C.: NEA, 1973] p. 15)

When black children go off to school, it is likely to be an inferior and segregated school because of white flight to the suburbs, increased white enrollment in private schools, and a reduced commitment by the power structure to public education. Despite such problems and the fact that 25 percent of black students do not complete high school (the figure was 33 percent in 1970), the percentage of blacks twenty-five and older with high school diplomas doubled from 30 percent to 60 percent between 1968 and 1985. The number who go on to college has improved, with the number enrolled full-time in American colleges and universities almost doubling from 1970 to 1980: from 522,000 to over 1 million. At the same time, the percentage of blacks with college degrees nearly tripled, from 4 percent to 11 percent, between 1968 and 1985. It must be said, of course, that the percentage of whites who graduate from high school and from college rose at a faster rate, and that it has become more difficult in the 1980s for poor people, both black and white, to afford higher education.

Those who fail to graduate from high school, have only a high school diploma, or do not complete college are found among the 48 percent of unemployed black teenagers, or the 21 percent of unemployed black adults. These figures include only those who are actively seeking work, not those "discouraged workers" who have given up. They include many people in the declining steel industries, auto plants, and garment factories. Most of these unemployed are probably doomed to welfare, military enlistment, fast-food jobs, service employment, and the economic and social scrapheap. In the past, the major function of blacks was to provide cheap, unskilled labor. The need for such labor is steadily declining, and there are only so many highly skilled jobs for people with specialized abilities. Just as the earlier industrial revolution dislocated many, so will the computer and information revolution. If black men do not compete successfully with baby boomers and white women for jobs, their failure will have an impact in many areas, such as on the black family.

For many employed blacks, however, there is a much wider range of possibilities. When Malcolm X was writing, he ridiculed the idea of a black middle class: when a black man said that he was "in government," that meant that he was a postal clerk; when a black man said that he was "in banking," that meant that he was a janitor in a bank; when a black man said that he was "in railroading," that meant that he was a porter. Malcolm portrayed all of them as "forty- and fifty-year-old errand boys."

This has changed. Since the 1960s, the numbers of black lawyers, doctors, dentists, accountants, government employees, realtors, teachers, businessmen, and office workers has grown rapidly. For these people, it is a long way from the world of field laborers, cooks, washerwomen, ditchdiggers, and house servants. Black workers are more represented in white-dominated corporations, whether banking, insurance companies, industries, or universities. These are the "buppies" (black urban professionals) or "blue chip blacks." They are a minority within a minority. While the U.S. government counts 36 percent of the black population as impoverished, the top 20 percent of black incomes make up 55 percent of total black income. These are the people who began moving into suburbia in the 1970s, where over 6 million now live.

Fewer American blacks have established their own businesses. Although blacks are 12 percent of the U.S. population, black-owned businesses account for only 0.16 percent of all business revenue. This entrepreneurial deficit cannot be attributed solely to racist barriers, since black West Indians have been far more successful in the United States. Cultural and historical factors must be involved. Black spokesmen like Tony Brown point to West Indian and Asian successes bolstered by strong family and community support, in terms of labor, loans, and patronage. He has argued that while Jamaicans help Jamaicans, Chinese help Chinese, Haitians help Haitians, and Koreans help Koreans, too many blacks almost boycott black businesses, perhaps reverting to the adage that "if you want to die, go to a black doctor; if you want to go to jail, go to a black lawyer." While this may be an extreme interpretation, it is true that the leaders of the U.S. black community are, to an unusual degree, ministers, politicians, and some professionals, rather than businessmen.

These black economic classes have focused not on business but on politics, old-line civil rights organizations, and new organizations that represent them. By 1987 there were 295 black mayors (including those of Atlanta, Chicago, Detroit, Los Angeles, and Philadelphia), more than 6,000 elected black officials, publications ranging from the small *Black Scholar* to *Essence* (800,000 circulation) and *Black Enterprise* (250,000), and new groups such as the Council of Concerned Black Executives.

These people have prospered while the material conditions of many blacks have worsened. There is an economic chasm between the buppies and the black underclass. Amiri Baraka, a former black nationalist, bluntly described class differences in Newark, New Jersey:

We got a government run by Black folks. . . . So you have a similar syndrome of Black public officials and Black poverty at the same time. We began to see a handful of niggers with their Rolls Royces and Mercedes and the rest of us out there on the sidewalk. There's no change. Yet if you go to work and meet those people, they're young, speak Swahili, some of them got Muslim names. I mean, the President of our Board of Education . . . opens the [meetings] "Selam Aleyijuan" and then the next thing he tells us is he wants to put art, music and physical education out of the curricula because our children don't need it. So, we began to see the reality of the class struggle business. (Interview in *Unicorn Times* [Washington, D.C.], February 1981, p. 39)

If a majority of the 28 million blacks in this country become a permanent caste in the basement of society, will this diminish the general status of those who have escaped? Today the leading cause of death among black men is murder; blacks have a six times greater chance to die violently. Today, while black men constitute only 6 percent of the total population, they make up about half of the U.S. prison population. There are 719 black prisoners per 100,000 blacks, compared to 114 white prisoners per 100,000 whites. (This difference is more than twice as great as it was in 1925). Unless one believes that blacks are genetically or racially disposed to be criminals, this must be related to broader social pathologies within the United States. Many are trapped in rotting ghettos because of declining affirmative action, social services, and funding for public education. The existence of so many poor blacks is often seen as evidence of black inferiority, although the existence of many poor whites is not interpreted as a commentary on whites as a group. A racial double standard often remains.

Some whites argue, furthermore, that many immigrants have been successful in America. Why have blacks lagged behind? This question ignores the greater opportunities that earlier immigrants had to find unskilled work, at a time when black labor was severely limited, usually to agriculture. Today, when the legal barriers are removed, blue-collar jobs are no longer as abundant in such declining industries as autos, steel, rubber, and coal. Instead, there is greater emphasis on technical skills, and recent immigrants have been among the most ambitious, imaginative, and skilled members of their cultures, not average or unskilled stay-at-homes. The immigrant analogy further misses the peculiarly intense history of black-white conflicts in U.S. society.

Anyone who doubts the frustrations caused by this history will find it difficult to explain the broad enthusiasm within the black community for Jesse Jackson's presidential candidacy in 1984, despite the common arguments that it was unrealistic. Nor will it be easy to understand why over 90 percent of black voters endorsed one candidate in that election, while over 60 percent of white voters endorsed another candidate. Many also failed to predict that a Muslim orator like Louis Farrakhan could attract audiences of 10,000 to 15,000, despite the fact that he appalled most whites and many blacks. Indeed, part of his attraction rested upon that fact. As Malcolm X once said, "I'm an extremist because black people are in an extremely bad situation." White America may wish to believe that this is now an open society of equal chances for all, but many blacks are not convinced. The addition of Dr. King's birthday to the list of national holidays in 1986, while symbolically important, cannot substitute for money, power, and real equality.

Nonetheless, it is true that a young Frederick Douglass or a young Malcolm X would have more opportunities to realize his abilities. Perhaps Malcolm *would* become a lawyer today. While the United States may never be a color-blind democracy where success is based solely on personal ability, Americans have become more conscious that this is a multiracial and multiethnic society. It is commonly agreed that all members of society should have equal opportunities to make their contributions.

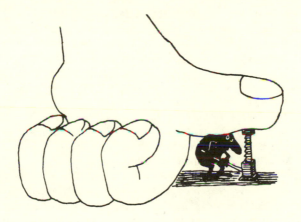

SOURCES OF FURTHER INFORMATION

Books and Articles

For references on black women, see the bibliography for Chapter 6. For references on black religion, see the bibliography for Chapter 8.

Anderson, Jervis. A. *Philip Randolph: A Biographical Portrait*. Foreword by A. H. Raskin. Berkeley and Los Angeles: University of California Press, 1986.

Anson, Robert S. *Best Intentions: The Education and Killing of Edmund Perry*. New York: Random House, 1987.

Aptheker, Herbert. *Herbert Aptheker's Afro-American History: The Modern Era*. New York: Citadel, 1986.

Ashmore, Harry S. *Hearts and Minds: The Anatomy of Racism from Roosevelt to Reagan*. New York: McGraw-Hill, 1983.

Bartley, Numan V. "In Search of the New South: Southern Politics after Reconstruction," in *The Promise of American History: Progress and Prospects*, Stanley I. Kutler and Stanley N. Katz, eds. pp. 150–63. Baltimore: Johns Hopkins University Press, 1982.

Bell, Derrick. *And We Are Not Saved: The Elusive Quest for Racial Equality*. New York: Basic Books, 1987.

Berry, Mary Frances, and John W. Blassingame. *Long Memory: The Black Experience in America*. New York: Oxford University Press, 1982.

Blackett, R.J.M. *Beating against the Barriers: Biographical Essays in Nineteenth-Century Afro-American History*. Baton Rouge: Louisiana State University Press, 1986.

Blassingame, John W. *The Slave Community*, rev. ed. New York: Oxford University Press, 1979.

Bloom, Jack M. *Class, Race, and the Civil Rights Movement: The Changing Political Economy of Southern Racism*. Bloomington: Indiana University Press, 1987.

Carson, Clayborne. *In Struggle: SNCC and the Black Awakening of the 1960s*. Cambridge: Harvard University Press, 1981.

Collins, Sheila D. *The Rainbow Challenge: The Jackson Campaign and the Future of U.S. Politics*. New York: Monthly Review Press, 1987.

Cruse, Harold. *Plural but Equal*. New York: Morrow, 1987.

Davis, David Brion. *Slavery and Human Progress*. New York: Oxford University Press, 1984.

Degler, Carl. *The Other South: Southern Dissenters in the Nineteenth Century*. Boston: Northeastern University Press, 1982.

Dewart, Janet, ed. *The State of Black America 1987*. New York: National Urban League, 1987.

Elliot, Jeffrey M., ed. *Black Voices in American Politics*. New York: Harcourt Brace Jovanovich, 1986.

Farmer, James. *Lay Bare the Heart: An Autobiography of the Civil Rights Movement*. New York: New American Library, 1986.

Faw, Bob, and Nancy Skelton. *Thunder in America: The Improbable Presidential Campaign of Jesse Jackson*. Austin: Texas Monthly Press, 1986.

Foner, Eric. *Nothing but Freedom: Emancipation and Its Legacy*. Baton Rouge: Louisiana State University Press, 1983.

Franklin, John Hope, and August Meier, eds. *Black Leaders of the Twentieth Century*. Urbana: University of Illinois Press, 1982.

Franklin, John Hope, and Alfred A. Moss, Jr. *From Slavery to Freedom*, 6th ed. New York: Alfred A. Knopf, 1988.

Franklin, V.P. *Black Self-Determination: A Cultural History of the Faith of Our Fathers*. Westport, Conn.: Lawrence Hill, 1984.

Fredrickson, George. *White Supremacy: A Comparative Study of American and South African History*. New York: Oxford University Press, 1981.

Garrow, David J. *Bearing the Cross: Martin Luther King, Jr., and the Southern Christian Leadership Conference, 1955–1968*. New York: Morrow, 1986.

Garvey, Marcus. *Marcus Garvey: Life and Letters*, Robert A. Hill and Barbara Bair, eds. Berkeley and Los Angeles: University of California Press, 1987.

Genovese, Elizabeth Fox, and Eugene Genovese. *Fruits of Merchant Capital: Slavery and Bourgeois Property in the Rise and Expansion of Capitalism*. New York: Oxford University Press, 1984.

Genovese, Eugene. *From Rebellion to Revolution: Afro-American Slave Revolts in the Making of the Modern World*. New York: Random House, 1981.

————. *In Red and Black: Marxian Explorations in Southern and Afro-American History*, 2d ed. Knoxville: University of Tennessee Press, 1984.

————. *The Political Economy of Slavery*. New York: Random House, 1967.

————. *Roll, Jordan, Roll: The World the Slaves Made*. New York: Random House, 1976.

————. *The World the Slaveholders Made*. New York: Random House, 1971.

Gutman, Herbert. *The Black Family in Slavery and Freedom, 1750–1925*. New York: Random House, 1977.

Hacker, Andrew. "American Apartheid," *New York Review of Books* 34 (December 3, 1987): 26–33.

Harding, Vincent. *There Is a River: The Black Struggle for Freedom in America*. New York: Random House, 1983.

Harlan, Louis B. *Booker T. Washington:* vol. 1, *The Making of a Black Leader* (1972); vol. 2, *The Wizard of Tuskegee* (1985). New York: Oxford University Press.

Harris, Robert L., Jr. *Teaching Afro-American History*. Washington, D.C.: American Historical Association, 1985.

Hill, George A. *Civil Rights Organizations and Leaders: An Annotated Bibliography*. New York: Garland, 1986.

Hine, Darlene Clark, ed. *The State of Afro-American History: Past, Present, and Future*. Baton Rouge: Louisiana State University Press, 1986.

Johnson, Timothy. *Malcolm X: A Comprehensive Annotated Bibliography*. New York: Garland, 1986.

King, Martin Luther, Jr. *A Testament of Hope: The Essential Writings of Martin Luther King, Jr.*, James Washington, ed. New York: Harper & Row, 1986.

Landry, Bart. *The New Black Middle Class*. Berkeley and Los Angeles: University of California Press, 1987.

Levine, Lawrence. *Black Culture and Black Consciousness: Afro-American Folk Thought from Slavery to Freedom*. New York: Oxford University Press, 1978.

Litwack, Leon F. "Trouble in Mind: The Bicentennial and the Afro-American Experience." *Journal of American History* 74 (September 1987): 315–37.

Love, Janice. *The United States Anti-Apartheid Movement: Local Activism in Global Politics*. New York: Praeger, 1985.

Lukas, J. Anthony. *Common Ground: A Turbulent Decade in the Lives of Three American Families*. New York: Alfred A. Knopf, 1985. See James Green's commentary "Searching for 'Common Ground'" in *Radical America* 20 (September-October 1986): 41–60.

MacLeod, Jay. *Ain't No Makin' It: Leveled Aspirations in a Low-Income Neighborhood*. Boulder, Colo.: Westview Press, 1987.

Marable, Manning. *Black American Politics: From the Washington Marches to Jesse Jackson*. New York: Schocken Books, 1985.

————. "Black Studies: Marxism and the Black Intellectual Tradition," in *The Left Academy: Marxist Scholarship on American Campuses*, vol. 3, Bertell Ollman and Edward Vernoff, eds., pp. 35–66. New York: Praeger, 1986.

————. *W.E.B. Du Bois: Black Radical Democrat*. Boston: Twayne Publishers, 1986.

Martin, Waldo, E., Jr. *The Mind of Frederick Douglass*. Chapel Hill: University of North Carolina Press, 1985.

Meier, August, and Elliott Rudwick. *Black History and the Historical Profession, 1915–1980*. Urbana: University of Illinois Press, 1986.

Morris, Aldon D. *The Origins of the Civil Rights Movement: Black Communities Organizing for Change*. New York: Free Press, 1984.

Murray, Charles. *Losing Ground: American Social Policy, 1950–1980*. New York: Basic Books, 1984.

Naison, Mark. *Communists in Harlem during the Depression*. Urbana: University of Illinois Press, 1983.

Nalty, Bernard C. *Strength for the Fight: A History of Black Americans in the Military*. New York: Free Press, 1986.

Nash, Gary. *Red, White, and Black: The People of Early America*, 2d ed. Englewood Cliffs, N.J.: Prentice-Hall, 1982.

Oates, Stephen. *The Fires of Jubilee: Nat Turner's Fierce Rebellion*. New York: New American Library, 1983.

————. *To Purge This Land with Blood: A Biography of John Brown*, 2d ed. Amherst: University of Massachusetts Press, 1984.

Painter, Nell Irvin. *The Narrative of the Life of Hosea Hudson: His Life as a Negro Communist in the South*. Cambridge: Harvard University Press, 1979.

Patterson, James T. *America's Struggle against Poverty, 1900–1985*, rev. ed. Cambridge: Harvard University Press, 1986.

Pinkney, Alphonso. *Black Americans*, 3d ed. Englewood Cliffs, N.J.: Prentice-Hall, 1987.

Quarles, Benjamin. *Black Mosaic: Essays in Afro-American History and Historiography*. Amherst: University of Massachusetts Press, 1988.

————. *The Myth of Black Progress*. New York: Cambridge University Press, 1986.

Rabinowitz, Howard N. "Race, Ethnicity and Cultural Pluralism in American History," in *Ordinary People and Everyday Life: Perspectives on the New Social History*, James B. Gardner and George Rollie Adams, eds., pp. 23–49. Nashville, Tenn.: American Association for State and Local History, 1983.

Reed, Adolph L., Jr. *The Jesse Jackson Phenomenon: The Crisis of Purpose in Afro-American Politics*. New Haven, Conn.: Yale University Press, 1986.

Schuman, Howard, Charlotte Steeh, and Lawrence Bobo. *Racial Attitudes in America: Trends and Interpretations*. Cambridge: Harvard University Press, 1985.

Shapiro, Herbert. *White Violence and Black Response: From Reconstruction to Montgomery*. Amherst: University of Massachusetts Press, 1988.

Sollors, Weiner. *Beyond Ethnicity: Consent and Descent in American Culture*. New York: Oxford University Press, 1986.

Sowell, Thomas. *Ethnic America: A History*. New York: Basic Books, 1981.

Stein, Judith. *The World of Marcus Garvey: Race and Class in Modern Society*. Baton Rouge: Louisiana State University Press, 1986.

Stewart, Jeffrey C., and Fath Davis Ruffins, "A Faithful Witness: Afro-American Public History in Historical Perspective, 1828–1984," in *Presenting the Past: Essays on History and the Public*, Susan Porter Benson, Stephen Brier, and

Roy Rosenzweig, eds., pp. 307–36. Philadelphia: Temple University Press, 1986.

Stuckey, Sterling. *Slave Culture: Nationalist Theory and the Foundations of Black America*. New York: Oxford University Press, 1987.

Takaki, Ronald, ed. *From Different Shores: Perspectives on Race and Ethnicity in America*. Berkeley and Los Angeles: University of California Press, 1987.

Wilkins, Roger. *A Man's Life: An Autobiography*. New York: Simon & Schuster, 1982.

Wilkins, Roy. *Standing Fast: The Autobiography of Roy Wilkins*. New York: Viking, 1982.

Wilson, William Julius. *The Truly Disadvantaged: The Inner City, the Underclass and Public Policy*. Chicago: University of Chicago Press, 1987.

Wolters, Raymond. *The Burden of Brown: Thirty Years of School Desegregation*. Knoxville: University of Tennessee Press, 1984. For a critical analysis by David Garrow, see "Segregation's Legacy," *Reviews in American History*, 13 (September 1985): 428–32.

Organizations and Publications

Requests for information should be accompanied by a stamped, self-addressed envelope.

American Visions: The Magazine of Afro-American Culture, P.O. Box 53129, Boulder, Colo. 80322-3129

Association for the Study of Afro-American Life and History, 1407 14th St., N.W., Washington, D.C. 20005

Black Enterprise, P.O. Box 3011, Harlan, Iowa 51593-2102

Black Scholar, P.O. Box 2869, Oakland, Calif. 94609

Congressional Black Caucus, H2-344 Annex 2, Washington, D.C. 20515

Ebony, 820 S. Michigan Ave., Chicago, Ill. 60605

Equal Employment Opportunity Commission, 2401 E St., N.W., Washington, D.C. 20506

Journal of Black Studies, Sage Publications, Inc., 2111 W. Hillcrest Drive, Newbury Park, Calif. 91320

Muslim Journal, 7801 S. Cottage Grove, Chicago, Ill. 60619 (major influence: Wallace Muhammad)

NAACP Legal Defense and Educational Fund, 99 Hudson St., Suite 1600, New York, N.Y. 10013

National Association for the Advancement of Colored People, 4805 Mt. Hope Drive, Baltimore, Md. 21215

National Black Caucus of State Legislators, 206 Hall of States Building, 444 N. Capitol, Washington, D.C. 20001

National Caucus and Center on the Black Aged, Inc., 1424 K St., N.W. Suite 500, Washington, D.C. 20005

National Council of Negro Women, 701 N. Fairfax St., Alexandria, Va. 22314

National Urban League, 500 E. 62nd St., New York, N.Y. 10021

Nation of Islam, 734 West 79th St., Chicago, Ill. 60620 (major influence: Louis Farrakhan)

PUSH (People United to Serve Humanity), 930 E. 50th St., Chicago, Ill. 60615

Rainbow Lobby, 236 Massachusetts Ave., N.E., Rm. 409, Washington, D.C. 20002

Southern Christian Leadership Conference, 334 Auburn Ave., N.E., Atlanta, Ga. 30312

Southern Exposure, P.O. Box 531, Durham, N.C. 27702

Southern Poverty Law Center, 400 Washington Ave., Montgomery, Ala. 36195

TransAfrica, 545 8th St., S.E., Washington, D.C. 20003

United Black Fund of America, 1012 14th St., N.W., Suite 300, Washington, D.C. 20005

United Negro College Fund, Inc., 500 E. 62nd St., New York, N.Y. 10021

U.S. Commission on Civil Rights, 1121 Vermont Ave., N.W., Washington, D.C. 20425

O, rise, shine for Thy Light is a' com-ing.
(Traditional.)

5

Why Don't They Speak English Like Everyone Else?

There were about 19 million people in the United States who had Spanish last names in 1987. About 11 million of these people spoke Spanish. Much of what the Anglo majority thinks that it knows about this group is inaccurate.

Cultural and racial stereotypes that have been common include the images of banditos in sombreros; Latin lovers strumming guitars to señoritas on balconies; lazy peasants dozing through long siestas; "greasers," "wetbacks," and "spics"; "superstitious Catholics"; padres and fatalistic peons working at a grand hacienda (a kind of Great White House, like the plantation for blacks); and garishly dressed bullfighters performing before an arena of frenzied enthusiasts. It is "common knowledge" that they are quick-tempered—when they are not placidly bovine.

The facts do not fit these cartoons. The Spanish-surnamed population, the second largest minority in the United States after blacks, is extremely diverse. There are Mexican-Americans (60 percent), Puerto Ricans (14 percent), Cubans (6 percent), Filipinos, Salvadorans, and many others. It is difficult to find a single name for this spectrum of people. "Hispanic" is not exact because of Indian and African intermixture. "Latino" would not cover Filipinos. Even for specific groups, such as those of Mexican origin, there is controversy about an overall name, with some favoring "Chicano," and others "Mexican American" or Mexican.

Large numbers of Spanish-surnamed people are found in many regions of the United States. Although Los Angeles may be the second largest Mexican town after Mexico City, New York has the third largest Latino population in the world, Miami is one of the economic and cultural capitals of Latin America, and there are more Hispanics in Illinois than in all of New Mexico and Arizona. In some areas, they are majorities, and, in such places, it is possible to live one's entire life in Spanish.

Since the 1960s, there has been talk that these people are a sleeping giant, an emerging minority, or an awakening giant. We can judge the validity of these characterizations by focusing on the largest groups, Mexican Americans and Puerto Ricans. While the facts will discredit any images of a giant or a unified minority, each group does have growing power and there are a few shared interests among most Spanish-speaking people.

A SHIFTING BORDER WITH MEXICO

Mexicans, like Indians, blacks, and Puerto Ricans, were incorporated into the United States by conquest. When Mexico overthrew Spanish rule in 1821, ending three centuries of foreign domination, it encouraged U.S. immigrants to fill its northern provinces. The Mexican government allowed Stephen Austin to bring 300 U.S. families into that area in 1822. The male head of each family received a generous grant of land. The settlers were required only to become citizens of Mexico and to adopt the Catholic religion.

While the Anglos were hungry for land, most learned only a few words of Spanish, were rebellious, and frequently expressed contempt for the darker-skinned Mexicans. The American settlers were annoyed when Mexico abolished slavery in 1830; some responded by "freeing" their slaves while requiring them to sign lifetime work contracts.

There were about 30,000 Americans in northern Mexico by 1835. The central government doubted their loyalty as Mexican citizens. When further immigration was cut off, the Americans overthrew the legal state in their region and declared the independent Lone Star Republic. Some of this has entered the mythology of American history, such as the battle of the Alamo, where rather dubious adventurers, like Davy Crockett and onetime slave-runner James Bowie, have been metamorphosed into national heroes.

When the Lone Star Republic asked to be annexed to the United States in 1838, many white Southerners were delighted by the prospect of cotton fields tilled by black slaves. Many Northerners, however, feared that Texas could be divided into as many as nine to ten slave states the size of Massachusetts. They blocked the admission of Texas. A compromise was reached when a free area, Oregon, was legally acquired in 1845. Texas was then occupied in 1846.

Mexico angrily broke off diplomatic relations, reinforced its army, and refused to recognize the new border. When the U.S. president, James Polk, sent 4,000 troops into the disputed area and they were fired upon, he announced that Mexico had aggressively "invaded our territory and shed American blood on American soil."

Polk sent orders to U.S. naval officers in the Pacific to seize the ports of California in the event of war, and he dispatched a heavily armed "scientific expedition" to California by land. Although most Americans were unaware of these moves, some Northerners suspected that the slaveowners wanted new territory. Abraham Lincoln, who was then a first-term representative from Illinois, introduced a resolution in the House that urged the president to identify the exact spot where American blood had been spilled. This "spot resolution" did not pass. It would have proven that the war began on what were commonly considered Mexican lands.

The war was a disaster for the Mexican armies, which were badly organized, badly led, and badly equipped. Texas was quickly subdued, California was declared the Bear Flag Republic, and Mexico City was captured in mid-September 1847.

While some Americans wanted to absorb all of Mexico, most were opposed. Many Northerners objected to an increase in southern territories. Some people feared that guerrilla warfare would continue if such annexation took place. Others doubted that white America would benefit racially. As Senator John C. Calhoun complained, "To incorporate Mexico would be the very first instance . . . of incorporating an Indian race; for more than half of the Mexicans are Indians, and the other is composed chiefly of mixed races. I protest against such a union as that! Ours, sir, is the government of a white race."

When the Treaty of Guadalupe Hidalgo was signed in February 1848, Mexico received $15,000,000 for loss of lands and $3,200,000 to settle various debts, whereas the United States took 40 percent of the territory of Mexico, an area larger than all of France, Italy, and Spain. It would eventually become Nevada, Arizona, California, Texas, New Mexico, and Utah, along with parts of Colorado and Wyoming. The 80,000 Mexicans who lived on these lands were guaranteed that, even if they did not become U.S. citizens, their religious liberty and property rights would be protected.

Following the conquest, these agreements were no more honored than were white America's treaties with the Indians. White Americans saw themselves as a superior people, and many felt that military victory was a sign from heaven that the United States was destined to conquer the continent. One popular image was the American buffalo getting its salt from either

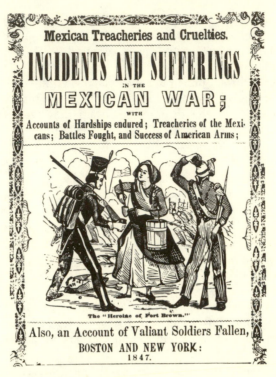

Blaming the victim.

ocean and finding its pasture throughout the middle of the nation. A more aggressive symbol was the American eagle with its wings stretched from coast to coast, its beak in Canada and its talons gripping Mexico.

Many bled from those claws. The *californios, tejanos,* and *nuevo méjicanos* were required to verify their land titles by a lengthy and expensive process that could be abused by the Anglos. In New Mexico, the Anglo governor used most of the state archives for wrapping paper, and many duplicates in Guadalajara mysteriously disappeared. In California, one-fourth of Mexican claims were invalidated under the Land Law of 1851, and administrative and legal costs during the average case of seventeen years forced the sale of other property.

Further efforts were made to prevent Mexicans from voting by limiting the ballot to whites. Mexicans were hindered from mining by the Foreign Miner's Tax, in 1850. White America wanted Mexicans primarily in one role: cheap labor. Mexicans became strangers in their own land.

Much of the Southwest was built with their labor. They planted, hoed, and harvested crops. They raised cattle and sheep. They loaded cargo on the docks of America's new Pacific ports. They laid track for the railroads. They worked in the mines. They usually made money for others.

PLUCKED:
THE MEXICAN·EAGLE BEFORE THE WAR!   OR,   THE MEXICAN EAGLE AFTER THE WAR!

Ridiculing the victim.

Although some employers posted signs that declared "Only White Labor Employed" or "No Niggers, Mexicans, or Dogs," the use of Mexican labor grew after the immigration laws excluded Chinese (1887) and Japanese (1907). Many Mexicans fled into the United States during the turbulent decade that followed the revolution of 1910. Their labor was cheap, non-unionized, and easily exploited. If they were illegal immigrants, it was a simple matter to intimidate them, or to call the immigration authorities to take them away before payday. They were kept divided, if necessary, by beatings, guards, local sheriffs, strikebreakers, arrests, deportations, "criminal syndicalism laws" (against labor organizing), and the pervasive powers of such large associations of growers as the United Farmers of the Pacific Coast, founded in 1936.

Mexican workers were imported when they were needed, such as during World War I, World War II, and the Korean War. The U.S. government even sponsored the importation of *braceros* (hired hands) from 1948 to 1964, bringing in about 4,500,000 "legal" workers. In addition to these people, most of whom returned to Mexico after their jobs were completed, employers continued to use illegal immigrants, since it was not a crime for them to do so. Illegals were cheaper and more readily controlled. In 1954 alone, the U.S. government rounded up and deported over 1 million such workers.

Many native Mexicans still find work in the United States attractive because of the economic problems of their own country. Millions of Mexicans and Mexican-Americans work as migratory farm laborers—which some have called rented slaves—from Texas to North Dakota, and from California to Maryland's Eastern Shore. Many more work in garment industries, restaurants, hotels, factories, and other urban occupations.

Some responses to exploitation have been violent, such as the nineteenth-century banditry of Joaquín Murieta in California and Juan Cortina in Texas, or the vigilante justice of La Mano Negra in New Mexico during the 1880s.

The dominant programs of Mexican-American groups, however, have been structured around reform and assimilation. This moderation was expressed by two early groups: the League of United Latin American Citizens (LULAC), founded in 1929, and the American GI Forum of the United States, founded in 1948. LULAC adopted English as its official language, repudiated any "radical and violent demonstrations," and announced that its highest goal was "to develop with members of our race the best, purest and most perfect type of true and loyal citizens of the United States." Although its original constitution declared "a respectful reverence for our social ori-

A fraudulent 1853 poster for an exhibit that claimed to display the severed head of Murieta. The entrance fee was $1.

"FOLLOW THE LULAC BANNER
TO BETTER CITIZENSHIP"

gins of which we are proud," LULAC did not promote cultural pluralism or
nationalism. Rather, it encouraged voter registration and financed legal challenges to educational segregation and job discrimination.

Some GI's felt that LULAC did not serve their particular needs. In 1948,
when the Texas city of Corpus Christi refused to bury a Mexican GI in a
"whites only" cemetary, Mexicans in the U.S. military and Mexican veterans
established an organization to insure their civil rights. The American GI
Forum tried to speak for over 300,000 Mexicans who served in the U.S.
forces during World War II, and to inspire them to participate in GI programs for education, loans, training, and jobs.

However, neither LULAC nor the GI Forum attempted to organize Mexican labor in the cities or in the countryside. Although there were efforts by
previous groups, such as the Industrial Workers of the World, these efforts
had been defeated. By the 1960s some people became dissatisfied enough
with the older moderate groups to begin their own independent projects.
The general environment was more encouraging; this was the era of civil
rights struggles, the War on Poverty, the Office of Economic Opportunity,
the Great Society, antiwar organizing, and heightened social and political
consciousness among significant sections of the U.S. public. César Chavez
left the Community Service Organization to form the National Farmworkers
Association in 1962. His combination of strikes, picketing, and boycotts,
coming fortuitously at the end of the *bracero* program that had been useful
for strikebreaking and union-busting, led to the first contracts with growers
in 1968. Although the National Labor Relations Act did not cover farm-

workers and employers were not obligated to recognize an elected bargain-
ing agent, Chavez firmly established his organization, now called the United
Farm Workers. Still, many problems continue: Most farm labor is unorganized (especially in the East and Midwest), child labor is heavily used,
dangerous pesticides have not been eliminated, unions such as the Team-
sters have sought to sign overly generous "sweetheart" contracts with major
growers, and mechanization on huge corporate "factory farms" eventually
will reduce the number of agricultural jobs.

Chavez's red flag with the black Aztec eagle was symbolic of a militancy
that influenced older, civil rights groups and stimulated the creation of new
ones. Moderates in the 1960s were likely to be characterized as *"vendidos"*
(sell-outs), coconuts (brown on the outside, but white on the inside), and *"tío
tacos"* (Uncle Tacos, like Uncle Toms). New heroes arose to call themselves
the sons of Zapata and to proclaim Brown Power. These "chieftains" included Reies López Tijerina, José Angel Gutiérrez, and Rodolfo "Corky"
Gonzales. Most of them, like the young Indian leaders of that period, called
for the return of ancestral lands, and the renewal of their distinctive culture.

Tijerina, for example, established the Alianza Federal de Mercedes
(Federal Alliance of Land Grants) in 1963. A fiery Pentecostal minister, he
urged his people to claim their ancient lands in New Mexico that had been
granted by Spanish and Mexican laws, protected by the Treaty of Guadalupe
Hidalgo, and taken fraudulently by the Anglos. In 1967, Tijerina and forty
armed *aliancistas* seized the Tierra Amarilla courthouse in northern New
Mexico. They claimed that vast territories, including the Kit Carson National Park, should be incorporated into a Republic of San Joaquín del Rio de
Chama. This episode publicized Chicano claims to millions of acres of land in
central and northern New Mexico. Although Tijerina and nine associates
were tried for kidnapping, assault on a county jail, and false imprisonment,
they defended their right to make "citizens' arrests" of authorities since, in
land grant areas, the *alianza* should be the law, not the state. A jury found
that Tijerina and his followers were not guilty on all three charges. Whether
Tijerina was a Don Quixote, or really "el Tigre," his vision had some historical merit, and the issues will surface again.

Gonzalez's Crusade for Justice began in Denver in 1965, and La Raza
Unida (the United People) party was formed in 1969. Although both had a
strongly nationalist and separatist character, even talking of a República de
Aztlán that would cover Texas, Colorado, New Mexico, Arizona, and California, they demonstrated the potential for bloc voting and interest group
politics, and they vigorously protested anti-Mexican prejudice. Some critics
grumbled that these Chicanos were biting the hand that fed them, but
others replied, "I bite it because it feeds me slop." Even though such groups
were small, they were potentially powerful. Peter Camejo, a Chicano militant, ominously noted in the 1970s,

Right: pre–World War I graphic from the Industrial Workers of the World;
left, and below: from the United Farm Workers.

It is true that we are a minority, but the Democratic Party in California or Texas can only win if we vote for it. Think of that. We have the potential to wipe it off the face of the map as a political institution. And on a national scale, in alliance with black people, we *could* have the power to make it impossible for the Democratic Party to win another election in this country.

Most Chicano groups now consider this stance extremist, and groups like La Raza Unida have declined in the 1980s. The largest organizations that speak for the 9 million or more Chicanos focus on issues of cultural identity, civil rights, and economics.

Culture is important because it is a basic element of our identity, whether positive or negative. Racial prejudice, for example, is seldom justified today by biology ("they" are "inferior people"), but by cultural arguments ("they" have an inferior, primitive, submissive culture).

The school is a vital institution for transmitting dominant ideas. In the past, the Spanish language was forbidden, and there were often "Spanish monitors" who, if they caught students speaking Spanish, could impose fines, detention, or paddling. (One educator justified this by saying, "A gentle whack or two does them good.") Anglicized education was a way of putting young Chicanos in a cultural prison, de-educating them of one language, and using a new language as a form of social control.

Spanish was common in the Southwest for centuries before English. It is not an inferior language, nor is English spoken with a Spanish accent a sign of a person's backwardness. If Mayor Koch of New York can have his Bronx nasal twang, Ted Kennedy his Bostonese, and Southerners their drawl, why should Chicanos speak a television newscaster type of English?

It has been asserted that if Spanish receives legal recognition, ranging from simple use in street signs and official notices to elevation as the second language of the United States, the United States may be threatened by a Hispanic Quebec that secedes from the rest of the country. A less disturbing prophecy was offered by Theodore Roosevelt. He predicted that the United States would become a "polyglot boarding house" if non-English languages were allowed or encouraged. If one accepts this view it would be logical for society to make a determined effort, such as placing tutors in the schools, to promote linguistic assimilation. Bilingualism, on the other hand, might create sensitivity among all Americans to other cultures, along with fostering a genuine sense of Pan-Americanism.

Whether or not the language of instruction is Spanish, Chicano groups often insist upon a recognition of cultural assumptions in educational materials. A child's education may begin with an IQ test based upon Anglo experiences, resulting in the immediate labeling of that child as mentally deficient. His or her schoolbooks are likely, from the earliest years, to be full of blond and blue-eyed strangers. Mexican contributions to the building of this country are seldom mentioned, and if they are, it is frequently implied that such Mexicans are white Spaniards, rather than people of mixed Indian, African, and Spanish origins.

Two of the mottoes of a large demonstration against the cultural chauvinism of the Los Angeles school system in 1968 are still relevant: "Education, not Eradication" and "Education, not Contempt." Biases in the schools, as in the media, not only degrade those who are stereotyped or dismissed, but cheapen the consciousness of all. The Supreme Court recognized that the language of instruction in the public schools may promote discrimination. The Court's landmark ruling in the case of *Lau v. Nichols* in 1974 did not require bilingual instruction in schools with diverse populations, but it did require special attention for people with special language problems.

In some urban areas, such as New York City, Los Angeles, and Washington, D.C., classrooms can be miniature Ellis Islands. Programs for these students may provoke a backlash from citizens who favor only English. In a 1986 vote in California, 74 percent urged that English be made the official language of the state, and that any effort to diminish its use be prohibited. By 1988, thirteen states had declared English their official language and thirty-three other states were considering such proposals. These laws may violate federal court rulings and statutes, along with the common feeling that it is not fair to tell a frightened child in an alien environment to "sink or swim." By the late 1980s, Spanish-speaking children were a majority of the first grade students in Houston and Los Angeles, and almost 80 percent in San Antonio. Educational and social problems are such that 45 percent of Hispanics drop out past the ninth grade in Texas (compared to 34 percent for blacks and 27 percent for non-Hispanic whites), 47 percent drop out in Illinois (versus 35 percent for blacks and 17 percent for whites), and 62 percent drop out in New York state (versus 53 percent for blacks and 30 percent for whites). This wasted human potential justifies special programs, such as federal spending of $150 million for bilingual education in 1987.

A second major issue for modern Chicano organizations has been social and political organization for the economic improvement of their people. Organized Chicanos are now courted by politicians, treated more fairly in government programs, and better acknowledged by business. The millions of illegal aliens who remain a subclass have been aided by some court rulings, such as one that forbids denial of public schooling to their children. There have been some positive changes in laws, such as an amnesty program for as many as 4 million that began in 1987. These people, many of whom are Chicano, had been a significant part of America's "Third World" of low-paid labor. President Reagan asserted that they could now "come into the sunlight." Meanwhile, employers are expected to ask for residency documents and can be fined $2,000 to $10,000 for each illegal alien that they employ. This was the biggest revision of immigration law in two decades. Overall, there has been enough progress for these Mexican Americans, and for others, to feel some hope for the future.

WHO CONTROLS PUERTO RICO?

Another large group of Spanish-speaking people, Puerto Ricans, have a complicated future. There are fundamental divisions among the 2 million Puerto Ricans on the mainland and the over 3 million in Puerto Rico. Should their island homeland become the fifty-first state, an independent country, or should it retain its ambiguous condition as a commonwealth? What will be the status of Puerto Ricans in the continental United States?

The United States acquired Puerto Rico by military conquest during the Spanish-American War in 1898. Although the war began with the announced goal of freeing oppressed Cuba from its Spanish tyrants, American newspapers soon reported naval battles in the Philippines, half a world away, and fighting in other locations closer to home. When the war ended, the United States was an international power with economic, political, and military influence in areas formerly controlled by Spain. Cuba was officially independent but remained an economic satellite until the revolution in 1960 that brought in the government of Fidel Castro. There is still a U.S. military base in Communist Cuba, at Guantánamo.

The Philippines were freed later, in 1946, but the United States received military bases and special privileges for U.S. citizens and businesses. Our government has given money and weapons to undemocratic elements to protect these privileges, such as generous U.S. support for the dictator Ferdinand Marcos until the rigged election of 1986 made it too embarrassing to retain him as a client. Clark Air Base and the naval center at Subic Bay are enormous U.S. military facilities, making the U.S. government the third largest employer of Filipinos within their own country, and U.S. corporations own central elements of the Filipino economy. By the end of 1987 U.S. military aid had doubled since the departure of Marcos.

Likewise, Puerto Rico has been a semicolony for all of this century. When a civilian government was installed in 1900, the governor, the cabinet, and most of the legislature were appointed by the U.S. president. In 1917 the United States gave Puerto Ricans some rights, such as the power to elect the Executive Council but not the governor or the lower house of the congress. In return for this, military service was imposed on Puerto Rican youth. In 1948 Puerto Ricans were allowed to elect their governor, and in 1953 Puerto Rico ceased to be a territory and was proclaimed a commonwealth. This is a unique rank within the American system. It stands above a territory, but below the powers of a state. Under the commonwealth arrangement, Puerto Rico controls most internal matters, but the U.S. government directs foreign relations, currency, external trade, and the military draft.

Puerto Rican unrest was the cause for many changes. Imagine how we would react if a foreign power invaded and occupied our country. How would we respond:

UNITED STATES

CUBA

MEXICO

PUERTO
RICO

SANTO
DOMINGO

WELL, I HARDLY KNOW WHICH TO TAKE FIRST!

—if the invaders had a language different from ours and required that it be used in important proceedings like federal court hearings;

—if the invaders used over 12 percent of the land for military forces, paid no rent, and used some land for shelling practice;

—if the invaders had a history unlike the four centuries of our own, and made our children study primarily their history and pledge allegiance to their flag;

—if the invaders drafted our young people to fight in distant wars, even as far away as Vietnam;

—if the businesses of the invaders were almost tax-free, while our local businesses struggled to survive;

—if the invaders often felt that we were "mongrels" because we were racially and culturally different from them;

—if the invaders reduced the local rights that we had gained earlier to control our own currency, trade agreements, foreign policies and media; and

—if the invaders wanted to use us primarily as cheap labor.

This would be as deeply offensive to us as it is to many Puerto Ricans.

Some people respond that Puerto Ricans are natural welfare bums and that "we" would be better off without them. Someone using this argument might point to the over $3 billion a year that the U.S. government spends in Puerto Rico (with over one-half of the population receiving food stamps) and welfare problems in New York City. But if Puerto Rico is such a burden, why has the United States held on to it for almost nine decades?

Besides the military value of the island, it has been an American success story for business. Especially after 1948, with the initiation of Operation Bootstrap, there were efforts to profit from Puerto Rico and to present it as a showcase of Caribbean democracy.

Its first major asset has been its people. Puerto Rico has one of the highest population densities in the world, on territory that is no larger than Long Island. In 1898 most people lived by agriculture, with 93 percent of all farms being owned and occupied by Puerto Ricans. Today, only 6 percent of labor is in farming. Urban labor is readily available to assemble raw materials for export.

Of course, this is not the only incentive for business to locate in Puerto Rico. The same human assets are found in Taiwan, Hong Kong, the Dominican Republic, and Mexico. Because Puerto Rico is a U.S. possession, however, U.S. businesses are not haunted by the spectres of nationalization and government instability.

Furthermore, the Puerto Rican government has offered "sugar cubes" of tax incentives to lure $24 billion of mainland investment. For years, Puerto Rico has been an investment paradise. U.S. companies were free of all federal taxes, received buildings at low costs or low rent in forty-six industrial parks, got land and services for small sums, and were given a 90 percent

break on local taxes for five years, followed by small tax increases over the next twenty years. If profits were sent to the mainland, there was a slight tax, but this did not prevent 90 percent of such profits from being exported, totaling $2.5 billion a year in the early 1980s. In addition, Puerto Rico has become the ninth largest customer of the United States, buying $6 billion in goods and services during 1983 and owing $7 billion to mainland banks. The overall result is that some jobs have been created, there is little capital accumulation in Puerto Rico, and there are comfortable profits for a few. This system has been called welfare for the rich. Just as the general taxpayer bears the burden of supporting those on relief, the general taxpayer underwrites these corporate free-loaders.

Some Puerto Ricans have benefited from this arrangement. Puerto Rico is one of the twenty most industrialized areas in the world, and there are significant managerial and technical classes. Most of these middle- and upper-class people are "Americanophiles." The average income is the highest in Latin America, although it is only one-half the level of the most squalid mainland state, Mississippi. It is also true that the cost of living is higher because most food is imported. Because of the emphasis on industry, Puerto Rico does not feed itself, despite its rich soil and an ideal climate.

This industrialization has displaced more people from agriculture than it has created jobs. This contributes to an unemployment rate that is three times higher than that of the mainland, and three of every five families fall below the official poverty line.

Large numbers of these people escape to the mainland with hopes of a better life. From 1899 to 1944, there were 75,000; from 1944 to 1960, as many as 1 million. Because air and ship fares are cheaper between San Juan and New York than between San Juan and Miami (which is much closer), the largest community was established in New York, which now has more Puerto Ricans than San Juan. Since they are legally U.S. citizens, there are no barriers to their settling in New York, Chicago, Philadelphia, or elsewhere in the United States. People are one of the biggest exports of Puerto Rico.

It is sometimes said, usually by those who have never lived in poverty, that Puerto Ricans come here to get on welfare. In fact, most Puerto Ricans are a boon to business, working as maids, orderlies, janitors, attendants, busboys, cleaners, dishwashers, migrant farm labor, seamen, construction help, and garment labor. For most of them, America has not been a pot of gold.

Immigrants in the past had similar problems, but modern society makes success more elusive. There are fewer unskilled or semiskilled jobs at which to begin working; large corporations compete with little businesses like grocery stores; contemporary urban life is more complex; racial prejudice hinders nonwhite immigrants; and Puerto Ricans, as U.S. citizens, have been less willing to abandon their old culture completely in order to be "naturalized." A poisonous world of poverty has been the result. For someone born into a Puerto Rican ghetto, it is too often a school for unemployment, alcoholism, drug addiction, and family problems. Education, one possible avenue of improvement, is conducted generally in English. It is not surprising that Puerto Ricans have the highest drop-out, or push-out, rate in the school system of New York City. Those who fail to complete high school will have a future as bleak as that of their parents. Only 1 percent of all Puerto Ricans have the training and the resources to attend college.

Since the 1960s, various groups have sought to organize mainland Puerto Ricans to gain bilingual education, vocational training, improved housing, equal legal treatment, and political influence. Such group politics has aroused the opposition of other racial or ethnic groups, such as blacks, Chicanos, and poor whites, on the grounds that the more one group gets, the less there will be for others. Coalitions based upon common interests have been rare.

Key sectors within Puerto Rico agree that there will be changes in the future, but they differ on the nature of those changes.

The Partido Popular Democrático (PPD) is the largest party favoring continuance of the commonwealth status, although with modifications. The PPD, which was in power for over three decades, wants increased local rights under its "New Thesis" program. It advocates the right to impose tariffs on other Caribbean imports, controls on immigration from other areas of the region, lower minimum wages than the mainland, independent Puerto Rican membership in some international cultural and technical groups, and a larger political voice in Washington (at present, Puerto Rico has one "resident commissioner" who has no vote in Congress). This is

| PARTIDO POPULAR DEMOCRATICO | PARTIDO NUEVO PROGRESISTA | PARTIDO INDEPENDENTISTA PUERTORRIQUEÑO | PARTIDO SOCIALISTA PUERTORRIQUEÑO |

From a sample ballot in the *San Juan Star*.

sometimes called the "perfecting" or the "maturation" of the commonwealth.

Many voters abandoned this position in the 1970s and surged toward statehood. Many felt that the commonwealth was an inferior situation that was not a middle road to freedom but a legally ambiguous swamp. The Partido Nuevo Progresista (PNP) elected a governor in 1980 on a pro-statehood position. As the fifty-first state, Puerto Rico might receive greater mainland investment and jobs, would be eligible for all federal spending programs, and would have two senators and seven representatives to speak for it in Congress. Supporters of statehood claimed that, after a transitional period, Puerto Rico would no longer be a dependency of the United States, but a "dignified" state of the union.

Many in Puerto Rico and in the United States are fearful that the reality would be a Spanish-speaking beggar state where U.S. business would no longer have special federal privileges. The mirage of Puerto Rican prosperity (limited as it already is) might vanish. Would many Puerto Ricans be willing to make sacrifices for the dignity of statehood? It is significant that the PNP did not procede with its earlier plans for a popular vote on the issue of statehood.

Some critics of statehood identify it with 100 percent Americanism, which they reject. Instead, they urge the creation of the Republic of Puerto Rico, which would join the other Caribbean ministates. Independence, they say, would be a blessing for U.S. taxpayers, and, under it, Puerto Rico would be able to make favorable trade agreements, even if it would probably lose free access to U.S. markets.

The two major groups of *independentistas* have recently polled less than 10 percent of the vote and are not on good terms with each other. The Partido Independentista Puertorriqueño essentially represents the liberal middle classes and favors a moderate socialism that is similar to that of Sweden. While it seeks independence, it promotes continued economic ties to the United States.

Far more radical is the Partido Socialista Puertorriqueño (PSP) that was established in 1972 from the Movimiento pro Independencia. PSP has adopted a Marxist-Leninist ideology and a party structure of "democratic centralism" (the Soviet political model). It sought to plead its case before the United Nations, and encouraged "solidarity committees" in the United States to build support for Puerto Rican independence. Its goal is a Cuban-style transformation of the island.

There is also one tiny but renowned grouplet that has resorted to nonelectoral means to achieve independence: the Armed Forces of National Liberation for Puerto Rico (FALN), begun in 1974. The newspapers will mention it now and then when it bombs some "imperialist agency," such as a bank. This violence is not new. In 1950 some *independentistas* began an armed uprising that became known as the Nationalist Revolution of 1950. In that same year, two nationalists tried to murder President Harry S. Truman in Blair House, where he was then living. In 1954 nationalists shot five representatives in the U.S. Congress.

The U.S. government has often pointed to the extra-legal tactics of a few Puerto Ricans to justify its own illegal harassment of Puerto Rican critics. According to a 1975 congressional investigation, the FBI had sent anonymous mailings accusing people of the fraudulent use of funds, inspected tax and bank records, made illegal wiretaps, opened mail, and used U.S. tax money to pay for spies.

Despite the fears of some U.S. officials, Puerto Rico is unlikely to become a second Cuba. An internationally supervised vote probably would demonstrate that a large majority favors ties to the United States while maintaining the Spanish language. There are few practical options to integration with mainland markets. An attempt at a Caribbean Common Market (CARICOM) was an embarassing failure because of political and economic rivalries among the small nations in the region. Trade ties to Cuba or other socialist nations would provoke U.S. retaliation. Talk of statehood or of sovereignty is both stirring and cheap. Neither Puerto Rican business interests nor the general public of the island seems willing to pay the price of basic change.

The status of Puerto Ricans and Chicanos, along with that of other Spanish-speaking minorities within the United States, is likely to remain uncertain. Their growing numbers, along with the reluctance of the Anglo majority to plan seriously for a multicultural, multilingual, and multiracial society,

insures resentment and controversy. What is a realistic expectation of our future together? Should our goal be a melting pot that produces a standard brand American? Or does the immigrant history of the United States, along with the continuing tide of immigrants, guarantee that we will be, happily or not, a "rainbow people"?

SOURCES OF FURTHER INFORMATION

Books and Articles

Abalos, David T. *Latinos in the United States: The Sacred and the Political.* Notre Dame, Ind.: University of Notre Dame Press, 1986.

Acosta-Belen, Edna, ed. *The Puerto Rican Woman: Perspective on Culture, History and Society,* 2d ed. New York: Praeger, 1986.

Acuña, Rodolfo. *Occupied America: A History of Chicanos,* 3d ed. New York: Harper & Row, 1988.

Bloomfield, Richard J. *Puerto Rico: The Search for a National Policy.* Boulder, Colo.: Westview Press, 1985.

Bonilla, Frank, Ricardo Campos, and Juan Flores. "Puerto Rican Studies: Promptings for the Academy and the Left," in *The Left Academy: Marxist Scholarship on American Campuses,* Vol. 3, Bertell Ollman and Edward Vernoff, eds., pp. 67–102. New York: Praeger, 1986.

Browning, Rufus, P., Dale Rogers Marshall, and David H. Tabb. *Protest Is Not Enough: The Struggle of Blacks and Hispanics for Equality in Urban Politics.* Berkeley and Los Angeles: University of California Press, 1984.

Caballero, Cesar. *Chicano Organizations Directory.* New York: Neal-Schuman, 1985.

Cafferty, Pastora San Juan, and William McReady, eds. *Hispanics in the United States: A New Social Agenda.* New Brunswick, N.J.: Transaction Books, 1985.

Camarillo, Albert, ed. *Latinos in the United States: A Historical Bibliography.* Santa Barbara, Calif.: ABC-Clio Press, 1986.

Carr, Raymond. *Puerto Rico: A Colonial Experiment.* New York: Random House, 1984.

Carrion, Arturo Morales. *Puerto Rico: A Political and Cultural History.* New York: Norton, 1984.

Cevallos, Elena. *Puerto Rico.* Santa Barbara, Calif.: ABC-Clio Press, 1985.

Chávez, John R. *The Lost Land: The Chicano Image of the Southwest.* Albuquerque: University of New Mexico Press, 1984.

Cockroft, James D. *Outlaws in the Promised Land: Mexican Immigrant Workers and America's Future.* New York: Grove Press, 1984.

Conover, Ted. *Coyotes: A Journey Through the Secret World of America's Illegal Aliens.* New York: Vintage, 1987.

Cornelius, Wayne A. *Building the Cactus Curtain: Mexican Immigration and U.S. Responses from Wilson to Carter.* Berkeley and Los Angeles: University of California Press, 1980.

De la Garza, Rodolfo O., et al., eds. *The Mexican American Experience: An Interdisciplinary Anthology.* Austin: University of Texas Press, 1985.

Dietz, James L. *The Economic History of Puerto Rico*. Princeton, N.J.: Princeton University Press, 1986.

Elsasser, Nan, Kyle MacKenzie, and Yvonne Tixier y Vigil. *Las Mujeres*. Old Westbury, N.Y.: Feminist Press, 1981.

Falk, Pamela S., ed. *The Political Status of Puerto Rico*. Lexington, Mass.: Lexington Books, 1986.

Fitzpatrick, Joseph P. *Puerto Rican Americans: The Meaning of Migrating to the Mainland*, 2d ed. Englewood Cliffs, N.J.: Prentice-Hall, 1987.

Flores, Estevan T. "The Mexican-Origin People in the United States and Marxist Thought in Chicano Studies," in *The Left Academy: Marxist Scholarship on American Campuses*, Vol. 3, Bertell Ollman and Edward Vernoff, eds., pp. 103–38. New York: Praeger, 1986.

Foster, David William. *Puerto Rican Literature: A Bibliography of Secondary Sources*. Westport, Conn.: Greenwood Press, 1982.

Gann, L.H., and Peter J. Duignan. *The Hispanics in the United States: A History*. Boulder, Colo.: Westview Press, 1986.

García, Eugene E., Francisco A. Lomeli, and Isidrio D. Ortiz. *Chicano Studies: An Interdisciplinary Approach*. New York: Teachers College, Columbia University, 1984.

García, Jesus. "Hispanic Perspective: Textbooks and Other Curriculum Materials," *The History Teacher* 14 (November 1980): 105–20.

García-Passalacqua, Juan M. *Puerto Rico: Equality and Freedom at Issue*. New York: Praeger, for the Hoover Institution, 1984.

Gonzales, Juan L. *Mexican-American Farm Workers: The California Agricultural Industry*. New York: Praeger, 1985.

Gonzales, Sylvia Alicia. *Hispanic American Voluntary Organizations*. Westport, Conn.: Greenwood Press, 1985.

Griswold del Castillo, Richard. *La Familia: Chicano Families in The Urban Southwest, 1848 to the Present*. Notre Dame, Ind.: University of Notre Dame Press, 1984.

Guerrero, Andrés G. *A Chicano Theology*. Maryknoll, N.Y.: Orbis Books, 1987.

Hammerback, John, Richard J. Jensen, and José Angel Gutierrez. *A War of Words: Chicano Protest in the 1960s and 1970s*. Westport, Conn.: Greenwood Press, 1983.

Horowitz, Ruth. *Honor and the American Dream: Culture and Social Identity in a Chicano Community*. New Brunswick, N.J.: Rutgers University Press, 1983.

Jennings, James, and Monte Rivers, eds. *Puerto Rican Politics in Urban America*. Westport, Conn.: Greenwood Press, 1984.

Johansen, Bruce, and Robert Maestras. *El Pueblo: The Gallegos Family's American Journey, 1503–1980*. New York: Monthly Review Press, 1983.

Kruszewski, Z. Anthony, Richard L. Hough, and Jacob Ornstein, eds. *Politics and Society in the Southwest: Ethnicity and Chicano Pluralism*. Boulder, Colo.: Westview Press, 1982.

Lopez, Alfredo. *Dona Licha: A History of Puerto Rico*. Boston: South End Press, 1985.

Lotchin, Roger W., and David J. Weber. "The New Chicano Urban History: Two Perspectives," *The History Teacher* 16 (February 1983): 219–47.

Martinez, Julio, and Francisco Lomeli, eds. *Chicano Literature: A Reference Guide*. Westport, Conn.: Greenwood Press, 1985.

Meier, Matt S., comp. *Bibliography of Mexican American History*. Westport, Conn.: Greenwood Press, 1984.

———, ed. *Mexican American Biographies: A Historical Dictionary, 1836–1987*. Westport, Conn.: Greenwood Press, 1988.

Meier, Matt S., and Feliciano Rivera, eds. *Dictionary of Mexican American History*. Westport, Conn.: Greenwood Press, 1981.

Melville, Margarita, ed. *Twice a Minority: Mexican American Women*. St. Louis: C. V. Mosby, 1980.

Meyer, Michael C., and William Sherman. *The Course of Mexican History*, 3d ed. New York: Oxford University Press, 1987.

Mirandé, Alfredo. *The Chicano Experience: An Alternative Perspective*. Notre Dame, Ind.: University of Notre Dame Press, 1985.

Mirandé, Alfredo, and Evangelina Enriquez. *La Chicana: The Mexican American Woman*. Chicago: University of Chicago Press, 1981.

Mora, Magdalena, and Adelaida Del Castillo, eds. *Mexican Women in the United States: Struggles Past and Present*. Los Angeles: Chicano Studies Research Center, UCLA, 1980.

Morales Vergara, Julio. *Puerto Rican Poverty and Immigration*. New York: Praeger, 1986.

Muñoz, Carolos, Jr. "Chicano Politics: The Current Conjuncture," in *Year Left 2*, Mike Davis, et al., eds. London: Verso/New Left Books, 1987, pp. 35–52.

———. *Youth, Identity, Power: The Chicano Generation*. London: Verso/New Left Books, 1987.

Ortiz, Isidrio, ed. *Chicanos and the Social Sciences: A Decade of Research and Development (1970–1980)*. Santa Barbara: Center for Chicano Studies, University of California, 1983.

Padilla, Felix M. *Latino Ethnic Consciousness: The Case of Mexican Americans and Puerto Ricans in Chicago*. Notre Dame, Ind.: University of Notre Dame Press, 1985.

Ramírez de Arellano, Annette B., and Conrad Seipp. *Colonialism, Catholicism, and Contraception: A History of Birth Control in Puerto Rico*. Chapel Hill: University of North Carolina Press, 1983.

Riding, Alan. *Distant Neighbors: A Portrait of the Mexicans*. New York: Knopf, 1984.

Romo, Ricardo. *East Los Angeles: History of a Barrio*. Austin: University of Texas Press, 1983.

Ruiz, Vicki L. "Teaching Chicano/American History: Goals and Methods." *The History Teacher* 20 (February 1987): 167–77.

Sánchez-Jankowski, Martin. *City Bound: Urban Life and Political Attitudes among Chicano Youth*. Albuquerque: University of New Mexico Press, 1986.

San Miguel, Guadalupe, Jr. *Let All of Them Take Heed: Mexican Americans and the Campaign for Educational Equality, 1929–1981*. Austin: University of Texas Press, 1987.

———. "Status of the Historiography of Chicano Education: A Preliminary Analysis," *History of Education Quarterly* 26 (Winter 1986): 523–35.

Stevens-Arroyo, Antonio M., ed. *Prophets Denied Honor: An Anthology on the Hispanic Church in the United States*. Maryknoll, N.Y.: Orbis Books, 1982.

Valdez, Armando, et al., eds. *The State of Chicano Research in Family, Labor and Migration Studies*. Stanford, Calif.: Stanford Center for Chicano Studies, Stanford University, 1983.

Vega, Bernardo. *Memoirs of Bernardo Vega: A Contribution to the History of the Puerto Rican Community in New York*, Cesar Andreu Iglesias, ed. New York: Monthly Review Press, 1984.

Wagenheim, Olga Jimenez de. *Puerto Rico's Revolt for Independence: El Grito de Lares*. Boulder, Colo.: Westview Press, 1985.

Weisskoff, Richard. *Factories and Food Stamps: The Puerto Rico Model of Development*. Baltimore: Johns Hopkins University Press, 1985.

Weyr, Thomas. *Hispanic USA: Assimilation or Separatism?* New York: Harper & Row, 1988.

Zanella, Patricia. *Women's Work and Chicano Families: Cannery Workers of the Santa Clara Valley*. Ithaca, N.Y.: Cornell University Press, 1987.

Zavala, Iris M., and Rafael Rodriguez, eds. *The Intellectual Roots of Independence: An Anthology of Puerto Rican Political Essays*. New York: Monthly Review Press, 1980.

Zinn, Maxine Baca, ed. "Chicanos" (entire issue), *Social Science Journal* 19 (April 1982).

Organizations and Publications

Requests for information should be accompanied by a stamped, self-addressed envelope.

American GI Forum of the United States, P.O. Box 7515, 621 Gabaldon Rd., N.W., Albuquerque, N.M. 87104

Aspira of America, 1112 16th St., N.W., Suite 340, Washington, D.C. 20036

Congressional Hispanic Caucus, H2-557, Washington, D.C. 20515

Council on Hemispheric Affairs, 1612 20th St., N.W., Washington, D.C. 20009

Cuba International, P.O. Box 3603, Havana 3, Cuba

Diario Las Américas, 2900 N.W. 39th St., Miami, Fla. 33142-5193

El Diario-La Prensa, 143-155 Varick St., New York, N.Y. 10013

Journal of Mexican Studies, 340 Humanities Office Bldg., University of California, Irvine, Calif. 92717

La Opinión, 1436 S. Main St., Los Angeles, Calif. 90015

League of United Latin American Citizens (LULAC), 400 First St., N.W., Suite 721, Washington, D.C. 20001

Mexican-American Legal Defense and Educational Fund (MALDEF), 634 S. Spring St., 11th Fl., Los Angeles, Calif. 90014

Mexican-American Opportunity Foundation, 670 Monterey Pass Rd., Monterey Park, Calif. 91754

Mexican-American Women's National Association, 1201 16th St., N.W., Suite 420, Washington, D.C. 20036

Mexican Embassy, 2829 16th St., N.W., Washington, D.C. 20009

NACLA's Report on the Americas, North American Congress on Latin America, 151 W. 19th St., 9th Fl., New York, N.Y. 10011

National Association for Puerto Ricans Civil Rights, P.O. Box 524, Hub Sta., Bronx, N.Y. 10455

National Conference of Puerto Rican Women, 1010 Vermont Ave., N.W., Washington, D.C. 20005

National Council of La Raza, 20 F St., N.W., 2nd Fl., Washington, D.C. 20001

National Puerto Rican Coalition, 1700 K St., N.W., Suite 500, Washington, D.C. 20006

National Puerto Rican Forum, 31 E. 32nd St., 4th Fl., New York, N.Y. 10016

Partido Independentista Puertorriqueño, 963 Roosevelt Ave., San Juan, Puerto Rico 00907

Partido Neuvo Progresista, Box 5192, Puerta de Tierra Sta., San Juan, Puerto Rico 00906

Partido Popular Democrático, 403 Ponce de León Ave., Puerta de la Tierra, San Juan, Puerto Rico 00906

Partido Socialista Puertorriqueño, 256 Padre Colón St., Rio Piedras, San Juan, Puerto Rico 00925

Permanent Mission of Cuba (at the United Nations), 315 Lexington Ave., New York, N.Y. 10016

A view of the Cuban revolution from the top and from the bottom by the Mexican cartoonist "Ruiz" (Eduardo del Rio).

Puerto Rican Family Institute, 116 W. 14th St., New York, N.Y. 10011

Puerto Rican Legal Defense and Education Fund, 99 Hudson St., 14th Fl., New York, N.Y. 10013

Puerto Rico Federal Affairs Administration, Public Affairs and Communication, 1100 17th St., N.W., Washington, D.C. 20005

United Farm Workers, La Paz, Keene, Calif. 93531

U.S. Hispanic Chamber of Commerce, Board of Trade Center, 4900 Main, Suite 700, Kansas City, Mo. 64112

Part III
SEXUAL DIVERSITY

While sexual organs are a simple matter of biology, sexual desires and behaviors are governed by complex social rules. Much of what we consider facts of nature are assumptions of a particular culture at a specific moment in time. These assumptions may not be shared by other cultures.

Our education begins in the crib. Male babies are placed in blue blankets and given masculine names. Female babies are placed in pink blankets and given feminine names. Later, both are taught various truths about little boys: they shouldn't cry; they should play with toy cars, tools, trucks, rockets, and guns; they should be active in competitive games. Girls are encouraged to play with dolls, stuffed animals, and babies; they are expected to be quiet, gentle, and sensitive. Both boys and girls are taught, in effect, that boys are naturally superior to girls because they are more independent and assertive.

These roles are not biological destiny. Although humans are animals, they are not geese, rats, mice, baboons, or chimpanzees. Unlike simpler forms of life, humans are characterized by intellect, language, and culture. Ashley Montagu, an anthropologist, maintains that human-animal analogies are often false. The human infant has only a few instinctive reactions, such as responding to loud noises or sucking at the mother's breast.

Nor are sex roles absolutely determined by hormones. Roles vary widely throughout history and between civilizations. It is one's own society that defines what it means to be a man or a woman. People are trained to respond to men and women within certain acceptable patterns of behavior, just as whites may be taught racist attitudes toward all blacks and gentiles toward all Jews.

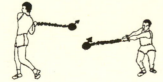

This sex-role conditioning oppresses both women and men. The women's liberation movement has condemned the old models of passive women and aggressive men for limiting the development of our humanity. The gay liberation movement has challenged the stereotypes of gay men as womanly (and therefore contemptible) and lesbians as manly (and therefore unnatural). These sexual prejudices are no more rational than racial prejudices.

6

The Longest Revolution:
Female Equality

We do as much, we eat as much, we want as much.
SOJOURNER TRUTH at Seneca Falls, New York (1848)

Women are the oldest oppressed group. In most societies, throughout recorded human history, they have been what the French feminist Simone de Beauvoir called "the second sex." Male dominance has been the rule generally, although there have been societies that worshiped female deities and some that accorded superior or equal status to women.

One common explanation for this situation, especially in the past, was that God Himself ordained the secondary role of women. Male-dominated religions commonly have preached that women are dangerously emotional, unreasonable, and childlike. Although many people still believe that this is the will of God the Father, contemporary churches in industrialized countries have tended to emphasize a new revelation that women are equal in rights and privileges with men.

A second argument has been that biology determined the inferior condition of women. Because they have been burdened with childbearing and childrearing and because they are physically weaker than men, they have been limited in their opportunities.

The British philosopher John Stuart Mill relied upon this theory when he wrote his classic statement of liberal feminism, *The Subjection of Women*, in 1869. He concluded that the modern subordination of women was a relic of the primitive childhood of humanity. Mill hoped that an enlightened society would treat women as free individuals who had a full range of choices in life. Nonetheless, he thought that most women would choose to be homemakers.

The sexual balance of power has shifted further since Mill's day: birth control frees both women and men to engage in sexual activity without reproduction; machines reduce or eliminate the importance of male strength; and technological change has removed such domestic drudgery as canning, making clothes, and doing laundry by hand.

A third interpretation of women's oppression is prevalent in Communist countries. It was first systematically formulated by Friedrich Engels in his book *The Origins of the Family, Private Property, and the State* (published in 1884 and revised in 1891). Engels rejected the assumption that woman had always been "the slave of man." Rather, he asserted that in primitive communal societies men and women had been approximately equal, since each performed work that was essential for the survival of all. Engels felt that men had created and controlled the first surpluses through their jobs as hunters, stock raisers, and farmers. These surpluses eventually became private property; then women and children began to be considered a form of private property (to assure that one's wealth was inherited by legitimate offspring); and, finally, the state was necessary to protect all private property. In brief, "The first class oppression is that of the female sex by the male." Even if this interpretation is correct, sexism has continued in Communist countries after the means of production have been socialized. Sexism, like racism, may have been primarily economic in origin, but it now pervades even "revolutionary" societies.

The American Revolution of 1776 did not immediately change the second-class status of women. Little education was available for girls. Few careers were possible but that of wife. If a woman didn't marry, she was legally a minor. If she married, she passed from the custody of her father to that of her husband, and was "civilly dead." A married woman had no right to her own property, no right to money that she earned, no right to protection from physical abuse by her husband, and no right to initiate a divorce. An adult woman could not vote, could not sit on a jury, and could not hold office. The legal status of women was little better than that of children, mental defectives, criminals, and slaves. This discrimination was justified by appeals to God, nature, English common law, and custom.

Yet, the first women's rights convention in the world was held in the United States in 1848, heralding here the first mass movement. It emerged out of greater freedoms in some frontier and urban areas, Enlightenment and revolutionary ideals, expanded definitions of women's active moral role in society, basic education for women throughout the North by the 1850s (female literacy in the North doubled from 1780 to 1840), the voluntary associations that were common in America, economic changes that created job opportunities, and the visions of a few early leaders.

By the 1830s some women who were active in helping others to improve their conditions in life began to reevaluate their own limited rights. These women had aided the rights of slaves, orphans, prisoners, and the poor. In doing so, they gained skills in organizing, writing, petitioning, speaking, and chairing meetings.

Women who worked to abolish slavery were the most likely to have their own consciousness raised. As Angelina Grimké said in the 1830s, "In investigating the rights of the slave, I have come to a better understanding of my own." Such women felt that they were being kept servile and ignorant.

The first women's organization to oppose black slavery was begun in Providence, Rhode Island, in 1832. The first woman antislavery speaker, Maria Stewart, a black woman from Boston, also became prominent in that year. The number of female abolitionists expanded rapidly. They appealed to traditional arguments that slavery denied blacks the institution of marriage, corrupted the bodies and souls of those involved, and maimed the lives of slave children. Many men, including abolitionist men, nonetheless objected to women entering this controversy. In 1839 the American Anti-Slavery Society bitterly fought over the issue of women members, reluctantly admitting them by a vote of 180 to 140.

European male reformers were even less willing to agree. When American women delegates appeared at the World's Anti-Slavery Convention in London in 1840, they were officially silenced. Although Lucretia Mott, Elizabeth Cady Stanton, and others had been elected by women's abolitionist societies in the United States, they were not seated. As one woman remembered, "Our mere presence produced an excitement and vehemence of protest and denunciation that could not have been greater if the news had come that the French were about to invade England." The women were forced to retire to a balcony, behind a curtain. Stanton and others were stung by this rejection. Stanton recalled, "My experience at the World's Anti-Slavery Convention, all I had read of the legal status of women, and the oppression I saw everywhere, together swept across my soul, intensified now by many personal experiences." Some men were disturbed by this injustice. A few, such as William Lloyd Garrison, left their seats on the convention floor to join the women in the balcony.

When the women returned to America, they continued their antislavery work, but some had a clearer vision of the slavery of sex. Male abolitionists, in the opinion of Stanton, "had manifested their great need for some education on that question."

But women like Stanton and Mott were not free to do as they wished. Stanton was burdened with a large home and a family that eventually numbered seven children. Although her antislavery husband was sympathetic and she had the assistance of servants, she carefully budgeted her time.

Stanton was not alone in wanting reforms for women, even though the motives for reformers were diverse. Some older men wanted property laws changed so that their daughters would not lose property because of a profligate husband. Some reformers, such as Margaret Fuller, the author of the first American feminist classic, *Woman in the Nineteenth Century* (1845), were more purely idealistic. Fuller sought to liberate individual women from bondage to any rigid standard of Woman, and individual men from any rigid standard of Man. People who were free from "the slavery of habit" could develop their own unique gifts.

Stanton seized an opportunity to promote her cause in 1848. New York had passed a married women's property bill that aroused public commentary. Stanton and others announced a Woman's Rights Convention. It would be held in the Wesleyan Chapel in Seneca Falls, New York, on July 19 and 20.

About 300 daring people attended. For many, such as Lucretia Mott, a militant Quaker, and Frederick Douglass, an ex-slave, the meeting was a logical extension of the abolitionist struggle and American democratic values.

The convention adopted a Declaration of Sentiments that was modeled after the Declaration of Independence. It began, "We hold these truths to be self-evident, that all men and women are created equal." The meeting rapidly passed eleven of twelve resolutions, calling for the right of women to make contracts, testify in court, sue, have equal wages, acquire property, have equal status in marriage and child custody, and enter the professions, schools, and churches.

The twelfth resolution nearly suffered defeat. Stanton believed that women should be allowed to vote. Mott and others objected that this was too radical and would make the conference seem "ridiculous." Stanton, Douglass, and others responded that the ballot was essential to gain many of the other desired reforms, and their views won a small majority. This was the first time that the vote for women had been publicly demanded.

Popular comment was limited and usually negative. The *Oneida Whig* reported the event as "the most shocking and unnatural incident ever recorded in the history of womaninity" and feared that, if women neglected the home, no one would tend "our domestic firesides and the holes in our stockings." Douglass, as the most prominent man, became a "hermaphrodite," "Aunt Nancy Man," and "woman's rights man." He was shocked that

a discussion of the rights of animals would be regarded with far more complacency by many of what are called the 'wise' and the 'good' of our land, than would a discussion of the rights of women. . . . Many who have at last made the discovery that negroes have some rights as well as other members of the human family, have yet to be convinced that women are entitled to any.

Most of those who agreed with the work of Seneca Falls were abolitionists.

Other conventions followed, and some European progressives noticed this radical innovation. John Stuart Mill and Harriet Taylor anonymously published "On the Enfranchisement of Women" in an 1851 issue of *Westminster Review*. They recognized that while there had been feminist authors, there had never been public meetings and political actions that championed women's rights. They added that, in democratic America, the movement against "the aristocracy of color" (white) had given birth to another movement against "the aristocracy of sex" (male).

Some of the most powerful testimonies of the tiny movement came from black women like Sojourner Truth (1797–1883) and Harriet Tubman (1821–1913). Both had been born into slavery; Truth in New York State and Tubman in Maryland. Both were strong and independent people. When a minister belittled women's rights at a conference in Akron, Ohio, in 1851, Sojourner Truth was long remembered for her answer:

That man over there say that a woman needs to be helped into carriages, and lifted over ditches, and to have the best place everywhere. Nobody ever helped me into carriages, or over mud puddles, or gives me a best place. . . . And ain't I a woman? Look at me. Look at my arm! I have plowed and planted and gathered into barns, and no man could head me. And ain't I a woman? I could work as much and eat as much as a man when I could get it, and bear the lash as well. . . . And ain't I a woman? I have borned thirteen children and seen them most all sold off into slavery. And when I cried out with a mother's grief, none but Jesus heard. . . . And ain't I a woman? (In *The Feminist Papers*, ed. Alice Rossi [New York: Bantam Books, 1974], p. 428; some spelling standardized)

She concluded by instructing the minister that Jesus was the product of God and a woman. Man didn't have anything to do with it!

How could one argue with such compellingly direct imagery? Nor was it easy to dismiss Harriet Tubman's logic for supporting women's rights: "I've suffered enough to believe in them."

Nonetheless, the movement for women's rights grew slowly. It was often ridiculed when it was noticed at all. Its female supporters were verbally abused as loathsome spinsters, lewd ladies, or bubble-headed idealists. Cartoonists were likely to depict its male supporters, like Horace Greeley, wearing petticoats. Critics were fond of emphasizing the exotic, especially the "bloomer" costume worn by some feminists as a way of freeing women from heavy and confining layers of skirts. Although the short skirt and pantalettes of the bloomer attire were a reasonable kind of dress reform, most of the public considered them bizarrely mannish. Since "bloomerism" diverted attention from other social, political, and economic questions—like the popular image of bra-burning in the 1960s—feminists abandoned their bloomers.

Despite the scorn or indifference of most of the public toward women's rights, the cause attracted more adherents throughout the 1850s. The resounding debate over slavery inherently asked, "What is freedom?" In the case of women, were they free if they could not vote, hold property, or be equal in the family? The movement for black freedom added to the ranks of this and other movements for democratic reform.

POPPING THE QUESTION.

Superior Creature. "SAY! OH, SAY DEAREST! WILL YOU BE MINE?" &c., &c.

Punch, 1851

Harriet Tubman

"BLOOMERISM,"
OR THE
NEW FEMALE COSTUME OF 1851.

As it has appeared in the various Cities and Towns.

BOSTON · S. W. WHEELER 66 Cornhill · 1851.

Woman's Emancipation

A description of the smoking, bulldog women that would result from the wearing of bloomers. Polite women have turned their backs and averted their eyes. (*Harper's Monthly*, August 1851)

A crowd of jeering men in the balconies overlooking a rather odd collection of women's rights people. (*Harper's Weekly*, June 11, 1859)

This was illustrated by the formation of the American Equal Rights Association in 1866. The *New York Herald* spoke for conventional opinion when it said:

All of the isms of the age were personated there. Long-haired men, apostles of some inexplicable emotion or sensations; gaunt and hungry looking men, disciples of bran bread and white turnip dietetic philosophy; advocates of liberty and small beer, professors of free love in the platonic sense, agrarians in property and the domestic values; infidels, saints, negro-worshippers, sinners and short-haired women . . . women in Bloomer dress to show their ankles, and their independence; women who hate their husbands and fathers, and hateful women wanting husbands. . . . Altogether the most long-necked, grim-visaged, dyspeptic, Puritanical, nasal-twanged agglomeration of isms ever assembled in this or any other state. (November 21, 1866)

This reform coalition did not collapse because of such criticism, but because of a split between the abolitionists and the women's rights advocates. As the Civil War ended, some demanded that it was "the Negroes' hour." Women were not lynched because they were women, and they had more protection from insults and injuries. Black (male) rights had to be secured first, and then reformers could turn to women's rights. Elizabeth Cady Stanton, Susan B. Anthony, and others were angrily insistent that both groups should achieve legal and political equality simultaneously.

When the Fourteenth Amendment to the Constitution was proposed in 1866 to insure black citizenship, the association was thrown into turmoil. The amendment included the statement that "when the right to vote at any election . . . is denied to any of the male inhabitants of such a state . . . the basis of representation [in the Congress] shall be reduced in the proportion [to such voting denial]." For the first time in American history the Constitution endorsed discrimination on the basis of sex. Previous references to the rights of Americans had spoken of "citizens" and "the people."

In 1868 women like Stanton and Anthony responded by forming the National Woman Suffrage Association in New York. These were the militant feminists. Only women could join, and only women could be officers. They immediately raised the banner of the vote, but they had many other demands related to marriage, professional training, and equal pay. Their newspaper, *The Revolution*, began with this declaration:

The ballot is not even half the loaf; it is only a crust, a crumb. The ballot touches only those interests, either of women or men, which take their root in political questions. But woman's chief discontent is not with her political, but with her social and particularly her marital bondage. The solemn and profound question of marriage . . . is of more vital consequence to woman's welfare and reaches down to a deeper depth in woman's heart and more thoroughly constitutes the core of the woman's movement than any such superficial and fragmentary question as women's suffrage. (January 8, 1868)

These women had wanted the American Equal Rights Association to focus not on black male suffrage but on broader issues. Even on the suffrage question, the association was criticized for its narrowness. Sojourner Truth noted, "there is a great stir about coloured men getting their rights but not a word about coloured women; and if coloured men get their rights and not coloured women theirs, you see, coloured men will be the masters over the women. . . . I wish woman to have her voice."

A more conservative group, led by Lucy Stone, founded the American Woman Suffrage Association in 1869. The main office was in staid Boston; its membership and officers included men; its first president was a man, Henry Ward Beecher. This organization stressed local organizing for the vote and avoided controversies over the family, the church, and social customs.

The Fifteenth Amendment, in 1869, agitated both groups by *not* mentioning sex. It stated that "the right of citizens of the United States to vote shall not be denied or abridged by the United States or by any State on account of race, color, or previous condition of servitude." Some women responded that since they were citizens who had been in servitude they should be considered politically liberated by this amendment. Susan B. Anthony tested this theory when she and twelve other women marched to the polls in Rochester, New York, in 1872. Armed with a copy of the Constitution, she successfully demanded the right to vote. However, she was later arrested, convicted, and fined for this criminal outburst. The Supreme Court ruled unanimously in 1876, in the separate case of *Minor v. Happersett*, that the citizenship of women did not automatically entitle them to vote.

The first political victories came in the West, where the hardships of frontier life encouraged greater independence among women and more respect from men. Wyoming Territory allowed women to vote in 1869; Utah, in 1870. Colorado and Idaho later followed, but such gains did not come easily. Seven states rejected proposals for female suffrage between 1867 and 1877.

As the struggle continued, it centered on voting rights, to the virtual exclusion of other concerns. When the two major organizations merged into the National American Woman Suffrage Association (NAWSA) in 1890, little remained of the broad idealism of Seneca Falls. NAWSA was designed to gain the vote, and in doing this it lost most of its soul. Its aspirations were limited. It did not allow black groups to join. It inveighed against the immigrant threat in the North. It refused black delegates. It glorified "high moral standards" that now seem prudish.

Radical and liberal women were isolated. Such black leaders as Ida Wells-Barnett and Mary Church Terrell began their own projects. Some like Frances Ellen Watkins Harper worked through the National Association of Colored Women, established in 1896. Radical white women like Victoria Woodhull (sometimes called "Mrs. Satan") and Emma Goldman ("the Red Queen") were frequently ostracized by liberals and conservatives. Women within radical organizations such as the Socialist party were generally treated as second-class members. Some of these felt that the vote was not important. For a labor militant and socialist like Mother Jones, female voting was a distraction from real questions of power:

I have never had a vote, and I have raised hell all over this country! You don't need a vote to raise hell! You need convictions and a voice! . . . The women of Colorado have had the vote for two generations and the working men and women are in slavery. . . . No matter what your fight, don't be ladylike! God Almighty made women and the Rockefeller gang of thieves made ladies.

Moderate and liberal women, however, usually supported the NAWSA or nonpolitical groups like the General Federation of Women's Clubs, which was founded in 1890 and had a membership of 1 million by 1910. While the General Federation did not endorse suffrage, it was active in such reforms as food inspection, public health, the abolition of child labor, and sanitation.

Politicians preferred to avoid the issue of women voting since there were powerful groups who were opposed. First, Southern politicians were ada-

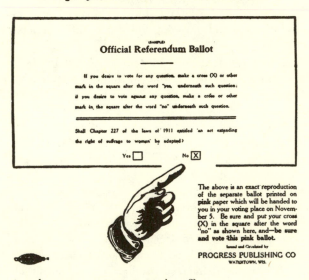

A male poster against women's suffrage.

mantly hostile. Women's suffrage raised the threat of black women voting. Some politicians also politely objected that the federal government should not decide this issue; it should be handled by individual states.

Second, many urban political machines feared that women voters might "clean house." Since women's groups often claimed that they had a purifying influence on American politics, big city bosses were wary of them.

Third, liquor interests suspected that women would vote for prohibition. There were hundreds of thousands of members in the Women's Christian Temperance Union who wanted to ban alcohol. They were a source of dread to those who made money from its sale.

Fourth, those who profited from child labor and cheap female labor donated money to defeat women's suffrage. If women could vote, they might limit or ban some of the employment practices of that day.

Fifth, there were women's antisuffrage groups. The Daughters of the American Revolution was among these antirevolutionary organizations.

Sixth, there were unorganized conservatives, moderates, and liberals who believed that God, nature, and custom destined women to occupy certain roles. If women could vote, their weak, sentimental, and unstable natures would create havoc in politics and encourage quarrels at home, juvenile delinquency, and divorce.

World War I, which President Woodrow Wilson pronounced "a war to make the world safe for democracy," highlighted the lack of democracy for women, even while they were asked to work for the war effort. Militant women, led by the National Women's party, picketed the White House, burned Wilson's speeches when they mentioned "freedom," and conducted sit-ins and hunger strikes. Wartime contributions by women, combined with

A myopic prediction by Rollin Kirby in 1920,
entitled "The End of the Climb."

Why We Oppose Votes For Men

1.

Because man's place is in the army.

2.

Because no really manly man wants to settle any question otherwise than by fighting about it.

3.

Because if men should adopt peaceable methods women will no longer look up to them.

4.

Because men will lose their charm if they step out of their natural sphere and interest themselves in other matters than feats of arms, uniforms and drums.

5.

Because men are too emotional to vote. Their conduct at baseball games and political conventions shows this, while their innate tendency to appeal to force renders them particularly unfit for the task of government.

—Alice Duer Miller, 1915

Feminist ridicule of male anti-suffrage arguments.

several decades of local, state, and national campaigns for women's suffrage, generated enough momentum to pass the Nineteenth Amendment in 1920, which granted women the right to vote throughout the United States. When this goal was reached, the organized women's movement all but vanished for the next half-century.

During the 1920s, a shrunken NAWSA evolved into the League of Women Voters, and the tiny National Women's party promoted the Equal Rights Amendment (ERA), which was first rejected by Congress in 1923. Even the League of Women Voters opposed the ERA, saying that it would destroy protections that had been legislated for working women. The National Women's Party tilted toward the right, endorsing Herbert Hoover in 1928 rather than the Catholic and antiprohibitionist Al Smith. The first wave of feminism was rapidly ebbing away.

Politics remained a man's game. Although Jeanette Rankin was elected the first congresswoman in 1917, she was a lonely figure. Other women became prominent because of their husbands, such as Eleanor Roosevelt and Ma Ferguson, who was elected governor of Texas in 1935. Some were appointed to high office, like Frances Perkins, the first woman to serve as secretary of labor in the 1930s. Despite such gains, however, the woman politician was an oddity.

While the 1920s recall the image of the "flapper"—a young and single woman who bobbed her hair, shortened her skirts, and danced the night away—life was not much freer for most women. The Great Depression of the 1930s further reinforced traditional sex roles: men should get available jobs and women should stay at home.

World War II was a burst of change. Six million women entered the labor force while many men were in the military. These women constituted more than one-half of those employed in the defense industries, and they were vital for the production of 12,000 ships, 87,000 tanks, and 300,000 airplanes. There were also about 220,000 women in various units of the military. It became patriotic to leave the home. A woman who worked in the shipyards—as did the poster character—"Rosie the Riveter"—or a woman who was a soldier could wear pants without being laughed at.

For black women, World War II was a second emancipation. In 1940, 62 percent of employed black women worked at jobs that could be classified as domestic labor. By 1946, this had fallen to 42 percent, a remarkable change in just a few years. War brought opportunities to escape from low-paid and low-status jobs.

When the war ended, it was assumed that returning male veterans would take these jobs. Many white and black women were fired or demoted, and child-care facilities at most businesses were closed. Nonetheless, some women tried to stay at their jobs. Not all wanted to move to the suburbs to have children, dress in high heels and skirts with cinched waists, watch "I Love Lucy" and "Father Knows Best," and read *Better Homes and Gardens*, *Family Circle*, *Good Housekeeping*, *Ladies Home Journal*, *McCall's*, *Redbook*, and *Woman's Day*. By 1954 the percentage of women in the work force began to rise steadily, reaching 42 percent by 1973, and over 50 percent by the mid-1980s.

Work-force participation was a central factor in the second wave of feminism that developed in the 1960s. Employed women with their own incomes were often more independent than housewives, and they provided different role models for their children. Still, many women resisted these changes. The Federation of Business and Professional Women's Clubs refused suggestions that it become a kind of NAACP for women, and in the 1950s it consciously changed the title of its magazine from the *Independent Woman* to the *National Business Woman* to avoid any implication that the organization was feminist.

The potential for a second wave of feminism (the first wave being the movement of the nineteenth and early twentieth centuries) was released by the civil rights revolution that became evident in the 1950s and by the revival of liberalism after the election of John F. Kennedy in 1960. These two factors were important in the rise of most social movements of the 1960s and 1970s. Although JFK was, in practice, a cautious political meter reader, his optimistic rhetoric about a New Frontier aroused expectations of social progress.

When Kennedy was criticized in 1961 for appointing only 9 women to the first 240 jobs that he filled, Kennedy modestly agreed with Eleanor Roosevelt's suggestion to create a Women's Commission on the Status of Women, with Eleanor as chairman. Although creating a commission is usually a polite way of doing nothing, this one brought together politically conscious women. They documented sex discrimination in their 1963 report, *American Women*, and created the hope of legal reforms. There were soon fifty state committees.

Consciousness was raised by this work as it was by the publication of Betty Friedan's *Feminine Mystique* in 1963, which inveighed against "the quiet desperation" of "the problem that has no name." Although Kennedy's reforms were minor, in 1963 Congress passed the Equal Pay Act. This was the first federal legislation prohibiting discrimination on the basis of sex. It amended the Fair Labor Standards Act of 1938 to encourage equal pay for men and women in the same federally related jobs.

The civil rights movement was essential to the next major advance, a section of the Civil Rights Act of 1965 that forbade sex discrimination. But the enforcing agency, the Equal Employment Opportunity Commission, considered the provision "a fluke" that was "born out of wedlock" (as one of its officials said) and refused to investigate such discrimination.

Some women were annoyed by the slowness of change and by the patronizing attitudes of men in the government, civil rights organizations, and liberal groups. Betty Friedan called for a separate women's lobby in 1966. Thirty-seven women and three men met to form the National Organization for Women (NOW). This would champion liberal feminism: the gaining of equal rights for women and men within the mainstream of U.S. society.

Radical elements of the new feminist movement were convinced that sex discrimination could not be ended by liberal reforms, but only by a wholesale restructuring of the United States. (This view was similar to that expressed in *The Revolution* in the nineteenth century.) These radical feminists developed within the context of the struggles of the early and mid-1960s: civil rights, the antiwar movement, and the countercultural lifestyle and press. Some women were offended by comments such as Stokely Carmichael's remark that the only position of women in SNCC was prone, or by the patronizing male liberalism of the National Conference for New Politics in 1967. Separate feminist organizations, both liberal and radical, multiplied in 1967 when six different women's groups started in six different cities, and the first modern feminist newspaper, *The Voice of the Women's Liberation Movement*, was published in Chicago.

National publicity came in 1968 when one group picketed the Miss American contest in Atlantic City. They portrayed it as a meatpacking enterprise, crowned a live sheep Miss America, and set up a "freedom trashcan" for high heels, bras, girdles, false eyelashes, conventional women's magazines, and other "instruments of torture." One male reporter invented a bra-burning, and the term "bra-burner" was used to label any feminist.

Feminism rapidly became a household word in the late 1960s, even if most women claimed that they were not in favor of it—or of what they imagined it to be. Conventional women's magazines began to include articles on single, divorced, and widowed women, rather than speaking only about idealized middle-class married women. NOW grew into a truly national organization. *Ms.* magazine was born in 1972. The Equal Rights Amendment finally got out of Congress in 1972, after almost fifty years, and was sent to the states for ratification.

Some of this was tokenism. Cosmetic changes were more likely to be tolerated than basic shifts of power. Resistance to the ERA and its narrow defeat in 1982 (three states within ratification) illustrated this hostility to fundamental change. The amendment was a statement of elemental justice: "Equality of rights under the law shall not be denied or abridged by the United States or by any State on account of sex." It was ridiculed as the Equal Restrooms Amendment and accused of being an insult to God, unnatural, a threat to laws that protected women, and a requirement for the military draft of women. Others claimed that it wasn't necessary because the courts and the federal government were already vigilant against sex discrimination. The ERA obviously struck a nerve, whether it was among people who believed sexual stereotypes or businessmen who profited because they paid female employees less.

Even though the ERA was defeated, women's progress did not end. Over a dozen states had their own ERAs; court cases continued; women's publications and organizations did not collapse. Although the membership of NOW fell from an early-1980s peak of 220,000 to a 1987 total of 150,000, it was still the largest independent feminist organization in the world.

As women became more politically organized, it was clearer that there were significant differences between them, as a political constituency, and most men. Since many women have jobs with little income, status, or security—such as the 9 million women in 1985 who were the sole support for their families—they have frequently endorsed government regulation of business and increased public assistance.

This potential was partially realized in 1984 when the Democratic party nominated the first woman vice-presidential candidate since the Constitution was written in 1787. While Geraldine Ferraro marked progress, there was considerable uneasiness. Commentators and pollsters disputed whether Walter Mondale was a "wimp" for having a woman on the ticket, along with his less "macho" military and foreign policies. The results were mixed: 63 percent of men voted for Reagan, but 56 percent of women did, too. Most of this difference, though, was based on class, not sex. One organizer for NOW conceded, "we have to give up our generic, Campbell's soup appeal to women and target instead."

Overall, there have been political successes. The 1986 elections marked the first time in history that a larger percentage of women than men voted;

in all, six million more women than men voted. By 1987 women were 16 percent of all state legislators, mayors of 96 towns with more than 30,000 inhabitants, 25 members of Congress, and 3 governors.

What is called the women's movement is, like all movements, fragmented. There are divisions based upon class, race, religion, ideology, ethnicity, culture, and region. Still, there have been pervasive changes since the 1960s. A 1986 Gallup Poll found that 56 percent of American women described themselves as feminists, and only 4 percent as antifeminists. Sexism is more recognized as a form of bigotry like racism: women should be treated as individual people rather than as the representatives of a sex.

Two of the major reasons for this overall change, besides the organization of a feminist constituency, have been the modern revolution in birth control and fundamental changes in the economy. Women, without control over their own bodies, would have been restricted in their gains; without more jobs, they would have been limited. And without organization they would not have benefited as fully.

REPRODUCTIVE RIGHTS

Nature controls population by brutally direct means such as famine, disease, and warfare. Some people believe that other types of control are not possible, either because they are contrary to God's will or because of the essential bestiality of the lower classes. The Rev. Thomas Malthus justified such views in a famous book published in 1798.

Many others reject the stark world of Malthusianism. They propose forms of contraception and, sometimes, abortion. These are more than legal and medical issues, but involve philosophy, religion, sex, race, and class. As a result, controversy has been inevitable.

It is important to begin with one simple fact: religious beliefs, medical practices, customs, and laws have varied considerably over the centuries. There has never been fundamental agreement on the basic question, "When does human life begin?" Aristotle believed that male fetuses were human at forty days and female fetuses at eighty days. Plato asserted that life began at birth. The Bible does not mention such practices as abortion. Islam considers life to begin fifty days after conception; early Judaism, at birth; and Shintoism, when the child first sees light.

On the issue of abortion, there have been divergent opinions. While the Hippocratic Oath forbade the practice, the early Catholic church did not. In the 1200s St. Thomas Aquinas claimed that a soul entered the fetus only at the moment of "quickening," the first movement of the fetus that is perceptible to the mother, after several months of gestation. The first recorded English legal case of an aborted child was in 1348. The judgment was that no murder had occurred because there was no baptismal name for the fetus. The official Catholic position from 1591 to 1869 was that abortion was acceptible to the fortieth day after conception. Some in the church added that abortion after that was still not murder, since the baby did not have a soul until it was born. Not until 1869 did the church rule that life began at conception and that abortion was more than a sexual sin; it was a mortal sin.

When the United States was founded, none of the major faiths condemned birth control or abortion. This changed in the early 1800s for medical rather than moral reasons. Danger to the health of the woman was the most potent reason.

Abortion, for example, was ten to fifteen times more dangerous than childbirth in the era before antiseptics. Some doctors were concerned that, by the mid-1800s, as many as one in five pregnancies in the United States was ended by abortion. Critics like Horatio Storer of Boston also feared that abortions threatened the Protestant white race, as opposed to the Catholic immigrant hordes. Although the first state law to change was in Connecticut in 1821, it was lobbying by the American Medical Association (AMA) after its founding in 1847 and recognition that abortions were a major cause of maternal deaths that caused the practice to be banned, with a few exceptions, by 1900.

Other forms of birth control were possible. Abstinence was successful, but of limited popularity. You could marry late and have infrequent marital sex. Withdrawal before ejaculation was not always dependable. Douches might be used to flush out sperm after intercourse. A sponge coated with olive oil or lemon juice could be used to block the opening to the cervix. Condoms were regrettably expensive before rubber ones were introduced in the 1850s. They were also uncomfortable, and they were likely to slip at unfortunate moments. Madame de Sévigné probably spoke for many knowledgeable people when she described them as "armor against pleasure and cobwebs against danger." The first diaphragms were developed in the 1850s, but they were costly, awkward, and of doubtful utility.

Americans were generally ignorant of these possibilities. The Comstock Law, passed in 1873, forbade the importing, mailing, or transporting of anything preventing conception or causing abortion. Anthony Comstock, the head of the Society for the Suppression of Vice, diligently enforced the law. He was personally responsible for 700 arrests and the confiscation of thousands of books, including medical texts. While upper-class women might avoid such limits, lower-class women resorted to dubious folk medicines, $5 back-alley abortionists, or infanticide.

Margaret Sanger was the first to challenge such laws effectively at the turn of the century. Sanger was a nurse in New York City, in the slums of Brownsville. She had wanted to be a doctor, but such opportunities were rare for women, especially poor women. Sanger had ten brothers and sisters. She remembered that her childhood was "one of longing for things that were always denied." When she was married, with two children of her own, she knew that many parents wanted fewer babies to prevent worse poverty for the family or to improve the opportunities of those children that they had. Sanger recalled one woman who had almost died from an illegal abortion. When that woman begged the doctor to tell her how to prevent unwanted pregnancies, he advised, "Tell Jake to sleep on the roof."

Everyone in this particular story was ignorant. The doctor had no training in this subject and may have considered birth control to be immoral. Sanger, as a nurse, had no useful advice to her patients. The woman may have resorted to remedies for pregnancy that were listed by Sanger: "herb teas, turpentine, steaming, rolling downstairs, inserting slippery elm (which would cause the uterus to contract, expelling the fetus), knitting needles, shoehooks." Sanger added:

The doomed women implored me to reveal the "secret" rich people had, offering to pay me extra to tell them; many really believed I was holding information back for money. They asked everyone and tried anything, but nothing did them any good. On Saturday nights I have seen groups of from fifty to one hundred with their shawls over their heads waiting outside the office of a five-dollar abortionist.

Some of these women suffered from perforated uteruses, bleeding, or infections.

In 1912 Sanger began to write a newspaper column entitled "What Every Girl Should Know." This was published in a New York socialist journal. The Post Office Department made regular efforts to censor it, and one issue of "What Every Girl Should Know" read simply "NOTHING! By order of the Post Office Department."

In 1913 she and her radical husband spent a year in France, where she studied the more enlightened ideas and practices of some Europeans. After she came home, she produced a monthly, *The Woman Rebel*, and a pamphlet called *Family Limitation*. The latter was printed after dark by someone who characterized it as a Sing-Sing job because it contained illegal information. When she was indicted, she left for another trip to Europe.

The government lost interest in prosecuting her. When she returned in 1915, she was able to speak extensively and to plan for the opening of a birth control clinic in Brownsville. She rented rooms for one month, painted them to look hospital-like, and printed 5,000 leaflets.

Her birth control clinic opened on October 16, 1916, about thirty-five years after the first such clinic in Holland. Although the women of the neighborhood seemed to appreciate its work, it was closed ten days later as a "public nuisance." When Sanger attempted to reopen it the following day, she was arrested by the vice squad.

She acquired the free services of a young Jewish lawyer, Jonah Goldstein, and proceeded to turn the trial into a political and moral play. The courtroom was crowded with Brownsville mothers, along with their many children. The witnesses recounted story after story of "eight children, and

MOTHERS!

Can you afford to have a large family?
Do you want any more children?
If not, why do you have them?
DO NOT KILL, DO NOT TAKE LIFE, BUT PREVENT
Safe, Harmless Information can be obtained of trained
Nurses at

46 AMBOY STREET
NEAR PITKIN AVE. — BROOKLYN.

Tell Your Friends and Neighbors.   All Mothers Welcome
A registration fee of 10 cents entitles any mother to this Information.

מומערס!

זייט איהר פערמעגליך צו האבען א גרויסע פאמיליע?

ווילט איהר האבען נאך קינדער?

אויב ניט, וואָרום האָם איהר זיי?

מערדערם נים, נעהמט נים קיין לעבען, נור פערהים זיך.

זיכערע, אונשעדליכע אינפאָרמאציע קענט איהר בעקומען פון ערפארענע נוירסעס אין

46 אמבאי סטריט ניער פיטקין עוועניו בּרוקלין

זאָגט דאָס בעקאנט צו אייערע פריינד און שכנות.   יעדער מוטער איז ווילקאמען

פיר 10 סענט איינשרייב־געלד וועט איהר בעקעממען צו דיעזע אינפאָרמיישאָן.

MADRI!

Potete permettervi il lusso d'avere altri bambini?
Ne volete ancora?
Se non ne volete piu', perche' continuate a metterli
al mondo?

NON UCCIDETE MA PREVENITE!

Informazioni sicure ed innocue saranno fornite da infermiere autorizzate a
46 AMBOY STREET   Near Pitkin Ave. Brooklyn
a cominciare dal 12 Ottobre. Avvertite le vostre amiche e vicine.
Tutte le madri sono ben accette. La tassa d'iscrizione di 10 cents da diritto
a qualunque madre di ricevere consigli ed informazioni gratis.

three who didn't live," and husbands who earned "ten dollars a week—when he works."

Sanger was guilty, of course, of distributing birth control information, and she was convicted. She refused to pay her fine and spent several weeks in a workhouse. There was a well-publicized "coming out" party when her sentence ended, complete with a band and many of her liberal and socialist friends.

As she continued her legal appeal, she turned from direct confrontation to education, organization, and legislation. In 1917 she founded the magazine *Birth Control Review* to educate the public and to change the laws.

While the Court of Appeals of New York upheld her conviction, it redefined the law so that a physician could dispense birth control information to married patients. This was the beginning of a number of legal victories.

In 1921 Sanger founded the American Birth Control League. Although some of her clinics were raided and closed by the police as late as 1926, progress was achieved for freedom of choice. In 1936 her organization took its present name, the Planned Parenthood Federation.

Critics were common, but their arguments were more emotional than logical. When a contraception bill was before Congress in 1934, a right-wing priest, Father Charles Coughlin, testified that the bill only meant "how to commit adultery and not get caught." He believed that birth control was "a Russian innovation" and that those who advocated its legalization were seeking to pull down motherhood and the family as had been done, supposedly, in Russia. Coughlin rejected all birth control as against nature, God, the Bible, the country's best interests, and morality. Despite such claimed allies, Coughlin and similar critics tended to lose their battles over the years.

As public opinion changed, technical progress was being made. In the 1920s, the first intrauterine devices (IUDs) were invented and used. A German gynecologist predicted that an object lying within the uterine cavity would "confuse" the woman's reproductive system by convincing it that an embryo was already present. The first IUDs were star-like objects made of silkworm gut, and then of pure gold and silver. When this doctor was driven from Germany in the 1930s, both because he was Jewish and because the Nazis wanted as many little Germans as possible, he came to the attention of Sanger. Nonetheless, many doctors feared malpractice suits, and IUDs were rarely tried in the United States for several decades. By 1962 the total number of women with IUDs was only a few hundred throughout the world. At that point, however, the use of plastics and stainless steel, along with new shapes, brought the device into general use.

At first, the IUD seemed to present no major problems for most women. It did not involve hormones or medications that disturbed the physiological balance of the body. The effect of an IUD was strictly local, and ovulation remained unaffected. Not all women could use IUDs, however, since they had to be inserted by qualified medical personnel, and some women experienced heavy periods and cramps. Still, there did not appear to be long-term difficulties.

Another advance was the development of a birth control pill. While a number of sex hormones had been isolated by the 1920s, they were enormously expensive. Progesterone cost as much as $40,000 a pound. Not until the 1950s, when such hormones could be manufactured synthetically, did the prospect of a widely used pill become realistic. After tests were conducted in the 1950s on poor women in Haiti and Puerto Rico, birth control pills were approved by the U.S. Food and Drug Administration in 1960. Their use grew rapidly, despite legal and moral barriers. The Supreme Court ruled in 1965, in *Griswold v. Connecticut*, that state laws banning the use of contraceptives by married couples violated their privacy.

Just as these birth control techniques were beginning to be commonly used in the 1960s, abortion became a major issue. In 1962, there was front-page coverage of the thalidomide scare. This tranquilizer, which had been given to pregnant women in Europe, was found to produce extreme birth defects, such as children who had only a head and a torso, but no arms or legs.

The most publicized case in the United States was that of Sherri Finkbine. In 1962 she was a television hostess on a children's show in Phoenix, Arizona, married to a schoolteacher, Robert Finkbine, and pregnant with her fifth child. To her horror, she learned that the tranquilizers she had been taking would probably cause a monstrously deformed child. Since abortions were not totally banned in Arizona, she decided to end this pregnancy. She checked into a Catholic hospital, St. Joseph's, and allowed some publicity for her case, thinking that she could alert other mothers to the potential dangers of bearing a thalidomide baby. Instead, there was a storm of controversy, and the hospital refused to perform the abortion. She was forced to travel to Sweden to end her three-month pregnancy. The fetus was defective.

Public reaction was both sympathetic and violently negative. On the negative side, she lost her television job immediately, and she and her husband were flooded with poison-pen letters, some of which even threatened the Finkbine children. Many other people identified with the plight of these middle-class people trapped in the irrationality of the law. Sherri Finkbine did not endorse all abortions, saying that it was "an ugly, horrible happening," but she concluded that "women should have the right."

There was another public discussion in 1964 when an epidemic of German measles, combined with the inability of women who were at risk to get abortions, resulted in the birth of over 20,000 severely deformed children in the United States.

Public opinion was shifting for many reasons. The existing law was too inflexible. There was growing concern, too, about overpopulation. It seemed more equitable for the individual woman to decide if she wished to have children. If this was a free society, why should any church or government dictate to a woman what to do with a fetus which was, after all, not a separately functional being? The women's movement of the 1960s emphasized such themes as "my uterus is not state property," "women must decide, not the church, not the state," and "our bodies belong to us, not to the government."

A final reason for change was that the law, whenever possible, was ignored. The more affluent could do this with probable impunity; the poor were more likely to suffer medical problems from quack abortionists. Estimates of illegal abortions ran as high as 1 million a year in the middle to late 1960s.

With the revival of the women's movement in the 1960s, advances in medicine, and greater social questioning and openness to new ideas, the issue of abortion was vigorously debated as part of the larger issue of women controlling their own bodies.

It was the courts rather than the legislatures that made contraception and abortion more available to those who wished to use them. Beginning in the 1960s, legal limits to birth control began to be struck down as hindrances to the right of privacy. It was asserted that birth control should be a personal decision, rather than a matter of law.

The most influential case was *Roe v. Wade*, in which the Supreme Court ruled in 1973 that American women have the right to legal abortions if they so choose. This was fifty-seven years after Sanger's first birth control clinic opened.

The Court declared that "the unborn have never been recognized in the law as persons in the whole sense" and refused to "resolve the difficult question of when life begins." Instead, it ruled that the state could not forbid abortion during the first trimester, could impose limits during the second trimester in the interest of the mother's health and medical standards, and could deny all abortions during the third trimester when the fetus might be viable outside the womb. With this legal ruling, the situation reverted to approximately that of the fourteenth century, except that abortions were now ten times safer than childbirth for the physical health of the mother.

Dissenters emphasized, however, the death of the fetus. Was it human? Did it have a soul? A minority condemned all abortions. If a woman was raped and conceived a child, that was unfortunate, but the woman should not kill the fetus. ("The victim of a rape survives. The victim of abortion does not.") The same was true if a pregnancy resulted from incest, or if a pregnancy was likely to produce a deformed infant, or if a pregnancy could damage the physical or mental health of the mother. For antiabortionists, a human being was created at the moment of conception and to destroy that being was murder. The hierarchy of the Catholic church was especially vocal in comparing abortion to infanticide.

The power of this minority seemed large in 1980 when it was crucial in the electoral defeat of liberal senators Birch Bayh, Frank Church, John Culver, and George McGovern. It became obvious by the mid-1980s that only about 20 percent of the adult population, including a similar percentage of all Catholics, endorsed the criminalization of all abortion. There were nineteen local votes on abortion from 1978 through 1986, and only one was negative and that by less than 1 percent. Given such facts, it is unlikely that a constitutional amendment banning abortion will succeed, since it would require sixty-seven votes in the Senate, two-thirds of the House, and three-fourths of all state legislatures. The percentage of those who want such an amendment declined in the late 1980s, despite the verbal encouragement of Ronald Reagan. The only reasonable hope seems to be the creation of an antiabortion majority on the Supreme Court, although in its 1986 upholding of *Roe v. Wade* there were seven justices who were opposed to any total ban on abortion. It is possible, however, that a majority could be gained for restrictions.

This would probably be acceptable to the large number of Americans who agree with limiting the availability of abortion. The courts have sometimes invalidated these restrictions, however, such as the requirement that a woman receive the consent of her parents if she is under the age of eighteen or that she gain the approval of the father of her child. Other restrictions have been successful, such as the Hyde Amendment to a congressional bill in 1976. This amendment denied Medicaid funds for abortions, which primarily limited the opportunities of the poor, while retaining freedom for the affluent. It was argued that without this amendment some taxpayers would be forced to pay for practices which they condemned. Of course, denying such funds also throttled the beliefs of many other taxpayers. In addition, if one accepted the principle that government programs could only be funded if virtually everyone agreed with them, government might well collapse.

Finally, some critics of abortion have promoted court cases that assert that the fetus is a "person" entitled to constitutional protection. This challenges the historic legal principle that live birth is necessary before any rights will be recognized. Although some isolated legal changes have been made, such as medical malpractice suits against doctors who harmed a fetus before birth or court-ordered feeding of a pregnant anorexic, the basic linkage of live birth to legal right is unlikely to be abandoned.

The 25 percent who favor no restrictions on abortion have been concentrated in the more educated and younger age groups. They have varying reasons for their position. Many believe that, since each person and each situation is unique, a decision involving abortion should be a pragmatic question of situational ethics. The right to choose should not be denied categorically.

Ninety-seven Catholics encouraged a similar idea in a large ad published in *The New York Times* in 1984. Their statement, entitled "A Catholic Statement on Pluralism and Abortion," forthrightly argued that "a large number of Catholic theologians hold that even direct abortion, though tragic, can sometimes be a moral choice." Although the church hierarchy demanded that all members of religious orders recant or be dismissed, it was obvious from all polls that most Catholics, and most people of all religions, found this a reasonable argument. Although many Americans have been uncomfortable with legal abortions, there has been no evidence that a majority would forbid abortion under all circumstances.

If a woman decides today that she does not want to carry a pregnancy to full term, she may have various options. If she has money, she has few if any problems. If she is poor or lives outside a major metropolitan area she may find that many hospitals refuse to perform abortions, less often because of scruples than because of negative publicity generated by the minority. If she goes to a clinic, she may run a gauntlet of picketers ("sidewalk counselors"), telling her that she is planning to become a murderer. They have magnified posters of pickled fetuses, tape recordings of crying babies, and signs declaring "God loves your baby even if you don't," "the second Holocaust," "aborting America," and "don't murder your baby." They imply that the fetus will feel great pain, which is disputed by the American Association of Obstetricians and Gynecologists. They say that the woman will experience sorrow and depression, although this may be culturally induced, since women following abortions are no more likely to have such feelings than women who have children ("postpartum depression"). Some critics of abortion, like the group Birthright, may try to convince the woman to have the child and surrender it for adoption.

Antiabortionists have become increasingly frustrated, and sometimes angry, at their inability to convince a majority of the rightness of their movement. This was a factor in the more than three dozen bombings and arson attacks at abortion clinics from 1982 to early 1985. There have also been workshops on "How to Disrupt an Abortion Clinic." Although some activists have claimed that "only" property would be destroyed, it is doubtful that they would have responded as mildly to the bombing of a ROTC center, a school, or their own church. Furthermore, life has been endangered: a January 1985 bombing in Washington, D.C., shattered over 230 windows in nearby apartment buildings. Any increase in violence will tend to discredit this movement further.

Some people predict that many abortions could be avoided if the public was better informed about birth control, but most antiabortionists oppose sex education and contraception. For many of them, sex is primarily for procreation, not recreation: "if you play, you've got to pay." The Catholic church bans all "artificial" birth control and favors only the rhythm method, in which a married couple have sex during the period of the month when the woman is infertile. Since this method can be unreliable, even a majority of Catholics use other means.

Americans of all backgrounds are using reproductive knowledge to increase both freedom and planning in their lives. Most people no longer assume that ignorance about sexuality is a virtue. In 1987 polls indicated that 85 percent of the public—including 89 percent of Catholics—supported sex education in the schools. Women are more aware of options; they are no longer automatically consigned to the role of baby-making machine. While this freedom has contributed to some problems, such as the herpes epidemic of the 1980s, there are few signs that the majority of Americans want to return to earlier limits.

A number of common means of contraception are now available. First, the pill. About 29 percent of those using contraception in the United States by the late 1980s, and a total of about 54 million worldwide, take contraceptive pills. Unfortunately, such hormones may increase the risk of blood clots, cancers, vision impairment, and high blood pressure. Such side effects caused their use to decline by one-half from 1973 to 1983. There continues to be scientific uncertainty about taking such hormones for many years, although a 1986 article in the *New England Journal of Medicine* concluded that the use of contraceptive pills did not increase the likelihood of breast cancer and produced "small" possibilities of other disorders.

Women suffer from these doubts and problems because there is no male contraceptive pill. Little research has been done to produce one. Even if a pill existed, men might complain about side effects that they consider minimal for women, and women might not trust men to tell them the truth if asked whether they had taken their pill.

A second common type of birth control is the use of condoms. After a 1977 Supreme Court ruling, they became easier to advertise and display in the United States. By the late 1980s over a half-billion condoms were sold each year in this country and, worldwide, about 40 million people used them as a regular form of birth control. Condoms have no side effects and are effective in preventing both disease and pregnancy. Although mass magazines and television once refused to carry ads for them because of moral critics, the first such ads began to appear in 1987, prompted mainly by the growing popular concern about Acquired Immune Defficiency Syndrome (AIDS) and the need for protection. As one woman in an ad sighs: "I'll do a lot for love, but I'm not ready to die for it."

Third, about 60 million people use IUDs throughout the world, with a relatively small percentage of them in the United States. IUDs may pose health hazards for some women, including permanent infertility, infection, hysterectomy, and toxic shock death. In 1985 the A. H. Robins Company, as the manufacturer of the Dalkon Shield, sought bankruptcy protection from lawsuits involving over 100,000 women and a half-billion dollars in damages. In 1986 the Searle Company also removed its IUD from the market. Only one IUD, Alza Corp's Progestasert, remained on the market, with another due out in 1988 from GynMed. Both companies require users to sign an informed-consent agreement stating that the user understands the risks of infection and sterility.

Fourth, other devices can be used, such as diaphragms, medicated vaginal rings, foams, douches, spermicidal creams and jellies, and suppositories. Some of these may vanish because of consumer liability suits and high insurance costs for their manufacturers.

Fifth, there were about 1.5 million abortions in the United States in 1986, 90 percent done during the first twelve weeks of pregnancy when the fetus could not live independently outside the womb. These facts may shock some people. Would they prefer 1.5 million unwanted children each year, with the social and economic consequences of that? Would they prefer that a desperate teenager or a young career woman turn to an illegal abortionist and suffer medical complications? People who have abortions are not numbers in a statistical table. They are real people with real problems.

It may be possible to resolve some of these dilemmas in a more private way than going to an abortion clinic. Within a few years, a woman may be able to take a once-a-month pill of the newly discovered RU 486. This pill, containing no harmful estrogen, would prevent a fertilized egg from becoming implanted in the uterine wall. Conception would be followed by regular menstruation. Such a medical possibility would allow abortion as simply the act of taking a pill in the privacy of one's own home. Critics nonetheless reject this as "chemical warfare against the unborn."

The sixth and most decisive form of birth control is sterilization. About 22 percent of women using contraception have had tubal ligations and hysterectomies, and 11 percent of such men have had vasectomies.

The future could see the addition of other methods, such as timed-release implants, morning-after pills, and reversible sterilizations. Of course, the final barrier would be crossed if sexuality is totally separated from reproduction through such processes as gynogenesis, cloning, and parthenogenesis. The common availability of such techniques would mean a new stage of human life.

The presence or absence of all forms of birth control will influence not only the lives of individual people but that of nations. When Paul Ehrlich wrote *The Population Bomb* in 1960, he predicted a grim future of poverty, malnutrition, mental retardation, and social chaos because of rising birthrates and the ability of medical science to save lives that would have perished in childhood during earlier eras. This is an international problem for which the opposers of contraception have no workable solutions. When the pope issued "Humanae Vitae" against contraception in 1968, it was met with such headlines as "Pope Denounces Birth Control as Millions Starve." From 1970 to 1980 the world's population grew by almost 20 percent to 4.4 billion people. By the year 2000, the total population may increase by another 40 percent. Despite this projection, the U.S. government cut all aid to the 140-member UN Fund for Population Activities in 1985 because the U.S. claimed that one government, the People's Republic of China, had allowed or encouraged forced abortions. The Reagan administration also attacked the family planning work of the International Planned Parenthood Federation and tried to cut off federal funds for Planned Parenthood in the U.S. in 1987. It is reasonable to suppose that without population controls, there may be standing room only for the children that we do have, in a crowded world of greater discontent and disruption.

WOMEN'S WORK

The best man for the job may be a woman.

1970s button

It was once easy to predict, when a female child was born, that the young woman would either be a wife, a schoolteacher, or a potential spinster. The same limiting assumptions were not made about a male child. Today, most women are still socialized to be less competitive than men; they are unlikely to be educated in scientific and managerial subjects; and they are expected to be satisfied with the lowest-paid tasks in American society. Nonetheless, all varieties of "women's work" have been altered during the last century and a half because of economic changes, educational advances, and the social and political organization of many women.

The major form of female labor has been the care of the home. It was assumed that a woman would pass from parental guidance to wifely obedience. Emma Goldman (1869–1940) remembered her father telling her that she did not need to be educated, since "girls do not have to learn much in order to prepare fish, cut noodles fine, and give a man plenty of children."

Goldman concluded that traditional marriage was little better than prostitution. If a woman had no training for an independent career, she was obligated to sell herself into marriage for money and security. She was a kept woman. To the indignant response that marriage was "sacred," a feminist like Charlotte Perkins Gilman (1860–1935) replied that "anybody can be a mother. An oyster can be a mother. The difficult thing is to be a person."

In the earlier home, women performed considerable unpaid labor. This included spinning, making cloth and clothes, baking, butter churning, candle and soap making, and producing many other things now bought in stores. The home also produced a kind of labor force: children. In early America, there were seven children in the average family, and a woman was pregnant or nursing about one-half of her time from the age of twenty to forty.

Today, the number of single people is the highest ever, rising almost 70 percent from 1970 to the mid-1980s (to over 18 million adults). Marriage may be approached more gradually. From 1970 to 1978 alone, the number of unmarried couples living together doubled, to well over 1 million. When people marry, they may decide not to have children. If they are unhappy with their marriage, they are freer to divorce, with most remarrying.

Married women generally live differently from their predecessors. In 1985, over 55 percent of married women had jobs outside the home. According to the 1980 census, only one in every seven families still consisted of the once-common model of an employed husband, children, and a stay-at-home wife.

The home itself is no longer a little factory; the industrial revolution ended most of its productive functions. The remaining housework has been transformed by the invention of canned and prepared foods, washing machines, refrigerators, gas and electric stoves, store-bought clothes, disposable diapers, baby formula, and other innovations.

This doesn't mean that the modern housewife necessarily has more leisure. Earlier standards of housekeeping were often sloppy, even for people with servants. Washing clothes is now a frequent task. A bath is more than a once-a-week affair. Housecleaning is not reserved for the spring and other

major seasons of the year. Servants are no longer common for the middle classes. Standards of child rearing may also be more demanding.

Even labor-saving inventions do not save much labor if they are used individually. There are no economies of scale if food is prepared in individual kitchens on individual stoves; if child care is still done by each mother; if washing is done at home; if housecleaning is an individual job. All of this is extremely inefficient, but most Americans find it hard to imagine communal arrangements.

Modest proposals have involved equal sharing of responsibilities between the man and the woman. Democracy would begin at home for the egalitarian family. Another moderate goal has been the greater availability of day-care centers, so that women would have more options in their lives. Mothers now are often compelled to remain at home, or if they work and cannot find day care or cannot afford to pay for it, their children may be left without supervision.

More fundamental proposals for cooperative housekeeping have been made by writers like Charlotte Perkins Gilman. She envisioned, in books like *Women and Economics* (1898) and *The Home* (1920), the possibilities of residential hotels. These kitchenless homes would have centralized, professional, and efficient facilities for the preparation of food, private dining rooms, areas for nurseries, and professional housecleaning services. Another writer of the same period, Alexandra Kollontai, predicted that the separation of the kitchen from the home would rival the historical significance of the separation of church and state! Although such theories have never gained a wide following, industrialization created some odd similarities in cafeterias and laundries, but without the cooperative spirit of Gilman's plans.

If the modern home contains children, they are likely to be present because their parents wanted them, rather than because they were "accidents" or automatic products of unreasoning biology. Motherhood is no longer compulsory for married women.

Other forms of traditional female labor outside marriage have included child care for others, health care, farm labor, needlework, domestic service, and keeping boarders. Black women, even when married, have always been more likely to have such jobs because it was impossible for a family to live on one income, or because of limited job opportunities for black men. In 1910, for example, 55 percent of black women worked for wages, compared to 23 percent of white women. Although this gap is now much narrower, it has not entirely vanished.

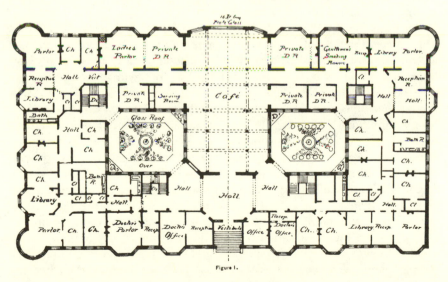

Figure I.

This plan for an apartment hotel is similar to Gilman's concept. It was done by John Pickering Putnam for an 1890 issue of *American Architect and Building News*. (From Dolores Hayden, *The Grand Domestic Revolution*, p. 193.)

When traditional jobs for women have changed, the new jobs often looked similar in content to the old:

—The expansion of education meant more jobs for women teachers, but they have constituted 99 percent of all kindergarten instructors, while they are rare at the level of full professor at a university.

—Changes in business expanded the number of woman secretaries, especially after it was proven that typewriters were not too complicated for them to use (as some men first thought).

—In medicine, women are nurses; men are doctors. In 1910, 93 percent of all nurses were women; in 1982, 95.6 percent were women. In 1910, 6 percent of all doctors were women; by 1982, this figure had only increased to 14.3 percent.

—The creation of airplane travel created a whole new female job, the stewardess. Pilots, of course, are men.

—The invention of the telephone eventually produced another type of job, the telephone operator, most of whom have been women.

According to the 1980 census, about 70 percent of female labor is confined to a relatively small number of sex-segregated, dead-end occupations, such as waitress, cook, librarian, elementary school teacher, nurse, secretary, clerk, and hairdresser. Fifty-two percent of all social workers and 79 percent of all librarians were women in 1910; in 1982 women did respectively 66.4 and 83.4 percent of these jobs. Women in such jobs have little ambition. What are the realistic chances for promotion from the rank of secretary? This is sometimes called "the pink-collar blues."

For some women, however, there are further options in the professions. Many people will point to a token woman pilot, woman astronaut, woman lawyer, or woman banker. Professional schooling and employment have improved. This process has grown from the days of the first secondary school for women in Troy, New York, in 1821; the first women's college, Mount Holyoke, in 1837; and the first woman graduate of Oberlin College in 1841. Momentum built slowly. By the late 1920s, only two out of every one hundred adult women went to college. By the 1980s, however, it would be uncommon to hear the ancient superstition that women's nervous systems were too delicate to bear the general strain of study, even though women might still be advised to forgo classes in science, math, and computers. This change is obvious in the professional schools: in 1985, 30 percent of medical school graduates and 37 percent of law school graduates were women.

Finally, the industrialization of the United States from the early 1800s created new options for female labor. Many jobs now de-emphasized strength and called for manual dexterity and mental quickness. Because women workers were generally cheaper and regarded as more pliable, their numbers increased in the early textile mills and factories.

Although many of these factories could be called sweatshops by modern standards, they did provide an independent income, however small. By 1880, 2 million women worked outside the home; by 1910, 4 million. The number and percentage of working women has increased constantly in recent decades, to comprise more than 50 percent of the total work force by the 1980s.

Various reform movements since the 1960s have encouraged the passage and enforcement of regulations that forbid discrimination against such working women. Feminists today can rely upon the Equal Pay Act of 1963, Title VII of the 1964 Civil Rights Act, the Age Discrimination Act of 1967, the Equal Credit Opportunity Act of 1974 (as amended in 1976), a congressional mandate in 1976 to open the enrollment in U.S. military academies to women, the Pregnancy Discrimination Act of 1978, several executive orders, many state ERAs, and the Supreme Court's interpretations of the Fourteenth Amendment, which declares that "no State shall . . . deny to any person within its jurisdiction the equal protection of the laws."

Although women still frequently earn less than men for the same or comparable jobs and have fewer encouragements for a wide range of choices in life (a pattern that eventually results in a larger number of elderly poor women), there are many trends for greater justice for women. The Supreme Court has continued its general support, ruling unanimously in *Meritor Savings Bank v. Vinson* (1986) that companies can be held liable for sexual harassment. Many local governments and about twenty state governments have also passed laws insuring that women will receive equal pay with men for comparable jobs. Even if the Reagan administration has verbally and administratively discouraged the Equal Employment Opportunity Commission, the U.S. Civil Rights Commission, and the other agencies of the federal government from promoting such change, the majority of public opinion has shifted remarkably in recent years. Even many self-identified conservatives today may endorse ideas about women's economic and social rights that would have been thought of as advanced twenty years ago.

Although middle-class white women have benefited the most, a 1987 poll found that 41 percent of upper-income women said that they were not feminists, whereas only 26 percent of lower-income women rejected the term, and a remarkable 64 percent of nonwhite women *affirmed* a self-description as feminists. The fifteenth anniversary issue of *Ms.* in the summer of 1987 outlined why there was still a need for feminism.

—The United States lacks a national policy that provides birth control information so that people can make informed decisions.

—The United States is the only industrialized country with no system of national health care for women, children, and all other citizens. This failing is reflected in the number of mothers who die in childbirth: the U.S. ranks eighteenth below the safest nation. More American children also die: the U.S. is seventeenth below the best nation.

—The U.S. is the only industrialized democracy with no national system of child care for those who choose to have children.

—There are many countries where women have better employment opportunities.

—The U.S. ranks twelfth in the world in percentage of women in government, after Norway, the USSR, Sweden, Finland, Denmark, Iceland, Australia, Canada, Ireland, Israel, and Italy.

Most women are still channeled into certain life patterns without the freedom that modern society could offer them. *Ms.* concluded that "we are just beginning to learn an important truth: the United States is *not* the best country in the world for women." Although this is a big and diverse nation, it is not so wretchedly poor that it has to accept inferior standards; we could do much better.

Reformers believe that equality for women would benefit all of society. As Frederick Douglass concluded, "This cause is not altogether and exclusively woman's cause. It is the cause of human brotherhood as well as human sisterhood, and both must rise and fall together. Woman cannot be elevated without elevating man, and man cannot be depressed without depressing woman also."

The problem of equality in an unjust society.

SOURCES OF FURTHER INFORMATION

Books and Articles

Aptheker, Bettina. *Woman's Legacy: Essays on Race, Sex, and Class in American History.* Amherst: University of Massachusetts Press, 1982.

Ariès, Philippe, and André Béjin, eds. *Western Sexuality: Practice and Precept in Past and Present Times.* New York: Basil Blackwell, 1985.

Balser, Diane. *Sisterhood and Solidarity: Feminism and Labor in Modern Times.* Boston: South End Press, 1987.

Banner, Lois M. *American Beauty.* Chicago: University of Chicago Press, 1983.

Bernard, Jessie. *The Female World from a Global Perspective.* Bloomington: Indiana University Press, 1987.

Berry, Mary Frances. *Why ERA Failed.* Bloomington: Indiana University Press, 1986.

"Black Women and Feminism," *Black Scholar* (entire issue) 16 (March-April 1985).

Bonar, Joy Walker, et al. *The Abortion Question.* New York: Columbia University Press, 1987.

Boston Women's Health Collective, eds. *The New Our Bodies, Ourselves: A Book by and for Woman,* 2d ed. New York: Simon & Schuster, 1984.

Brandt, Allan M. *No Magic Bullet: A Social History of Veneral Disease in the United States since 1880,* updated ed. New York: Oxford University Press, 1987.

Chafetz, Janet S., and Anthony G. Dworkin. *Female Revolt: The Rise of Women's Movements in World and Historical Perspective.* Totowa, N.J.: Rowman & Allanheld, 1986.

Clark, Judith. *Almanac of American Women in the 20th Century.* Englewood Cliffs, N.J.: Prentice-Hall, 1987.

Cott, Nancy F. *The Grounding of Modern Feminism.* New Haven, Conn.: Yale University Press, 1987.

Davis, Angela. *Women, Race and Class.* New York: Random House, 1981.

Dearborn, Mary V. *Pocahontas's Daughters: Gender and Ethnicity in American Culture.* New York: Oxford University Press, 1987.

Degler, Carl. *At Odds: Women and the Family in America, 1776 to the Present.* New York: Oxford University Press, 1980.

D'Emilio, John D., and Estelle Freedman. *Intimate Matters: A History of Sexuality in America.* New York: Harper & Row, 1988.

Demos, John. *Past, Present, and Personal: The Family and the Life Course in American History.* New York: Oxford University Press, 1986.

Ehrenreich, Barbara, Elizabeth Hess, and Gloria Jacobs. *Re-Making Love: The Feminization of Sex.* New York: Doubleday, 1986.

Filene, Peter G. *Him/Her/Self: Sex Roles in Modern America,* 2d ed. Baltimore: Johns Hopkins University Press, 1986.

Freedman, Estelle B. "Sexuality in Nineteenth-Century America: Behavior, Ideology, and Politics," in *The Promise of American History: Progress and Prospects,* Stanley I. Kutler and Stanley N. Katz, eds., pp. 196–215. Baltimore: Johns Hopkins University Press, 1982.

Friedlander, Judith, et al., eds. *Women in Culture and Politics: A Century of Change.* Bloomington: Indiana University Press, 1986.

Friedman, Jean, et al., eds. *Our American Sisters: Women in American Life and Thought*, 4th ed. Lexington, Mass.: D. C. Heath, 1987.

Gay, Peter. *The Bourgeois Experience: Victoria to Freud*. Vol. 1: *The Education of the Senses* (1984); vol. 2: *The Tender Passion* (1986). New York: Oxford University Press, 1984–.

Gelpi, Barbara C., et al., eds. *Women and Poverty*. Chicago: University of Chicago Press, 1986.

Gerson, Kathleen. *Hard Choices: How Women Decide about Work, Career and Motherhood*. Berkeley and Los Angeles: University of California Press, 1986.

Giddings, Paula. *When and Where I Enter: The Impact of Black Women on Race and Sex in America*. New York: Morrow, 1984.

Harevan, Tamara, and Andrejs Plakans, eds. *Family History at the Crossroads: A Journal of Family History Reader*. Princeton, N.J.: Princeton University Press, 1987.

Hartmann, Betsy. *Reproductive Rights and Wrongs: Global Politics of Population Control and Contraceptive Choice*. New York: Harper & Row, 1987.

Hawes, Joseph M., and N. Ray Hiner, eds. *American Childhood: A Research Guide and Historical Handbook*. Westport, Conn.: Greenwood Press, 1985.

Hayden, Dolores. *The Grand Domestic Revolution: A History of Feminist Designs for American Homes, Neighborhoods, and Cities*. Cambridge, Mass.: MIT Press, 1981.

———. *Redesigning the American Dream: The Future of Housing, Work, and Family Life*. New York: Norton, 1984.

Hewitt, Nancy A. "Beyond the Search for Sisterhood: American Women's History in the 1980s." *Social History* 10 (October 1985): 299–321.

Hiner, N. Ray, and Joseph M. Hawes, eds. *Growing Up in America: Children in Historical Perspective*. Urbana: University of Illinois Press, 1985.

Hobson, Barbara Meil. *Uneasy Virtue: The Politics of Prostitution and the American Reform Tradition*. New York: Basic Books, 1987.

Hoff-Wilson, Joan, ed. *Rights of Passage: The Past and Future of the ERA*. Bloomington: Indiana University Press, 1986.

Hull, Gloria, Patricia Bell Scott, and Barbara Smith, eds. *All the Women Are White, and All the Blacks Are Men, but Some of Us Are Brave*. Old Westbury, N.Y.: Feminist Press, 1982.

Hunter College Women's Studies Collective. *Women's Realities, Women's Choices: An Introduction to Women's Studies*. New York: Oxford University Press, 1983.

Jardine, Alice, and Paul Smith, eds. *Men in Feminism*. New York: Methuen, 1987.

Jones, Jacqueline. *Labor of Love, Labor of Sorrow: Black Women, Work, and the Family*. New York: Basic Books, 1985.

Katzenstein, Mary F., and Carol M. Mueller, eds. *The Women's Movements of the United States and Western Europe: Consciousness, Political Opportunity and Public Policy*. Philadelphia: Temple University Press, 1987.

Kerber, Linda, and Jane De Hart Mathews, eds. *Women's America: Refocusing the Past*, 2d ed. New York: Oxford University Press, 1987.

Leavitt, Judith Walzer. *Brought to Bed: Childbearing in America, 1750–1950*. New York: Oxford University Press, 1986.

Lerner, Gerda. *The Creation of Patriarchy*. New York: Oxford University Press, 1986.

_____. *The Majority Finds Its Past: Placing Women in History*. New York: Oxford University Press, 1982.

_____. *Women Are History: A Bibliography in the History of American Women*, 4th rev. ed. Madison: Graduate Program in Women's History, Department of History, University of Wisconsin, 1986.

Luker, Kristin. *Abortion and the Politics of Motherhood*. Berkeley and Los Angeles: University of California Press, 1984.

Mansbridge, Jane J. *Why We Lost the ERA*. Chicago: University of Chicago Press, 1986.

Masters, William H., Virginia E. Johnson, and Robert C. Kolodny. *Masters and Johnson on Sex and Human Loving*. Boston: Little, Brown, 1986.

Mathews, Glenna. *"Just a Housewife": The Rise and Fall of Domesticity in the United States*. New York: Oxford University Press, 1987.

May, Elaine Tyler. "Expanding the Past: Recent Scholarship on Women and Work," in *The Promise of American History: Progress and Prospects*, Stanley I. Kutler and Stanley N. Katz, eds., pp. 216–33. Baltimore: Johns Hopkins University Press, 1982.

Melosh, Barbara, and Christina Simmons. "Exhibiting Women's History," in *Presenting the Past: Essays on History and the Public*, Susan Porter Benson, Stephen Brier, and Roy Rosenzweig, eds., pp. 203–21. Philadelphia: Temple University Press, 1986.

Mintz, Steven, and Susan Kellogg. *Domestic Revolutions: A Social History of American Family Life*. New York: Free Press, 1987.

Mitchell, Juliet, and Ann Oakley, eds. *What Is Feminism? A Re-Examination*. New York: Pantheon Books, 1987.

Newman, Richard, comp. "A Bibliography of Bibliographies on Black Women," *Newsletter* of the Afro-American Religious History Group of the American Academy of Religion 9 (Spring 1985): 5–11.

Noonan, John T., Jr. *Contraception: A History of Its Treatment by the Catholic Theologians and Canonists*, enl. ed. Cambridge: Harvard University Press, 1986.

Norton, Mary Beth. "The Evolution of White Women's Experience in Early America," *American Historical Review* 89 (June 1984): 593–619.

Ogden, Annegret S. *The Great American Housewife: From Helpmate to Wage Earner, 1776–1986*. Westport, Conn.: Greenwood Press, 1986.

Olson, Ann, and Joni Seager. *Women in the World—An International Atlas*. New York: Simon & Schuster, 1986.

Pleck, Elizabeth H. *Domestic Tyranny: The Making of American Social Policy against Family Violence from Colonial Times to the Present*. New York: Oxford University Press, 1987.

_____. "Women's History: Gender as a Category of Historical Analysis," in *Ordinary People and Everyday Life: Perspectives on the New Social History*, James B. Gardner and George Rollie Adams, eds., pp. 51–65. Nashville, Tenn.: American Association for State and Local History, 1983.

Reinisch, June Machover, et al., eds. *Masculinity/Femininity: Basic Perspectives*. New York: Oxford University Press, 1987.

Riley, Glenda. *Inventing the American Woman: A Perspective on Women's History*. Arlington Heights, Ill.: Harlan Davidson, 1987.

Rix, Sarah E., for the Women's Research and Education Institute of the Congressional Caucus for Women's Issues. *The American Woman, 1987–1988: A Report in Depth*. New York: Norton, 1987.

Roth, Darlene. "Growing Like Topsy: Research Guides to Women's History." *Journal of American History* 70 (June 1983): 95–100.

Rothman, Ellen K. *Hands and Hearts: A History of Courtship in America*. New York: Oxford University Press, 1984.

Rubin, Eva R. *Abortion, Politics, and the Courts: Roe v. Wade and Its Aftermath*. Rev. ed. Westport, Conn.: Greenwood Press, 1987.

Ryan, Mary P. "The Explosion of Family History," in *The Promise of American History: Progress and Prospects*, Stanley I. Kutler and Stanley N. Katz, eds., pp. 181–95. Baltimore: Johns Hopkins University Press, 1982.

————. *Womanhood in America: From Colonial Times to the Present*, 3d ed. New York: Franklin Watts, 1983.

Rybczynski, Witold. *Home: The Short History of an Idea*. New York: Penguin, 1987.

Scott, Anne Firor. *Making the Invisible Woman Visible*. Urbana: University of Illinois Press, 1984.

Scott, Hilda. *Working Your Way to the Bottom: The Feminization of Poverty*. London: Routledge & Kegan Paul, 1985.

Scott, Joan. "Gender: A Useful Category of Historical Analysis," *American Historical Review* 91 (December 1986): 1053–75.

Sicherman, Barbara, and Carol Hurd Green, eds. *Notable American Women: The Modern Period*. Cambridge, Mass.: Harvard University Press, 1984.

Sidel, Ruth. *Women and Children Last: The Plight of Poor Women in Affluent America*. New York: Penguin, 1987.

Snitow, Ann, Christine Stansell, and Sharon Thompson, eds. *The Powers of Desire: The Politics of Sexuality*. New York: Monthly Review Press, 1983.

Sterling, Dorothy, ed. *We Are Your Sisters: Black Women in the Nineteenth Century*. New York: Norton, 1984.

Tetreault, Mary K. "Integrating Women's History: The Case of United States History." *The History Teacher* 19 (February 1986): 210–62.

Tomaselli, Sylvanna, and Roy Porter, eds. *Rape*. New York: Basil Blackwell, 1987.

Vinovkis, Maris A. "American Families in the Past," in *Ordinary People and Everyday Life: Perspectives on the New Social History*, James B. Gardner and George Rollie Adams, eds., pp. 115–37. Nashville, Tenn.: American Association for State and Local History, 1983.

Vogel, Lise. "Feminist Scholarship: The Impact of Marxism," in *The Left Academy: Marxist Scholarship on American Campuses*, Vol. 3, Bertell Ollman and Edward Vernoff, eds., pp. 1–34. New York: Praeger, 1986.

Washington, Mary H. *Invented Lives: Narratives of Black Women, 1860–1960*. New York: Doubleday, 1987.

Weiner, Lynn Y. *From Working Girl to Working Mother: The Female Labor Force in the United States, 1820–1980*. Chapel Hill: University of North Carolina Press, 1985.

Wertz, Richard W., and Dorothy C. Wertz. *Lying-In: A History of Childbirth in America*. New York: Schocken Books, 1982.

Woloch, Nancy. *Women and the American Experience*. New York: Alfred A. Knopf, 1984.

Zelizer, Viviana. *Pricing the Priceless Child: The Changing Social Value of Children*. New York: Basic Books, 1986.

Women who seek to be equal to men lack ambition.
Placard in a West Hollywood parade, July 1987

military   political activism   building maintenance   medicine   religion

CAREER OPPORTUNITIES FOR WOMEN

Organizations and Publications

Requests for information should be accompanied by a stamped, self-addressed envelope.

American Association of University Women, 2401 Virginia Ave., N.W., Washington, D.C. 20037

American Civil Liberties Union, 132 W. 43rd St., New York, N.Y. 10036 (has many relevant committees on reproductive rights, children's rights, and women's rights)

Berkeley Women's Law Journal, Boalt Hall School of Law, University of California, Berkeley, Calif. 94720

Catholics For a Free Choice, 2008 17th St., N.W., Washington, D.C. 20002

Changing Men: Issues in Gender, Sex and Politics, 306 N. Brooks, Madison, Wisc. 53715

Children's Defense Fund, 122 C. St., N.W., Washington, D.C. 20001

Coalition of Labor Union Women, Center for Educational Research, 2000 P St., N.W., #615, Washington, D.C. 20036

Congressional Caucus for Women's Issues, 2471 Rayburn House Office Bldg., Washington, D.C. 20515

Connexions, 4228 Telegraph Ave., Oakland, Calif. 94609

Equal Employment Opportunity Commission, Office of Public Information, 2401 E St., N.W., Washington, D.C. 20506

Federally Employed Women (FEW), 1010 Vermont Ave., N.W., Washington, D.C. 20005

Feminist Issues, Transaction Periodicals Consortium, Rutgers University, New Brunswick, N.J. 08903

Feminist Press, City University of New York, 311 E. 94th St., New York, N.Y. 10128

Feminist Studies, c/o Women's Studies Program, University of Maryland, College Park, Md. 20742

Frontiers: A Journal of Women Studies, Women Studies, Campus Box 325, University of Colorado, Boulder, Colo. 80309

Genders: Art, History, Literature and Film, University of Texas, P.O. Box 7819, Austin, Tex. 78713-7819

Harvard Women's Law Journal, Publications Office, Harvard Law School, Cambridge, Mass. 02138

Heresies, P.O. Box 766, Canal St. Sta., New York, N.Y. 10013

Iris: A Journal About Women, B5 Garrett Hall, University of Virginia, Charlottesville, Va. 22903

League of Women Voters, 1730 M St., N.W., Washington, D.C. 20036

Lilith: The Jewish Women's Magazine, 250 W. 57th St., New York, N.Y. 10107

Mexican American Women's National Association (MANA), 1201 16th St., N.W., Suite 420, Washington, D.C. 20036

Ms., Subscription Dept., P.O. Box 50008, Boulder, Colo. 80321-0008

National Abortion Rights Action League (NARAL), 1101 14th St., N.W., Washington, D.C. 20005

National Center on Women and Family Law, 799 Broadway, Rm. 402, New York, N.Y. 10003

National Committee on Pay Equity, c/o National Education Association, 1201 16th St., N.W., Rm 420, Washington, D.C. 20036

National Conference on Puerto Rican Women, 1010 Vermont Ave., N.W., Washington, D.C. 20005

National Council of Jewish Women, 15 E. 26th St., New York, N.Y. 10010

National Council of Negro Women, 701 N. Fairfax St., Alexandria, Va. 22314

National Federation of Business and Professional Women's Clubs, 2012 Massachusetts Ave., N.W., Washington, D.C. 20036

National Organization for Women, 1401 New York Ave., N.W., Suite 800, Washington, D.C. 20005 (There is also a separate NOW Legal Defense and Education Fund at 99 Hudson St., New York, N.Y. 10013.)

National Task Force on Prostitution, P.O. Box 26354, San Francisco, Calif. 94126 (Earlier name: Call Off Your Old Tired Ethics [COYOTE])

National Women's Health Network, 224 7th St., S.E., Washington, D.C. 20003

National Women's Law Center, 1751 N St., N.W., Washington, D.C. 20036

National Women's Political Caucus, 1275 K St., N.W., Suite 750, Washington, D.C. 20005

New Directions for Women, 108 W. Palisade Ave., Englewood, N.J. 07631

Off Our Backs, 2423 18th St., N.W., Washington, D.C. 20009

Older Women's League (OWL), 1325 G St., N.W., Lower-Level B, Washington, D.C. 20005

Planned Parenthood Federation of America, 810 7th Ave., New York, N.Y. 10019

Project on the Status and Education of Women, Association of American Colleges, 1818 R St., N.W., Washington, D.C. 20009

Religious Coalition for Abortion Rights, 100 Maryland Ave., N.E., Washington, D.C. 20002

SAGE: A Scholarly Journal on Black Women, P.O. Box 42741, Atlanta, Ga. 30311-0741

Signs: A Journal of Women in Culture and Society, University of Chicago Press, Journals Division, 5801 S. Ellis Ave., Chicago, Ill. 60637

13th Moon: A Feminist Literary Magazine, Box 309, Cathedral Station, New York, N.Y. 10025

Womanews, P.O. Box 220, Village Sta., New York, N.Y. 10014

Women Against Pornography, 358 W. 47th St., New York, N.Y. 10036

Women's Bureau, U.S. Department of Labor, 14th and Constitution, N.W., Washington, D.C. 20210

Women's Equity Action League, 1250 I St., N.W., Suite 305, Washington, D.C. 20005

Women's Institute for Freedom of the Press, 3306 Ross Place, N.W., Washington, D.C. 20008 (Publishes an annual *Index/Directory of Women's Media*)

Women's Legal Defense Fund, 2000 P St., N.W., Suite 400, Washington, D.C. 20036

Women's Occupational Health Resource Center, 117 St. John's Place, Brooklyn, N.Y. 11217

Women's Review of Books, Wellesley College Center for Research on Women, Wellesley, Mass. 02181

Women's Rights Law Reporter, Rutgers Law School, 15 Washington St., Newark, N.J. 07102

Women's Studies International Forum, Pergamon Press, Fairview Park, Elmsford, N.Y. 10523

Women's Studies Quarterly, 311 E. 94th St., New York, N.Y. 10128

Yellow Silk; Journal of Erotic Arts, P.O. Box 6374, Albany, Calif. 94706

7

"We Are Everywhere":
Gay Men and Lesbians

Everyone has gay friends, neighbors, relatives, and coworkers, but usually they are hidden because of society's prejudices. A lesbian who placed a photo of her lover on the office desk, a man who publicly kissed another man, or someone who chatted about a date with a person of the same sex would be regarded as flaunting a perversion, although these are perfectly normal activities for heterosexuals. For the vast majority of homosexuals, it is easier to remain silent or to lie, whether out of fear of controversy and job loss, or merely because it seems impossible to explain their lives to heterosexuals.

Recently, growing numbers have broken this silence, and the deep prejudices of thousands of years have been challenged dramatically by the appearance of gay liberation throughout the West, but most comprehensively in the United States. Americans have suddenly learned that homosexuals constitute a large and diverse minority, that they have a cruelly long history of persecution, and that they offer special insights into the nature of sexuality and living arrangements in this society.

The size of this population compels attention. The Kinsey Reports (1948; 1953) indicated that no more than 50 percent of men and 72 percent of women were totally heterosexual. Large minorities in a more repressive era than ours admitted to having erotic attractions to members of their own sex. Indeed, 37 percent of men and 21 percent of women had some overt homosexual experience, ranging from single instances of mutual masturbation to repeated sexual encounters. Approximately 13 percent of men and 7 percent of women engaged in more homosexual than heterosexual activity for at least three years of their lives between the ages of sixteen and fifty-five. Thus, millions are exclusively homosexual, and a much larger group may be predominantly one way or the other, but not totally so. Allen Ginsberg's poem is truer than public opinion once assumed:

```
Everybody's just      a little
      bit homo        sexual
        whether they like it or not
Everybody feels       a little bit
      of love for their sex
              even if        they almost forgot
```

Since the people with homosexual experience are of every age, occupation, educational level, ethnic background, class, and region, it is obvious
that stereotypes of "the homosexual" cannot be accurate. Despite the popular images of lesbian truck drivers, limp-wristed decorators, and timid flo-
rists with wavering voices, there is no more a typical homosexual than there
is a typical heterosexual. Just as racial bigotry is expressed in comments on
typical Jews and blacks, "kikes and niggers," sexual bigotry is found in
comments on typical homosexuals, "faggots and dykes." The study of gay
liberation, is important not only for the numbers of people involved but for
what can be learned of the rich diversity so often obscured by labels. Rita
Mae Brown outlined this complexity for lesbians:

There are lesbians whose politics are to the right of Genghis Khan. There are lesbians
who make Maoists look moderate. There are lesbians who can only be described as
dowdy dykes. There are lesbians who can't be described, they simply knock you out
with their beauty. There are lesbians who love cats and would never be seen without
one. There are lesbians who like dogs. There are lesbians who like men (no parallel
intended) and there are lesbians who barely know that men as a group exist. There
are Baptist lesbians, born again; there are Catholic lesbians who certainly never
violate papal procedure regarding birth control. There are Jewish lesbians and Zen
ones, Shinto and all the other religious possibilities. There are even lesbians who
don't believe in any religion at all. There are poor lesbians and rich lesbians. There
are dumb lesbians (yes, I hate to admit it but there are) and there are smart lesbians.
(Foreword to Our Right to Love, ed. Ginny Vida et al. [Englewood Cliffs, N.J.:
Prentice-Hall, 1978], p. 13)

Gay liberation has raised basic questions about sex roles in this culture.
These roles are confined to the basic dichotomies of "acting like a man" or
"acting like a woman," "straight or gay" (with little recognition of gradations), and "active or passive." Gay liberation has sensitized many people to
the life-denying aspects of these categories, making it an important struggle
for individual freedom and expression.

Having said this, where does one begin the history of an "invisible people," or find the sources for it? These problems were confronted by gay
organizations in the 1950s. On one hand, they felt the need to learn about
the hidden history of their brothers and sisters. Like other minorities who
are self-conscious, such as Jews, blacks, and women, they wanted to rescue
their past from suppression and neglect.

This proved to be an enormous task. How does one reconstruct the history of a people from anonymous martyrs, burned letters and scrapbooks, writings with the pronouns changed, suppressed autobiographies, and silenced voices? Little was recorded, most of that was destroyed, and almost all of the remainder has been filtered through heterosexual biases. The conventional history of homosexuality focuses on the scandalous: heretic burnings, sex arrests, prison records, exposés, and gossip-mongering. Homosexuals of the past are generally faceless; one sees only the masks that society has put on them.

What remains is a record of intolerance that one historian has called "a heterosexual dictatorship":

During the four hundred years documented here, American homosexuals were condemned to death by choking, burning, and drowning; they were executed, jailed, pilloried, fined, court-martialed, prostituted, fired, framed, blackmailed, disinherited, declared insane, driven to insanity, to suicide, murder, and self-hate, witch-hunted, entrapped, stereotyped, mocked, insulted, pitied, castrated and despised. (Jonathan Katz, in *Gay American History*, p. 17)

This contempt is rooted in such Old Testament books as Leviticus, carried forward into the Roman world by such disciples as St. Paul, and turned into law when Christianity became the state religion in A.D. 323. Homosexuality was a damnable sin, and those guilty of it could be legally murdered from that time until the days of the founding of the colonies in the New World. The bundles of wood stacked around the people burned alive were called faggots.

The ferocity of the antihomosexual taboo in Western society is difficult to explain rationally. While other cultures have tolerated and even encouraged homosexual experimentation, those of the West have not. The Jews, at least, had a good reason: as a small and persecuted people, any sex that would not produce children was a social threat meriting the severest penalties. Curiously enough, this attitude continued into the Christian era. St. Thomas Aquinas amazingly claimed that masturbation was a more serious offense than forcible rape, since the latter included the possibility of conception.

With increasing secularization, enlightened people called for modernization of the old laws. For Thomas Jefferson, this meant that the Virginia death penalty against sodomy should be replaced by the humane punishment of castration. In the context of history, this was progress. Also, with urbanization, gay people more easily met one another, and subcultures began to form in larger cities.

At first, there were only scattered and veiled writings by American and foreign authors like Walt Whitman (d. 1892), John Addington Symonds, (d. 1893), and Edward Carpenter (d. 1929). The earliest works to achieve some respectibility were efforts to create a scientific interpretation of homosexuality. Writers like Havelock Ellis spoke of it neither as a sin nor a sickness, but as an anomaly. This literature described "inverts" who were men with women's "souls" and vice versa, and Uranians, after a reference in Plato's *Symposium* to male-male love. Other terms included Urnings, the third sex, the intermediate sex, simisexuals, and the intersexes. These writings, such as Dr. Krafft-Ebing's *Psychopathia Sexualis* (1887), the works of Dr. Magnus Hirshfeld's Scientific-Humanitarian Committee (founded in 1897), and the publications of the British Society for the Study of Sex Psychology (founded in 1914), began to be known by some in the United States.

Still, the first major nonfiction book by an American on this subject was printed in Italy under a pseudonym: Xavier Mayne (Edward I. Stevenson), *The Intersexes: A History of Similsexualism as a Problem in Social Life* (1908). This massive, 641-page commentary was published in a meagre edition of 125 copies. While the accepted wisdom was being criticized by a tiny number of educated professionals like Dr. Hirshfeld, along with audacious writers such as Carpenter and ultra-left radicals like Emma Goldman, they were opposed by an array of censoring individuals and groups. Typically, in 1927 the state legislature of New York forbade the depiction of homosexuality on any stage; this law persisted until 1967. In 1929 a lesbian novel by Radclyffe Hall, *The Well of Loneliness*, was flayed by critics and widely banned throughout the United States.

THE END OF INVISIBILITY: ORGANIZATIONS

Despite this repression, and sometimes because of it, new forces were beginning to coalesce. Margaret Sanger knew and approved of the British Society for Sex Psychology, and others were aware of the work of various German groups. In 1925 an American who had been in Germany shortly after World War I and had learned of the pro-homosexual *Bund für Menschenrecht* set up the first documented homosexual organization in the United States.

This group, the Society for Human Rights, Inc., was founded in Chicago by Henry Gerber and incorporated under the laws of the state of Illinois. Its purpose was to "combat public prejudice" against those "who by reasons of mental and physical abnormalities are abused and hindered in the legal pursuit of happiness . . . guaranteed them by the Declaration of Independence." It gathered only ten members and published two issues of *Friendship and Freedom* before its leaders were arrested, their materials confiscated, and Gerber fired from his job. Although they had broken no laws, the organization was fatally wounded. It died because of newspaper comments on a "strange sex cult" in Chicago, the cost of legal fees ($800, which was Gerber's entire savings), job losses, and public contempt.

Gerber retreated to New York City where he created a mimeographed newsletter for pen pals, *Contacts*, in 1930, and a literary magazine, *Chan-*

ticleer, in 1934. He was, in some ways, a budding social critic. He not only condemned antihomosexual laws and prejudices, but also pro-gay literature that embodied clichés (such as the masculine lesbians in *The Well of Lone-liness*, which he called "ideal anti-homosexual propaganda").

Other groups came and went without much notice, but society was changing in ways that would make it more receptive to the emergence of gay liberation. Urbanization allowed escape from the suffocatingly small worlds of farms and villages; the decline of extended families lessened social restrictions; and industrialization produced more jobs and relative independence for some women. World War II was a catalyst that brought together these factors. Millions of men and women went through the induction centers—sometimes jokingly called "seduction centers"—and went into military units where they were separated from the opposite sex. Many passed through seaports containing bars that the California Penal Code once referred to as "resorts for sex perverts." Sexual morals and sexual practices may have loosened during the war.

Still, almost no homosexuals would have expected that the 1950s would bring three national organizations for their social and legal justice. Jim Kepner, who became a gay activist in the early 1950s, bleakly portrayed the opening of that decade:

In 1950 there were no gay publications or organizations or churches; . . . no identified gays on any public platform; no gay novels describing sex or having happy endings; . . . no gay vote; no demonstrations; no gay cycle clubs; virtually no gay social activities; no gays who were arrested pleading not guilty, and hence no cases appealed; and almost no mention of homosexuality in the press except for accounts of bar raids and murders, and occasional McCarthyite screams that homosexuality was a Communist plot. (Jim Kepner, "Gay Heritage," in *A Selection of Gay Liberation Essays, 1953–1973* [Torrance, Calif.: Kepner, 1973], p. 6)

Popular myths about sexuality were challenged in 1948 with the publication of Dr. Alfred Kinsey's *Sexual Behavior in the Human Male* (selling 200,000 copies in two months), followed in 1953 by *Sexual Behavior in the Human Female*. Here, for the first time, was a scientific survey. It avoided open moralizing and attempted to depict things as they were. One admirer claimed that Kinsey had done for sex "what Columbus had done for geography." Among his shocking discoveries was evidence that nine of every ten men had committed heterosexual or homosexual acts that were, by law, sex crimes.

His study was remarkable for its rejection of absolutes. He refused to characterize people as *either* heterosexual *or* homosexual. Rather, he used a scale ranging from "0", where all of the individual's fantasies and activities were directed toward the opposite sex, to "6," where all fantasies and activities were directed toward the same sex. For Kinsey, a person could be a

Crackdown On Deviate Nests Urged

How L. A. Handles Its 150,000 Perverts

(Second In A Series)

By JACK W. ROBERTS
Miami Daily News Staff Writer

Is Greater Miami in danger of becoming a favorite gathering spot for homosexuals and sexual psychopaths?

It happened in Los Angeles and it could happen here. In California the homosexuals have organized to resist interference by police. They have established their own magazine and are constantly crusading for recognition as a "normal" group, a so-called "third sex."

They number 150,000 in Los Angeles, their leaders say. They claim kinship by nature with some of the leading literary and business figures in the nation.

The Los Angeles homosexuals are apparently well aware of the situation in Miami.

In the January issue of their magazine, Miami Beach Police Chief Romeo Shepard was roasted to a turn for a raid on homosexuals gathered at the 22nd Street bathing beach.

Urge Suit On City

The cover of the magazine showed a young man in bathing trunks facing Biscayne Bay with his arms lifted up in supplication.

Beside the figure was this headline:

"Miami Junks The Constitution."

The article urged homosexuals living in the Miami area to get together and sue the City of Miami Beach for their arrest.

Dan Sullivan, operating director of the Greater Miami Crime Commission, also was lambasted in the same issue for calling all homosexuals "sex criminals."

Due For Roasting

Last Thursday Chief Shepard pulled another raid at 22nd Street and probably will get another roasting from the magazine published in Los Angeles.

Perverts Seized in Bar Raids

'Disguised' Detectives Visit Beaches

Great Civilizations Plagued By Deviates

Pervert Colony Uncovered In Simpson Slaying Probe

By MILT SOSIN
Miami Daily News Staff Writer

A colony of some 500 male homosexuals, congregated mostly in the near-downtown northeast section and ruled by a "queen," was uncovered in the investigation of the murder of an Eastern Air Lines steward.

MIAMI HERALD   8/13/54

Deviate Drops Charge Against His Accuser

Not-so-Gay Life in Miami, Florida, 1954

"2," an ambisexual "3," or a "5." He concluded that millions of people had experienced both homosexual desires and acts.

Although his critics doubted the representativeness of the people that he interviewed as well as the wording of his questionnaires, it was commonly agreed that he was a pioneer investigator of the actual sex lives of Americans. His conclusions, even when disputed, stimulated public discussion about sexual beliefs and laws in this society, including those related to homosexuality.

This discussion encouraged the publication and success of the first widely read defense of homosexuality in the United States. Although the author, Edward Sagarin, wrote under the pseudonym Donald Webster Cory, he boldly stated that *The Homosexual in America* (1951) was based upon a quarter-century of his own life. It was a forthright polemic for a persecuted minority. It drew upon both contemporary society and the works of Edward Carpenter, John Addington Symonds, Walt Whitman, André Gide, Radclyffe Hall, Christopher Isherwood, Gertrude Stein, and many others. "Addressed to all the gay people of America," it implored them to become conscious of themselves as a community and it included a plea for heterosexuals to cast off their ignorant fears of those different from themselves.

Although some libraries filed the book under the history of pornography or abnormal psychology, some of its readers found the book a revelation. This book changed the lives of those people in the same way that many proto-feminists were intellectually enriched and stirred to action by the American edition of Simone de Beauvoir's *The Second Sex* in 1953.

Both the Kinsey Report and the Cory book reflected the changing times. The first successful gay organization in U.S. history, the Mattachine Society, was about to appear in Los Angeles. Henry Hay, a member of the Communist party for over a decade and a half, decided in 1948 that he should do something for his own oppressed people. He was afraid that in a future crisis gays would become "America's Jews," the scapegoats for social troubles. He composed a plan for a new organization, drawing upon some knowledge of the Chicago Society for Human Rights. He approached members of Bachelors for Wallace, which had supported the Progressive party candidate for president, Henry Wallace, in 1948. Later, Hay distributed leaflets at gay bars and beaches in Santa Monica. By November 1950 he had convinced only two other people that his dream was possible, and these three, with considerable audacity, founded a preliminary committee that warned of "encroaching fascism" as a danger to all minorities. The founding date: April Fool's Day, 1950.

Hay, then left the Communist party (out of concern that he would be a security risk to it!) and turned to creating "a service and welfare organization devoted to the protection and improvement of society's Androgynous Minority." Because Hay and others felt that heterosexuals required them to wear masks, they adopted the name Mattachine in 1951, after medieval jesters who were allowed to speak the truth in public because of their costumes. They would be professional fools.

The first meetings in 1950 and 1951 began the long process of overcoming the social isolation and intellectual confusion of gay people. Under the slogans of "to unify; to educate; to lead," the directors of the society proposed meetings and publications that would encourage self-understanding, regulation of "the social conduct of our minority," "social analyses" of others, "progressive sexual legislation," and "alliances" with other minorities. Each member pledged himself or herself "in every way possible, to respect the

mattachine
society
inc.

rights of all radical, religious, and national minorities, since I realize I also am a member of a persecuted minority."

Mattachine started cautiously with promises of secrecy and a "guild" structure of cells so that those who joined did not know the entire membership of the society. The number of guilds grew quickly. In 1952 the group won a publicized legal case involving one of its members, Dale Jennings, who had been arrested falsely by a police decoy for "solicitation." By 1953 the society held approximately fifty meetings with a total attendance of several thousand. There were Mattachine discussion guilds in Los Angeles, San Diego, San Francisco, and New York. The Los Angeles group began such novel activities as sending questionnaires to metropolitan political candidates requesting their views on sexual legislation and enforcement. The Los Angeles leaders also distributed 20,000 copies of an article on Mattachine in the Los Angeles *Mirror*, although it implied Communist influences.

Their expansion was too rapid and flawed. There were not enough experienced leaders, the cell structure was not democratic, basic principles were not clear to all, and there were severe social and political tensions. The potential threat of an investigation of Mattachine by the House Un-American Activities Committee (never actually carried out but a fearful thought in 1953) unnerved many members and supporters. Recognizing that the society could be destroyed by a split or an investigation, Hay dissolved the parent foundation at a meeting in the summer of 1953 and allowed different leaders to reorganize the group. The new Mattachine actively opposed communism, supported evolution not revolution, and proclaimed that it had "no connection whatever with the Mattachine Foundation."

This was not true in terms of membership and some goals, but Hay's radical theories were no longer welcome. The purged Mattachine emphasized coat-and-tie respectability, and general enthusiasm declined both because of its timidity and because of fears generated by various controversies. In 1957 the society moved to San Francisco, where it had no more than 100 members and 500 subscribers to the *Mattachine Review* (begun in 1955). There were also tiny chapters in Boston, Chicago, Denver, New York, and Los Angeles that were affiliated with this central office. By 1961 the corporation ceased to handle the administration of the far-flung outposts and refused to accept any responsibility for what they did. Each chapter went its own way.

Given the limited size of the groups, they were astonishingly active in their publications and meetings. Even in 1955, a reader of the *Mattachine Review* would learn about American activities, along with foreign literature such as *Futur, Arcadie, Der Weg, Der Ring, Vennen,* the *International Journal of Sexology, Vriendschap,* and the *Newsletter* of the International Committee for Sexual Equality. While gay liberation lacked numbers in the 1950s, it did not lack ambition or energy from a dedicated and tenacious few.

One can measure the influence of Mattachine on individuals like Frank Kameny. With a Harvard Ph.D. in astronomy, he was employed by the Army Map Service in Washington, D.C., until he was fired in 1957. There were secret allegations of homosexuality in his private life. It was not disputed that he was a competent worker who had not interjected his sexuality at the office. Despite numerous appeals and job searches, he remained unemployed for twenty months. He concluded that a gay organization was needed to supply legal aid to victims, to lobby for change, and "to pick up the pieces after society has done the smashing." In 1961 he founded the Mattachine Society of Washington, D.C., which in the 1960s picketed the White House, the Pentagon, the UN, and Independence Hall. Gays were like blacks, Kameny said. As long as blacks sat quietly in the back of the bus and accepted their inferiority they got nowhere. Even polite educational work was not sufficient. Militant public demands were the main engine for basic change. In 1962 Kameny was the first open homosexual to appear on Washington television without wearing a bag over his face or speaking from the shadows. Viewers could see a human being rather than that bizarre abstraction, The Homosexual. In 1964 he convinced the Washington Mattachine Society to reject the "sickness" and "abnormality" theories of homosexuality, although the conservative members asserted that they were not qualified to reach a scientific judgment. In 1968 he proposed the motto "Gay Is Good" at the North American Conference of Homophile Organizations; it was unanimously accepted. A few gays had now rejected an assumption that was once common, even among gays, that it was wrong to love someone of the same sex. By 1980 Kameny was an official member of the Human Rights Commission of the District of Columbia.

Turning back to the opening days of the movement, the second and third oldest gay organizations were established in the 1950s in California: ONE in 1952, and the Daughters of Bilitis in 1955.

The first was begun by several members of Mattachine and a grouplet called the Knights of the Clock, created by a black man in 1950 as an interracial club concerned with issues of unemployment, housing, and democratic equality between the races and sexes. Members of the new organization would focus on educational work, such as a high-quality magazine that espoused homophile rights and the fundamental unity of humanity. The name "ONE" was suggested by a young black man, Guy Rousseau. While Mattachine continued its efforts to generate a broad movement, ONE centered on educational forums, classes, and "a real magazine" that was not a tract or a sex-tease journal. The premier issue of America's first openly gay magazine, *ONE*, appeared in 1953; an Institute for Homophile Studies was set up in 1956; and a more scholarly journal was added in 1958.

ONE, Inc., was dedicated to the "Higher Homosexuality." Through it, an individual learned about the past and present of his or her people, foreign movements, recent publications, contemporary struggles within a civil

rights context, and some vision of a democratic and just order. As one author expressed his hopes for human rights in 1954:

The homosexual minority can play a very creditable role in the evolution of human rights and in the fulfillment of the democratic ideal—not because it is homosexual, and certainly not if it is under the delusion that sexual rights are humanity's chief or only rights, but because its individual members have been compelled, like the members of many other minorities, to visualize the full nature of human rights perhaps more clearly than those who are complacently entrenched in traditional conceptions and majority attitudes. Thus this group can, if it will, make a distinct contribution to the social discovery and revaluation of human rights on all levels, a discovery and revaluation which stands as the issue of greatest human importance during this apocalyptic era. (R. H. Crowther, "Democracy," *ONE*, October 1954, p. 9)

Already in 1954, ONE, Inc., received several pages of publicity in *People Today*. This was a magazine with a somewhat larger audience than *ONE:* approximately 2 million. Although photos showed only the backs of people's heads, and the article was condescending and bigoted by later standards, *People Today* did publicize the early work of an emerging minority. By 1965 ONE's Institute of Homophile Studies had conducted 1,000 public lectures and the magazine circulated in yearly runs of several thousand copies. It presented an image that was not primarily sexual (as in homosexual), but intelligent and unsensational. Thus, it preferred the word "homophile" to awkward medical terms like homosexual, or underground slang that it dismissed as frivolous and demeaning, such as "gay."

ONE, Inc. had a remarkable record for its size. It laid the foundations for an international reference library. It published its own literature, counseled people, held meetings, conducted travel tours, and supported one major legal victory for the homosexual press. In the early 1950s, some Americans had objected that if homosexuality was illegal then *ONE* must be a magazine for criminals. After several complaints to the Post Office were reported, the magazine deleted some of Whitman's poems, and the corporation's attorney read every issue before it was printed and sent out. When the entire press run of October 1954 was seized, a three-and-a-half-year battle was waged in the courts, at considerable expense. A fund appeal regretted that "Principles are often expensive!" National support was mobilized, including Dr. Kinsey. In January 1958, the Supreme Court overruled the opinion of the Ninth Circuit Court of Appeals that *ONE*, as a pro-homosexual publication, was inherently "filthy and obscene." This helped to open the door toward an honest and diverse gay literature.

While this was a victory for both homosexual self-worth and freedom of the press, it attracted public attention that disturbed some members. In August 1958, *ONE* shocked many of its subscribers with a cover that declared "I'm Glad I am Homosexual." Just as some black readers of *The Crisis* had once complained that W.E.B. Du Bois printed pictures of people who

BOOKS

Notices and reviews of books, articles, plays and poetry dealing with homosexuality and the sex variant. Readers are invited to send in reviews or printed matter for review.

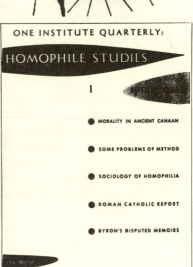

were *too* black (in the days when the highest status went to the lightest-skinned), some subscribers and members dropped out of ONE.

Lesbians who were aware of this homophile movement often looked at it from the outside. They sometimes asserted that a principal weakness of both Mattachine and ONE was a failure to attract women or to incorporate them into leadership roles. Sexism among gay men was probably a key factor, although the general discrimination against women throughout this culture meant that women were less likely to have the organizational skills, money, or time to participate. They also may have feared losing whatever they had by public exposure of their lesbianism. Mattachine and ONE did not transcend most of the common sexism of U.S. society or vigorously encourage women's participation and development within their groups. Although Ann Carll Reid was editor of *ONE* for several years in the 1950s, and a journal section entitled "Feminine Viewpoint" was apparently popular, women were seldom found in either of these male-dominated societies, nor did they tend to stay.

This was the background for a 1955 meeting of eight people in San Francisco that began the earliest effort to organize American lesbians. Del Martin and Phyllis Lyon, a couple who had been together for several years, wanted an alternative to a gay bar culture where police commonly raided bars as "houses of ill repute," decoys were sometimes used to entrap customers for "lewd and lascivious behavior," and the bars themselves were dreary and repressive. A Filipina at the first meeting suggested an obscure and therefore protective name: the Daughters of Bilitis (DOB). Bilitis was supposed to have been one of the lovers of Sappho (600 B.C.) on the island of Lesbos. As Martin and Lyon explained this curious title years later: "We thought that 'Daughters of Bilitis' would sound like any other women's lodge—you know, like the Daughters of the Nile or the DAR. . . . 'Bilitis' would mean something to us, but not to any outsider. If anyone asked us, we could always say we belong to a poetry club."

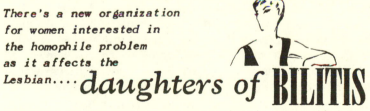

There's a new organization
for women interested in
the homophile problem
as it affects the
Lesbian.... daughters of BILITIS

DAUGHTERS OF BILITIS women's organization (parallel to but not affiliated with Mattachine Society) publishes a monthly news periodical, *THE LADDER*. Subscriptions: $1 per year, first class sealed in plain envelope.

Address inquiries and replies to:

DAUGHTERS OF BILITIS
Post Office Box 2183
SAN FRANCISCO 26, CALIF.

December 1956

Even this tiny society, however, suffered from divisions. Most wanted to exclude all men; others insisted on excluding nonlesbian women. There were disagreements about whether DOB should be a purely social club. Martin and Lyon, because of their personal values and their discovery of both ONE and Mattachine, seemed drawn to social activism. Although the group had only fifteen members after one year, it decided to publish a magazine to reach a broader public. The first issue of their historically important journal, *The Ladder* (out of the *Well of Loneliness?*) appeared in October 1956. Like *ONE*, it was a quiet, unsensational journal of news, analysis and fiction for its lesbian readers and friends. It would be fourteen years before there was a second lesbian journal.

DOB was recognized as a nonprofit corporation in California in 1957 and received federal tax-exempt status soon after. It provided a family-like social life that was separate from gay bars. Someone later dubbed it a lesbian YWCA. While the dress code of DOB and some of their rules urging a dignified respectability seem fainthearted, the existence of the group was daring. Its founders rebelled against the lesbian reputation as "semi men" and freaks. Del Martin announced in 1956, "The salvation of the Lesbian lies in her acceptance of herself without guilt or anxiety, in her awareness of her capabilities and her limitations, and in pursuit of a constructive way of life without misgivings or apology." Lesbians were what Kinsey called "variants," not monsters.

These were novel ideas that attracted only fifty members by 1958. Still, DOB was responsible for an influential publication that lasted until 1972, and autonomous branches in other cities like Los Angeles, Boston, and New York. In San Francisco the Mattachine Society and the Daughters were instrumental in forming the Council on Religion and the Homosexual in 1964 to educate the churches about homophile society. When police harassed a New Year's party of the council on January 1, 1965, their tactic backfired. They had ringed the building with squad cars, floodlights, photographers, and fifty policemen, and expected that the partygoers would be frightened away. Instead, over 500 entered despite the glare of lights, and the nongays were shocked at this display of police power. At a news conference the next day, seven clergymen damned the police. Gay people and their supporters were beginning to be a conscious minority. This was acknowledged in 1966 when the fourth national convention of DOB in San Francisco was greeted by radio announcements, interviews, television taping, and mainstream newspaper coverage.

The activities of the Daughters of Bilitis, Mattachine, and ONE, along with the expanding atmosphere of social change in the early 1960s, fostered a growing consciousness among a minority of gays within enclaves or "ghettoes" in San Francisco, Los Angeles, and Greenwich Village. *Life* magazine took notice of the "new homosexual" by publishing a lengthy article in 1964. It reported that "today, especially in big cities, homosexuals are discarding their furtive ways and openly admitting, even flaunting, their deviation." The magazine added that the Los Angeles Police Department analyzed this menace in an educational pamphlet that decided that the secret goal of homosexuals was "a fruit world."

A gay social network evolved in major cities of the United States by the late 1960s. Within this population, a minority had begun to think of themselves as a "community." This world was outlined in local, national, and international guides like the *Gay Yellow Pages*, *Bob Damron's Address Book*, *Lavender Guide*, *Barfly*, *Guild Guide*, and *Le Guide Gris*, first published by the Mattachine Society in 1958.

The original militants were not highly visible even in the homosexual world, much less in the larger society, but they were soon joined by many others. While one poll in 1965 found that 58 percent of the overall population considered homosexuals a threat to the nation, surpassed only by the menacing presence of atheists and Communists, in that same year Barbara Gittings was refusing to be a polite and hidden lesbian. She compared herself to a Mississippi Negro told to adjust to a "nigger" role. She insisted that "there are times when revolt, not 'adjustment to society,' is the only mature and self-respecting course."

These activists sometimes lashed out at the older homophile organizations for being too quiet. They wanted to be heard. The East Coast Homophile Organization (ECHO) was begun in 1963, and the Society for Individual Rights (SIR) was founded in San Francisco in 1964 to counter the "sluggishness of other groups." SIR quickly became the largest homosexual organization by building a prototype of the "gay community center" later found in some cities: a meeting place for activities from educational forums to election nights for political candidates, a Sirporium (thrift shop), an auditorium for plays and dances, referral services for housing, legal aid, jobs, counseling and medical help, publications (such as *Vector*, a magazine), and individual social groups for activities like swimming and hiking.

Because of the growing range of local organizations, some people concluded that a national movement was possible. A planning meeting was held in Kansas City in February 1966. Thirty delegates, representing fourteen groups, formed a center for communication, to be called the North American Conference of Homophile Organizations (NACHO). This and later conferences were premature, however, because the miniscule membership was scattered in Ithaca, Syracuse, New York City, Dayton, Cincinnati, Rock Island, Kansas City, San Francisco, and Los Angeles. Despite its limitations, NACHO was a sign of the gradual creation of an identifiable gay lobby.

More successful was the invention of a national newspaper. After a 1968 raid on a gay bar in Los Angeles, one of those arrested was angered by police storming into a private club, randomly charging people, and closing the place. Although Dick Michaels considered himself a conservative, this experience, and $600 in legal expenses, prompted him to join PRIDE (Personal Rights in Defense and Education). He began a newsletter for the organization, the Los Angeles *Advocate*. The journal started as a twelve-page tabloid with a press run of 500 copies, $24 in advertising (two-thirds of which was never paid), and $200 in capital. It became a comprehensive newspaper with a nationwide readership. Another gay institution had been established.

By January 1969 *Time* magazine reported a new homosexual activism, and the early June issue of the *Advocate* editorialized about "signs of a new movement." The stage was set for the dramatic eclipse of the older and smaller homophile societies by a mass phenomenon, "gay liberation."

Quite unexpectedly, the symbolic event was a police raid on a New York gay bar. For about two years the Stonewall Inn on Christopher Street in Greenwich Village operated without a license, although it was within a few blocks of a precinct station. The police finally appeared at the Stonewall Inn on the evening of June 27, 1969. They evicted the patrons, beat up some of them, and arrested a few of the more flamboyant. A crowd of about 400 gathered, at first curious, but with rising anger as the arrested were brought out. Antigay harassment by the police had been declining, and people had not expected such actions. The police began to be taunted, coins were thrown, then bottles and cans. After the police retreated into the bar, the door was nearly smashed in with a parking meter ripped from the sidewalk, trash cans were beaten against the boarded-up windows, and matches were tossed into the room. Although the police were saved by reinforcements, they and public opinion were startled by homosexuals who defended themselves. On the other hand, closeted gays like the writer Merle Miller became activists and open gays may have agreed with Allen Ginsberg: "Gay power is great! We're one of the largest minorities, you know. It's about time

we did something to assert ourselves. [The demonstrators are] beautiful—
they've lost that wounded look that fags all had ten years ago."

Much had happened in the previous decade to promote gay liberation.
John F. Kennedy's "New Frontier" created a hopeful mood for change.
There were massive struggles by other minorities for full equality (first
blacks and, soon after, women) and the unsettling criticism by the antiwar
movement, the New Left, and the counterculture. Earlier advocates of free
sexuality, like Ginsberg, were now members of a new sensibility, including
androgynous rock stars and hippie romantics that said, "If it feels good, do
it." Left gay critics like Paul Goodman were no longer isolated but were
speakers for broad coalitions that advocated decentralism and pluralism.
There were alternative presses throughout the United States willing to report unconventional people, ideas, and news. This social and political fer-
ment stimulated the mass media to report, and perhaps help to form, the
new gay liberation movement.

Once this stage had been reached, there was a quantitative and qualitative
explosion of consciousness. Allen Young, a leftist writer working at Liberation News Service, realized that he hadn't even liberated himself so long as
he hid his gayness. Karla Jay, who became a major gay anthologist (with
Young), said that she was brought out by the women's movement which, in
turn, became progressively more supportive of lesbian rights. At first, some
leaders of the National Organization for Women, such as Betty Friedan,
warned of a "lavender menace" that might cause all feminists to be dismissed
as lesbians. These attitudes changed. In 1970 the radical black leader Huey
Newton condemned the use of words like "faggot" among Black Panthers
and praised gay liberation as the struggle of a minority against oppression.

He noted that "maybe they might be the most oppressed people in the society."

Stonewall marked the beginning of a movement interrelated with other movements. Within a few weeks, a radical Gay Liberation Front was formed in New York City, with its name suggested by an ex-member of the Mattachine Action Committee. It published an openly gay newspaper, *Come Out!* Later, there was a more reformist single issue group, the Gay Activists Alliance. In March 1970 the first Christopher Street parade of 5,000 to 10,000 was held in New York City to commemorate Stonewall. It summoned people to come "out of the closets and into the streets." The idea of a Gay Freedom Day quickly spread to other cities where significant numbers of gays were willing to "come out" publicly. Stonewall became a part of the historical memory of a newly conscious group. Nonetheless, there were many divisions among gay people between those who had opposing ideologies, those who hated other gay people of different races, those who disdained members of other classes or gays of the opposite sex, and those who wore leather and ridiculed others who preferred more "feminine" attire. Despite this, a vital sense of community had begun to replace the previous isolation of gays. The time of nearly complete silence was over.

WHAT DO THESE PEOPLE WANT?

Most gay organizations that favor social reform have worked to change sex stereotypes, the "sickness" theories of the psychiatric establishment, legal inequalities, and antiquated religious attitudes.

The first task of any minority is to overcome the demeaning stereotypes that a majority has forced upon it. Just as blacks had to fight against self-hating behavior like hair straightening and skin bleaching, admiration of lighter-skinned blacks, and copying white ways to try to "pass," gays had to conquer prejudices that had been glorified into "science" and "religion" before they could achieve a positive self-identity. The meetings of Mattachine, ONE, and DOB began with invitations to psychiatrists, ministers, and sociologists to address their explanations of gay life to gay people themselves. After overcoming some of the fear, doubt, ignorance, and aloneness that characterized homosexual life (and finding that many professionals were bigoted in their own complacent ways), some gays took the aggressive step of stating, from their own experience, that gay is, or could be, good. Just as most blacks came to ridicule the concept of "the Negro problem," saying that it was really "the white problem," many gays stopped blaming themselves and rebuked society for labelling them sick and forcing them to lead secretive lives. From this self-acceptance grew a willingness to make a generalized critique of the dominant sex roles in this society.

First, gender conditioning is a form of social control that limits the potentialities of everyone. "Real men" are strong, silent, and unemotional crea-

Artist: Rick Fiala. Courtesy of *Christopher Street*.

tures who learn from the cradle that only sissies, fags, and little girls cry and show intimate feelings toward others of the same sex. "Effeminacy" in men is a loathesome flaw.

"Real women" are expected to be the opposite of independent men: soft, passive, and unassertive, that is, "feminine". Women who don't comform may be intimidated by being called "dykes." Such ideas restricted the imagination of most people in the past. Many throughout society now question these roles as more women have independent careers, the women's movement has matured, and the gay movement has become accepted. A man who approves of the feminist movement or shares domestic responsibilities is less likely to be scorned as a pansy pervert. Sex-determined roles are no longer as rigid.

Second, gay liberation has meant erotic liberation. While every individual is born with sexual desires, it is society that attempts to determine the "proper" objects of those desires. In this and other Western societies, the ideal has been one of exclusive heterosexuality. Gay liberation has challenged this sexual conditioning as a denial of individuality, arguing that we cannot be fully human so long as we are forced to live in such narrow abstractions. The many people who deviate from the ideal suffer both guilt and doubt because they are not "real men" or "real women."

Gay liberation has disturbed many people, not only because of the newly perceived reality that "we are everywhere," but because of the possibility that "we are inside you." Once the simple polarities of straight or gay are abandoned, then one sees gradations, like Kinsey's "2" or "5", gay fathers and lesbian mothers, or other ambivalences. A narrow and comfortable mind-set cracks. Instead, there is the vast possibility that (as Ginsberg said) "we have many loves, many of which are denied, many of which we deny to ourselves," or the poignantly direct vision of one gay collective: "Love is not a scarce commodity. Everybody's got a lot and wants to give it all away."

As gay liberation contributes to the erotic and sex-role liberation of straights, it raises the third problem of sex stereotypes among gay people. Just as there is no role-free heterosexuality today, there is no role-free homosexuality. In the past, gays who became aware of their sexual orientation may have accepted society's masks: the bitchy, campy, fey man; the "butch" or "femme" lesbian. This was one way for homosexuals to identify themselves to others of their kind, or it might have reflected hostility toward an oppressive society. But was it "natural"? Was it really that person? Did it necessarily mean, for example, that gay men were more sympathetic and egalitarian with women? Del Martin complained that male-run homophile groups treated lesbians like "second-class homosexuals" and "niggers" who were fit to run the mimeograph machines or make coffee, but not to be equals in discussion or leaders in decisions. Many lesbians have asserted that gay men can be, and generally have been, as sexist toward women as straight males.

While gay society is more conscious of these issues today, it is still true that the highest status in that society is to the person, man or woman, who can "pass" as straight. Heterosexual society is closely imitated in most of gay society. Among men, for example, masculinism provides anonymity among homophobes, approval from liberal straights, rescue from street violence and the humiliation of verbal abuse, and job and housing preference. Full sexual liberation might mean an identity crisis among gays as much as in the general society. Free men and free women in a free society is a utopian aspiration, the dimensions of which are, perhaps, beyond the present imagination.

Given the centrality of sex role issues to the gay movement, its activists have centered much of their work on the methods by which these roles are transmitted and reinforced. The movement identified three basic rationales for codifying and perpetuating myths: psychiatric theory, legal proscription, and religious belief. Although gay militants might also consider the schools to be factories for drab conformity in sex as in everything else, and the mass media (in most cases) purveyors of prejudice, they have focused commonly on these three ultimate justifications for discrimination.

Psychiatry was rated of first importance, by the early movement. While many bigots justified their hatred of homosexuality by arguing its "sinful" nature, the official basis for criminalization was psychiatric. Psychiatry, as a self-announced science, provided theories to explain homosexuality: early

"We Are Everywhere": Gay Men and Lesbians					199

family life, a "close-binding mother and a detached-hostile father," sexual fears, or "arrested development." These assumptions dominated the public discussion more than medical possibilities of hormonal imbalances in the pregnant mother or young child, or genetic disposition. If any of these causes could be proven, then it might be possible to "cure" all of the afflicted and create a 100 percent heterosexual society. Homoeroticism would be stamped out.

By the early 1960s some gays were no longer willing to listen to these explanations quietly. Most generalizations were based upon studies of psychiatric patients or prisoners. Could one deduce the character of the typical heterosexual from those who went to psychiatrists or to prison? Was it fair to contrast some ideal model of heterosexuality against an open minority of a hidden minority? Why was it that many people had "close-binding mothers and detached-hostile fathers" and didn't become gay? Why was it that one boy or girl of identical twins would be gay and the other not? Why was love for someone of one's own sex abnormal?

Early gay activists conceded that some homosexuals, like some heterosexuals, were sick, but they criticized the analytical categories of psychiatrists as pseudoscientific excuses for prejudice. In 1964 the Mattachine Society of Washington, D.C., concluded that "in the absence of valid evidence to the contrary, homosexuality could not be considered a sickness, illness, disturbance, disorder, or other pathology of any kind." The North American Conference of Homophile Organizations asserted in 1966 that "we are not sick." The DOB surreptitiously paid for a study of mental health professionals in 1968. How did they actually treat homosexuals? According to this study, 96 percent of these professionals believed that gays could be happy, 97 percent said that they would not try to change a client's sexuality, and over 90 percent questioned the term "disease."

Few people predicted in the late 1960s that the American Psychiatric Association and the American Psychological Association would publicly agree with these views. The psychiatric industry was essentially a closed shop for an elite. It was very white, very male, very heterosexual, very middle-class, and very conventional in politics. In 1970 the national convention of the American Psychiatric Association was disrupted in San Francisco. One of the radical manifestos presented this critique:

[You have] a panel about American Indians which concentrates on suicide by them rather than genocide by us . . . learning about aversion treatment for homosexuals— but not considering whether homosexuality is really a psychiatric "disease" . . . hearings about drugs, new drugs and old drugs—but not the way drugs are used to tranquilize people who are legitimately upset . . . hearings about psychiatry and law enforcement—but not about how our society uses police to oppress people and prevent change . . . hearings discussing sexuality and abortion—but not the way sex roles are used to oppress women. . . . Women come to you suffering from depression. Women *ought* to feel depressed with the roles society puts on them. . . . Those roles aren't biological; those roles are learned. . . . It started when my mother threw me a doll and my brother a ball. (Quoted in Gary Alinder, "Off Dr. Bieber," in *The Gay Liberation Book*, ed. Len Richmond [San Francisco: Ramparts Press, 1973], p. 106)

This convention was followed by several years of protest against logical inconsistencies in theories of homosexuality, along with the low or virtually nonexistent "cure" rates, and such barbaric methods as electric shocks, nausea-producing drugs, lobotomies, castration, clitoridectomies, and hormonal injections.

In 1974 the governing board of the American Psychiatric Association voted 13 to 0 to drop the old listing of homosexuality as a mental disorder. They urged the abolition of all legal inequalities applied to gays. Later in the year, the membership of the association upheld this decision. This produced a sudden cure for about 20 million people, by a positive vote of 58 percent. Same-sex relations between consenting adults were no longer diseased. This vote had potential ramifications in legislatures, courts, the civil service at all levels, private employment, the military, and security clearances. The APA acknowledged this in a public statement:

We will be removing one of the justifications for the denial of civil rights to individuals whose only crime is that their sexual orientation is to members of the same sex. In the past, homosexuals have been denied civil rights in many areas of life on

the ground that they suffer from a "mental illness," the burden of proof being on them that they were competent, reliable, or mentally stable.

Two things are immediately clear. The APA was galvanized into speedy action not by genteel words but by confrontations, including the invasion of its conventions. It is also obvious that psychiatry is not a science, although it is capable of being pushed toward greater humanistic maturity. Despite this evolution there was one residue of the earlier homophobic interpretation. The APA continued to defend a "sexual orientation disturbance" category "for individuals whose sexual interests are directed primarily towards people of the same sex and who are either disturbed by, in conflict with, or wish to change their sexual orientation. . . . This diagnostic category is distinguished from homosexuality which, by itself, does not necessarily constitute a psychiatric disorder." To be consistent, the new manual should have included a "sexual orientation disturbance" category for exclusive heterosexuals who wish to be cured of their limited interests. The revised paragraph was nonetheless a giant step forward.

Modern psychiatry, psychology, and sociology no longer give much support to popular myths about homosexuality. They generally agree that gays

—are no more obsessed by sex than straight people;
—are unlikely to recruit children if, as many experts now believe, basic sexual identity is established by the ages of three to five;
—seem to influence their own offspring (since some are parents) mainly in their greater tolerance of role-model diversity;
—are unlikely to molest children (95 percent of cases are by heterosexuals);
—are rarely involved in coerced sex (98 percent of rapes are by heterosexuals);
—may be more promiscuous because society denies many respectible meeting places and refuses any kind of social or legal status to long-term same-sex relations;
—are better adjusted than one might expect, given society's limitations.

A second major gay concern has been reform of the laws concerning sexual activity and discrimination in housing and jobs. Although it is nowhere illegal to be gay, homosexual acts are, in many cities and states, criminal. It is important to remember, furthermore, that laws against "perverted sexual practices" (such as fellatio and cunnilingus) usually apply to heterosexuals. With the sexual revolution of recent years, it has been estimated that 80 percent of the adult population has been guilty, at some moment, of a sex crime. Jerry Wilson, when he was chief of police of the District of Columbia, remarked that because the local statutes forbid all sexual intercourse not conducted in the male-female "missionary position," he could arrest several hundred thousand people within the district.

Already in 1955 the American Law Institute, in its Model Penal Code, urged the decriminalization of any kind of sex between consenting adults in private. Since Illinois changed its law in 1961, twenty-six states modernized their bans on sexual "crimes against nature" by 1987. Less progressively, the Supreme Court has upheld state laws prohibiting same-sex acts in private between consenting adults, such as in a five-to-four vote in 1986 to sustain a Georgia law in *Bowers v. Hardwick*. It was significant that four justices concluded that the state should not invade the personal lives of citizens. In fact, over one-half of the states no longer had sodomy laws by 1986, no one had been prosecuted under the contested Georgia law for the last four or five decades (although it allowed a prison sentence of up to twenty years), and one of the majority justices believed that a successful appeal could be made under the constitutional protection against cruel and unusual punishment if anyone was sentenced harshly for sodomy. It remained true, of course, that the majority of the Court affirmed time-honored bigotry with a decision that may encourage discrimination within the court system and the general society.

Even when the laws have changed, police may continue their harassment under other excuses. In Illinois local police invaded gay bars after 1961, relying upon a nineteenth-century law against "disorderly houses." Since a disorderly house was defined as "any establishment in which any sort of physical contact of a sexual nature takes place," one wonders if this pristine ideal was applied equally to straight bars.

Another favorite police tactic in past years was the use of officers in tight-fitting civilian clothes standing around hoping to entice an act of "solicitation," and then arresting the victim. The use of decoys to incite a crime seems to have diminished in recent years, especially where the law requires a third-party witness (*not* police) who was offended by such a public solicitation.

There are further legal questions related to job and housing discrimination. In most of the United States, a citizen who has been fired, evicted, or denied some civil right merely because of affectional preference has no legal protection. Even the U.S. Civil Rights Commission has no authority in cases of gay discrimination.

The argument that laws should apply equally has touched the public conscience. Opinion polls indicate that most people think that individuals should be judged on the basis of personal merit rather than by some preconceived category. By the mid-1970s, the U.S. Civil Service Commission severely restricted any firing of gay people without a list of substantive reasons related to actual job performance; the Department of Defense was more willing to give security clearances to open gays (since, after all, if they were open, how could they be blackmailed?); major corporations such as CBS, IBM, AT&T, the Bank of America, and 130 of the Fortune 500 businesses had issued antidiscrimination statements; and many cities, churches, and unions expanded their civil right protections. Perhaps the Civil Rights Acts of 1964 and 1968 will one day be amended to include "affectional and sexual preference."

The general public, however, accepts discrimination in jobs such as teaching and the military. There is, of course, no documentation that gay teachers seduce their students (such incidents are remarkably rare), nor even that, as role models, they "convert" their naturally heterosexual students. There is no evidence that more gays in the military, who are already there now, would cause the collapse of the armed forces. Nonetheless, one reads of cases like that of Joseph Acanfora of Maryland, who was dismissed from his teaching job solely because he had belonged to a gay organization when he was a student at the University of Pennsylvania. Or the case of Sgt. Leonard Matlovich, who got a medal for killing two men and a discharge for loving others.

But times are changing. The National Education Association spent $25,000 to defend Acanfora in the 1970s, and Matlovich was featured on the cover of *Time* magazine. The military is much more generous in giving honorable discharges, and some major school systems have announced that hiring and promotion should depend solely on merit. In California, for example, school districts in Palo Alto, San Francisco, and Santa Barbara reject any sexual discrimination against teachers, while forbidding teachers from promoting any sexual life-style in the classroom.

A final case of legal inequality, highlighting much of the hypocrisy of society, is the ban against same-sex marriages. As one lesbian writer said:

Our relationships are often principally physical ones . . . because we are not allowed to bring them out of the bedroom. Our marriages, which are just as sacred to us as any religious ceremony, are constantly harrassed by "Be careful how you look at me in public," "Uncle John's coming to visit, push the beds apart so he won't suspect," "We can't buy a house together, how will I explain it to my folks," "Make sure you kiss Ed good-night, so he won't think anything's funny," "Don't wear your matching little-finger ring when you drop by the office today, someone might notice," and on and on. (Carol Bradford, "The Invisible Society," *ONE*, May 1962, p. 11)

This cultural taboo is reflected in the law. Marriage is not only a social rite that brings status and implies a long commitment. It has tangible material benefits, such as community property rights, income tax breaks, the capacity to inherit if there is no will, special rates for couples by credit unions, banks, and insurance companies, the ability to collect on disability insurance, Social Security, and veteran's benefits at the loss of the partner, and the right to recover damages for wrongful death. What rational basis is there for denying such advantages because both members of a union are of the same sex? Or, if such relationships are given no validity, is it fair to complain that gay relationships are transient?

Some litigation has attempted to expand the definition of family, domestic partner, and spouse. If a man and a woman can be related by marriage, adoption, or common-law practice, why not two men, or two women, or some alternative family? Such efforts assume that family rights should be available to all who want them. Other legal possibilities include the writing of relationship contracts or adopting one's lover. Progress will be slow because the institution is basic. Large majorities reject the idea of same-sex marriages. It is dismissed as "sick," "decadent," "disgusting," and a forerunner of a new Sodom. Some states, such as California, have specifically denied any legal status to gay marriages. Nevertheless, the American Civil Liberties Union endorsed the legalization of same-sex marriages in 1986. As a mainstream civil rights organization, it argued that such changes in the marriage laws were "imperative for the complete legal equality of lesbians and gay men."

A third bastion of antigay prejudice, besides psychiatry and the law, has been religion. Many current laws have hidden foundations in religious belief. For centuries, gay people have suffered mentally and physically from Judeo-Christian hate groups. Recent gay responses to this have included dropping out, staying in (angry or submissive), forming gay caucuses within established churches, and forming entirely new gay churches.

The reinterpretation of biblical passages on homosexuality seems to be the most common approach. Many people recognize that the Bible is not a legal document, like a collection of statutes. It is the spiritual anthology of ancient peoples thousands of years removed from us. Many of the Old Testament edicts, such as the dietary code (necessary before refrigeration) were reasonable in their day but are not life-or-death matters now. Who remembers that the Bible calls it a sin for a man to wear woolen pants or a cotton shirt, or for a woman to wear a red dress? Most Jews and Christians choose to ignore the Bible's praise of slavery, and few believers would kill adulterers (Leviticus 20:10).

In short, most people select from the Bible what they want. On the question of homosexuality, this raises typical problems: Are the translations accurate? What were the circumstances of the time? What was the context of the quotation in each book and in the Bible as a whole? One discovers, first, that lesbians are never mentioned, and, second, that male references are subject to more ambiguity than many people have assumed. The inhabitants of Sodom and Gomorrah may have been guilty of pride and inhospitality. Other quotes refer to male prostitutes and to unloving relationships generally. Even so, the sex phobias of much of the Bible are not completely offset by these interpretations by praise of David's love for Jonathan, or by references to the love and compassion of Jesus, who never married, said nothing about homosexuality, and consorted with twelve other men.

What about modern religions? It is certainly still a problem if you are Jewish and gay, although the radical decentralization of the faith allows the formation of gay synagogues. Israel, however, is not a promised land for gay Jews. It has few meeting places, and sectarian prejudices have been turned into laws.

The New Testament successor to this tradition, the Catholic church, has a record of centuries of intolerance against sexual minorities. Within the church, however, a gay caucus named Dignity was begun in 1968 by an Augustinian priest in San Diego. Dignity started the process of petitioning the hierarchy for change, educating the church's members, and providing social and intellectual support for gay Catholics. By the late 1980s, it had about 5,000 members in over one hundred chapters.

The Catholic church must be taken seriously for its reinforcement of sexual guilt. In 1986 the Vatican issued "A Letter to the Bishops of the Catholic Church on the Pastoral Care of Homosexual Persons." It bluntly restated the official doctrine that only marital sex is positive. This condemned not only homosexuality but, implicitly, masturbation (both harmless and nearly universal), premarital sex, extramarital sex, and "deviant" marital sex. It criticized gay organizations and added that their actions might lead to "irrational and violent reactions" by heterosexuals. Opponents of this letter said that it blamed the victims, demonstrated little "care" for "homosexual persons," and did not represent a religion of love.

Efforts to redeem the other mainline churches have been attempted through the organization of caucuses: Affirmation (Mormon), Emergence (Christian Science), SDA Kinship (Adventists), Integrity (Episcopal), Lutherans Concerned, Unitarian Gay Caucus, Committee of Friends, Lazarus Rising (Presbyterians), and the Brethren-Mennonite Council for Gay Concerns. Such activities seek to overcome the pain of separation within these churches by bringing about reconciliation among their members.

As an alternative to caucuses, some gays have promoted separate churches. In 1956 some members of ONE, Inc., established a First Church of One Brotherhood ("Archdiocese of Los Angeles") with elaborate plans, a

INTEGRITY/ Washington

...FOR GAY EPISCOPALIANS & THEIR FRIENDS

EUCHARIST/MEETINGS

few projects, and ultimate failure. Some later efforts were equally exotic, such as gynocentric religions (Wicce) or "high camp" episodes intended to be satirical, such as High Holiness Pope Morris (Kight) I renting a clerical costume in 1970 and making a pilgrimage to the First Congregational Church of Los Angeles to demand $90 billion in reparations, based upon $10,000 for each of the 9 million gays which he claimed had been killed by the Christian church over the centuries.

Less extravagant, and more influential, has been the Metropolitan Community Church (MCC). Its founder was the Rev. Troy Perry, a fundamentalist minister who had presided over churches in Florida and California. In 1963 he separated from his wife, two sons, and the church. His problem was his homosexuality, which neither his family nor his church could accept. By 1968 he concluded that the problem was not caused by a God of love, but by the immoral hatreds of many people. He began a study group with twelve others that eventually became a church with over 200 congregations in the United States and several foreign countries, and almost 42,000 members by 1987. Although MCC is not strictly a church for gay people, since that would be a denial of the universal message of Christianity, it is essentially gay because of the inhospitable atmosphere in most other churches.

Although Perry has remained a fundamentalist—or, as he prefers, a "primitive Christian"—the Metropolitan Community Church tends to be ecumenical. Congregational meetings vary greatly: they may be quietly formal or loudly charismatic; the politics may be subdued or aggressive. One common characteristic has been its effort to create a nonsexist religion: gender references have been eliminated from the liturgy, many women have been ordained, and parity has been attempted on all of the committees of the church. This trend disturbed some within the church, and some outside of

it, but the leadership of MCC has been committed to living out its egalitarian principles.

Other gays rejected religion entirely, believing that it is the problem rather than the solution. Organizations like the Gay Atheist League of America (GALA) assert that "a gay religionist is a gay dupe," since religion is both an illusion and an enemy of physical pleasure. GALA does not care whether God created the first heterosexual couple, or whether He/She/It approves of homosexuality. The league dismisses God as the essence of antihumanistic repression and insists that what we really need is freedom from religion. Such critiques have little influence among people who live within traditional Jewish and Christian symbol systems, and even many of those disenchanted with conventional religion find atheism too purely negative.

The mass media have been a powerful force for these changes in religion, law, and psychological theory. Television, films, magazines, and newspapers inform and shape how Americans see the world. A few informational centers, such as New York and Los Angeles, mold the imagination of the entire nation. This fact has been crucial for gay liberation, since most gays are still closeted and much of the general public's knowledge comes from the media.

IF YOU BELIEVE
organized religion is the greatest enemy of gay liberation,
we will send you a **free** copy of GALA Review
published by the Gay Atheist League of America

OUT OF SATAN'S SHADOWY WORLD OF HOMOSEXUALITY, IN A DISPLAY OF DEFIANCE AGAINST SOCIETY, THEY COME FORTH — THOSE WHO SUFFER THE AGONY OF REJECTION, THE DESPAIR OF UNSATISFIED LONGING — DESIRING — ENDLESS LUSTING AND REMORSE CRYING THAT GAY IS GOOD — THEIR TRAGIC LIVES PROVE THAT THERE ISN'T ANYTHING GAY ABOUT BEING GAY.

From a religious booklet reprinted in *GALA Review*.

Publicity fed the early movement. Television viewers may have been startled on April 8, 1971, when Walter Cronkite told them, "In Minneapolis, an admitted homosexual, Jack Baker, has been elected president of the University of Minnesota Student Association." Since the networks believed that people were curious about such events, the first specials were filmed and shown, such as a 1971 panel on David Susskind's program. Earlier, the subject had been generally taboo, and only the bad (such as sex crimes) had reached the mass audience. The rise and the reporting of gay activism began the process of transforming common prejudices, anxieties, and myths.

A result has been a more accurate understanding of the realities of American homosexual life. Even if stereotypes are common in the recent depictions in film, television, and print, millions of people have additional information and some opportunity to talk with others about what they either saw on television last night, read in *Newsweek*, or found in the bookrack at their drugstore or supermarket. Responses, of course, are mixed. They include, "I don't want to hear about it again," a belief that the number of homosexuals must have grown to explain their public emergence, or some fundamental education on the subject. Discussion means greater opportunity for gays and their supporters to pressure the Federal Communications Commission and the National Association of Broadcasters about false images of sexual minorities, to make calls, to send letters to media stations and publications, and to organize protests against negative and erroneous depictions. Both the National Gay and Lesbian Task Force and a caucus of the American Civil Liberties Union have been especially willing to act as homosexual anti-defamation leagues in cases involving the media.

The total number of specialized groups like these is remarkable. Although most of these local, regional, and national organizations are small in size and budget, some gay leaders predict that the late 1980s and early 1990s will bring more coalitions or networks between them. In some cities, this could mean a multipurpose center, like the one in Los Angeles that provides health care, legal aid, housing referrals, job counseling, speakers, and cultural and social activities.

Some have looked upon this diversity as a sign of weakness, since political groups range from the Alice B. Toklas Democratic Club and the Teddy Roosevelt Rough Riders to gay anarchists, communists, and Nazis; lobbying includes the "respectable" National Gay and Lesbian Task Force and the more voluble, ad hoc committees; there are elegant bookshops like the Walt Whitman in San Francisco and there are porno dives; journals include both *Christopher Street* (the gay *New Yorker*) and *Blue Boy;* and gay youth groups exist along with the National Association of Lesbian and Gay Gerontologists. Perhaps it is positive that there is no single organization run by a gay elite of "homocrats." Diversity may mean that each individual can find a comfortable support group and that such organizations have greater force by speaking for their own segment of society. The Stonewall Democratic Club may be recognized within a local Democratic party, Parents and Friends of Lesbians and Gays ("We love our gay children") can be very effective with many audiences, and Dignity has more influence within the Catholic church because it speaks as an organization of believers.

Despite such progress, antigay bias has won often in public votes on equal rights ordinances. Voters rejected ordinances in Dade County, Florida (by a 7-to-3 margin), St. Paul (2-to-1), Wichita (4-to-1), and Eugene, Oregon (2-to-1). Some interpreted these defeats as disasters for gay rights; others asked whether large minorities would have voted for legislation in, let us say, 1960. Furthermore, the voting politicized many gays, motivating them to contribute money and time to gay lobbies. The elections heightened the public's consciousness of sexual discrimination. Following these defeats, ordinances were approved in other cities, such as Atlanta and New York in 1986. In addition, there have been executive orders by mayors and governors, and several victories in public votes, most notably in Seattle (63 percent voting for ending antigay discrimination) and in California.

The California vote on the Briggs Amendment in 1978 was dramatic because it focused on the volatile issue of gay teachers. John Briggs, a right-wing state senator from the Republican party, got enough signatures for a referendum that, if successful, would have required school boards to investigate and dismiss any school employee "advocating, soliciting, imposing, encouraging, or promoting private or public homosexual activity directed at, or likely to come to the attention of, school children and/or other employees." Thus, a straight person who made a pro-gay comment in a private conversation could be fired, rumor-mongering and witch-hunts might have been promoted, and a form of open discrimination would have been legalized. As Californians became aware of these possibilities, public opinion changed from its initial 2-to-1 support. Opponents emphasized job security, civil liberties, fairness, the New Right champions of the referendum, and the violent harangues of homophobes like the Rev. Royal Blue, who frankly agreed that "Hitler was right about the homosexuals. . . . I think we should find a humane way to kill these people." Many voters decided that an anti-Briggs slogan was correct: "It's not just dumb—it's dangerous."

Briggs was unable to find a single case of child molesting to publicize; he was undermined by his unsupported assertions. Although 2.8 million voted for his proposition, 3.9 million voted against (58 percent to 42 percent). The referendum educated the public, and although it may have incited some violence and hatred against gays, the constituencies of the gay community were successful in winning what had seemed unwinnable.

Rather than discouraging the movement, these partial successes and partial failures had by 1979 produced the first national mass demonstration for gay rights—perhaps the first in the history of the world. On October 14, 1979, tens of thousands of people from all fifty states and thirty-three countries turned out for the National March on Washington for Lesbian and Gay

Rights, saying, "We want to be judged on our individual merits, not on some prejudiced notions about us." A similar march in 1987 drew at least 200,000 to Washington, with some estimates far higher. Events included The Wedding (with over 1,500 same-sex couples), Let Freedom Ring (a concert of gay bands), the placing of a wreath at the Tomb of the Unknown Soldier, a name-quilt the size of two football fields that was placed on the mall to memorialize those with AIDS, civil disobedience at the Supreme Court, and a four-hour-long procession representing the full spectrum of this community. As one banner read: "Diversity is American." The organizers sought various reforms, such as the repeal of laws that invade the sexual lives of consenting adults, civil rights protection against discrimination that is based solely on affectional preference, and legal recognition of gay marriage.

Perhaps the most stunning example of hostility occurred earlier, in 1978: the killing of Mayor George Moscone of San Francisco and a gay supervisor, Harvey Milk. Bizarrely enough, the assassin, Dan White, was a champion of law and order. White, a Vietnam veteran, former police officer, and one-time firefighter, had been elected to the Board of Supervisors in 1977 as a critic of unnamed "deviates" (sic) who were taking over the city. While on the council, he represented a rightist constituency. Unable to live on his official salary, he resigned his office, then reconsidered and asked for it back. Stymied by a liberal mayor and the opposition of Supervisor Milk, he loaded his .38 special with hollow-point bullets on November 27, 1978, took extra ammunition, slipped by metal detectors at City Hall, waited in an outer office (chatting with a secretary), entered Moscone's room, and shot him twice in the body and then twice in the head after Moscone had fallen to the floor. White then reloaded his gun, walked down the hall, and shot Milk three times in the chest, stomach, and back, and then twice in the head. When White surrendered, he showed no remorse and was allowed to give his confession to a friend and ex-coach. The final result was disturbingly ironic, since White had supported the death penalty for murder. White received a maximum sentence of seven years and eight months.

While liberals were prone to describe the murders as "a senseless tragedy" and depict White as disoriented, despite his purposeful actions, others asked whether he would have gotten off so lightly if he had been poor and black, or if he had not been the killer of two progressive leaders. James Denman, former undersheriff of San Francisco, commented that "to a lot of cops, Dan White was a hero."

At this point, however, violence is unlikely to vanquish so large and diverse a movement. In San Francisco, the White trial was central in the massive political defeat of the district attorney and the sheriff, along with forcing a run-off election in the mayoral race.

The primary threat to the continued progress of gay equality is a medical problem that may provoke political and social repression. In 1981 doctors in New York City identified what appeared to be a new or previously unrecognized disease, which they called Acquired Immune Deficiency Syndrome (AIDS). This viral disease attacked the body's natural defenses, resulting in various cancers, infections, and finally death.

The first categories of people affected by AIDS were intravenous drug users, people who had received blood transfusions, Haitians, and homosexual men. Later research indicated that AIDS had originated in equatorial Africa, and that it had been "discovered" as a new disease when Westerners had been stricken by it.

AIDS was publicized quickly by the mass media. Critics of homosexuality sometimes characterized it as a "gay plague" that was punishment for a depraved life-style. Others, such as the Rt. Rev. John T. Walker, Episcopal bishop of Washington, D.C., responded that if God destroyed all who sinned, humanity would have become extinct long ago.

AIDS is not a "gay disease." In Africa, the vast majority of victims are heterosexual. In the United States the infection rate has been growing among all groups, although not as explosively as had been feared originally. From June 1981 to late 1987, there was a cumulative total of about 50,000 cases, with over 27,000 deaths. While this could be compared with a yearly average of about 1 million deaths from heart disease, 450,000 deaths from all forms of cancer, or 45,000 deaths from car accidents, such statistics are of little comfort for those who hear of the ravaging effects of AIDS. Like the specter of syphilis in the era before penicillin, it arouses dark images of sexual sin and physical corruption.

The social consequences of AIDS are uncertain. Some proposals have been cruel or cynical, such as the 1985 solution offered by a mayoral candidate in Houston: "Shoot the queers!" He was defeated. A 1986 referendum in California suggested mass quarantines. This was defeated also, with 71 percent opposed.

Other people, including the surgeon general, C. Everett Koop, have advocated early sex education in the schools, public information programs on safe sex (such as the use of condoms as "life preservers"), and massive funding of AIDS research. These people emphasized that AIDS cannot be spread by casual contact, but only through the exchange of body fluids, such as blood during a transfusion or semen during sexual activity, or by using a contaminated needle for drug injections. It appears that the virus does not infect all those who come into contact with it, and that many of those infected do not develop AIDS, although the reasons for this are not known. For those who do become infected or ill, the Supreme Court ruled in 1987, by a vote of 7 to 2, that federal antidiscrimination laws protect AIDS victims. They cannot be fired or otherwise discriminated against because of unreasonable fears.

Will AIDS increase popular prejudices against all gays? Will it change sexual practices among gay men? Will it make gay men more monogamous? Will it strengthen the sense of community among gays? Will it create new alliances to encourage mass education on this medical problem and possible solutions to it? Will it educate the public to be more realistic about sexual practices and sexual diversity? Will people realize that even if AIDS is cured, some other viral or bacterial problem will occur eventually, meaning that there will never be a medically risk-free sex life?

By the late 1980s, it was improbable that American society would return to cartoon images of homosexuality as nothing more than sin, sickness, and crime. A new generation, both straight and gay, was coming to adulthood in a time when the general consciousness of society had expanded and many people had greater freedom to make real choices. Gay liberation is no longer a suppressed or isolated issue, the visibility of the movement has not declined, and there are literally thousands of local and national gay organizations. Failures and problems should not obscure this fundamental success. As with the case of feminism, gay liberation has moved us closer to a world where people are treated as individuals rather than as categories.

> We are born naked.
> Everyone is in drag.
>
> TED, in *Word Is Out*
> (a 1970s documentary)

SOURCES OF FURTHER INFORMATION

Books and Articles

Adam, Barry D. *The Rise of a Gay and Lesbian Movement*. Boston: Twayne, 1987.

Adelman, Marcy, ed. *Long Time Passing: Lives of Older Lesbians*. Boston: Alyson Publications, 1986.

Altman, Dennis. *AIDS in the Mind of America*. Garden City, N.Y.: Doubleday/Anchor, 1986.

Bayer, Ronald. *Homosexuality and American Psychiatry: The Politics of Diagnosis* (with a new afterword on AIDS). Princeton, N.J.: Princeton University Press, 1987 [1980].

Beam, Joseph, ed. *In the Life: A Black Gay Anthology*. Boston: Alyson Publications, 1986.

Beck, Evelyn T., ed. *Nice Jewish Girls: A Lesbian Anthology*. Trumansburg, N.Y.: Crossing Press, 1984.

Bell, Alan, and Martin S. Weinberg. *Homosexualities: A Study of Human Diversity* (a "Kinsey" report). New York: Simon & Schuster, 1978. (See Dr. Martin Duberman's review in *The New York Times*, [November 26, 1978], sec. 7, p. 1.)

Berger, Raymond M. *Gay and Gray: The Older Homosexual Man.* Urbana: University of Illinois Press, 1982.

Berzon, Betty, and Martin S. Weinberg, eds. *Positively Gay*, rev. ed. Studio City, Calif.: Mediamix, 1984.

Boswell, John. *Christianity, Social Tolerance, and Homosexuality: Gay People in Western Europe from the Beginning of the Christian Era to the Fourteenth Century.* Chicago: University of Chicago Press, 1980.

Boyd, Malcolm. *Gay Priest: An Inner Journey.* New York: St. Martin's Press, 1986.

Califia, Pat. *Sapphistry: The Book of Lesbian Sexuality*, 2d rev. ed. Tallahassee, Fla.: Naiad Press, 1983.

Clark, Don. *The New Loving Someone Gay*, 2d rev. ed. Berkeley, Calif.: Celestial Arts, 1987.

Clifford, Denis, and Hayden Curry. *Legal Guide for Lesbian and Gay Couples*, 4th ed. Berkeley, Calif.: Nolo Press, 1986.

Costello, John. *Virtue under Fire: How World War II Changed Our Social and Sexual Attitudes.* Boston: Little, Brown, 1986.

Cruikshank, Margaret, ed. *Lesbian Studies.* Old Westbury, N.Y.: Feminist Press, 1982.

Curb, Rosemary, and Nancy Manahan. *Lesbian Nuns: Breaking Silence.* New York: Warner Books, 1986.

Dalton, Harlon, Scott Burris, and the Yale AIDS Law Project. *AIDS and the Law: A Guide for the Public.* New Haven, Conn.: Yale University Press, 1987.

Darter, Trudy, and Sandee Potter. *Women-Identified Women.* Palo Alto, Calif.: Mayfield Publishing Company, 1984.

D'Emilio, John. *Sexual Politics, Sexual Communities: The Making of a Homosexual Minority in the United States, 1940–1970.* Chicago: University of Chicago Press, 1983.

Duberman, Martin B. *About Time: Exploring the Gay Past.* New York: Gay Presses of New York, 1986.

Duggan, Lisa. "History's Gay Ghetto: The Contradictions of Growth in Lesbian and Gay History," in *Presenting the Past: Essays on History and the Public,* Susan Porter Benson, Stephen Brier, and Roy Rosenzweig, eds., pp. 281–90. Philadelphia: Temple University Press, 1986.

Filene, Peter G. *Him/Her/Self: Sex Roles in Modern America*, 2d ed. Baltimore: Johns Hopkins University Press, 1986.

Freedman, Estelle B., et al., eds. *The Lesbian Issue: Essays from SIGNS.* Chicago: University of Chicago Press, 1985.

Grier, Barbara. *The Lesbian in Literature*, 3d ed. Tallahassee, Fla.: Naiad Press, 1981.

Hanscombe, Gillian, and Jackie Forster. *Rocking the Cradle: Lesbian Mothers, A Challenge in Family Living.* Boston: Alyson Publications, 1982.

Holbrook, Sara. *Fighting Back: The Struggle for Gay Rights.* New York: Lodestar/Dutton, 1987.

Institute of Medicine, National Academy of Sciences; Eve K. Nichols, writer. *Mobilizing against AIDS: The Unfinished Story of a Virus.* Cambridge, Mass.: Harvard University Press, 1986.

Katz, Jonathan, ed. *Gay American History: Lesbians and Gay Men in the U.S.A.* New York: Harper & Row, 1985 [1978].

————. *Gay/Lesbian Almanac.* New York: Harper & Row, 1983.

Kleinberg, Seymour. *Alienated Affections: Being Gay in America*. New York: Warner Books, 1982.

Licata, Salvatore, and Robert Petersen, eds. *The Gay Past: A Collection of Historical Essays*. New York: Harrington Park Press, 1985 [1981].

McWhirter, David P., and Andrew W. Mattison. *The Male Couple: How Relationships Develop*. Englewood Cliffs, N.J.: Prentice-Hall, 1984.

Martin, Del, and Phyllis Lyon. *Lesbian/Woman*, rev. ed. New York: Bantam Books, 1983.

Masters, William, and Virginia Johnson. *Homosexuality in Perspective*. Boston: Little, Brown, 1979. (See Dr. Martin Duberman's review in *The New Republic* 180 [June 16, 1979], pp. 24-31.)

Muchmore, Wes, and William Hansen. *Coming out Right: A Handbook for the Gay Male Beginner*. Boston: Alyson Publications, 1982.

Plant, Richard. *The Pink Triangle*. New York: Henry Holt & Co., 1986.

Rofes, Eric C., ed. *Gay Life*. New York: Dolphin/Doubleday, 1986.

Rowse, A. L. *Homosexuals in History*. New York: Carroll & Graf, 1983.

Russo, Vito. *The Celluloid Closet: Homosexuality in the Movies*, rev. ed. New York: Harper & Row, 1987.

Rutledge, Leigh W. *The Gay Book of Lists*. Boston: Alyson Publications. 1987.

Shilts, Randy. *And the Band Played On: Politics, People, and the AIDS Epidemic*. New York: St. Martin's Press, 1987.

Silverstein, Charles, and Edmund White. *The Joy of Gay Sex*. New York: Simon & Schuster, 1978.

Sisley, Emily L., and Bertha Harris. *The Joy of Lesbian Sex*. New York: Simon & Schuster, 1978.

Stoddard, Tom B., et al., for the American Civil Liberties Union. *The Rights of Gay People*, rev. ed. New York: Bantam Books, 1983.

Organizations and Publications

Requests for information should be accompanied by a stamped, self-addressed envelope. Additional lesbian-related publications can be found at the end of Chapter 6.

Contemporary National and International Guides

Bob Damron's Address Book, Box 14-007, San Francisco, Calif. 94114

Gaia's Guide (women), 132 W. 24th St., New York, N.Y. 10010

Gayellow Pages, Renaissance House, Box 292, Village Sta., New York, N.Y. 10014

Odysseus (international), Box 7605, Flushing, N.Y. 11352

Places of Interest, Places in Europe, Places for Men, Places for Women, Ferrari Publications, Box 35575, Phoenix, Ariz. 85069

Spartacus Guide (international) (order from Renaissance House; address under item #3)

Selected National Addresses

Advocate (newspaper), P.O. Box 4371, Los Angeles, Calif. 90078-4371

Alyson Publications, 40 Plympton St., Boston, Mass. 02118

Amazon Bookstore, 1612 Harmon Place, Minneapolis, Minn. 55403 (book catalog for two first-class stamps)

Black/Out; The Magazine of the National Coalition of Black Lesbians and Gays, P.O. Box 2490, Washington, D.C. 20013

Body Politic, Toronto, Canada (1971–1986)

Christopher Street (magazine), P.O. 1475, Church St. Sta., New York, N.Y. 10008

Common Lives/Lesbian Lives; A Lesbian Quarterly, P.O. Box 1553, Iowa City, Iowa 52244

Dignity (Catholic), 1500 Massachusetts Ave., N.W., Suite 11, Washington, D.C. 20005

Fag Rag, Box 331, Kenmore Sta., Boston, Mass. 02215

Gay Community News, 62 Berkeley St.. Boston, Mass. 02116

Human Rights Campaign Fund, 1012 14th St., N.W., 6th Fl., Washington, D.C. 20005

Knights Press, P.O. Box 454, Pound Ridge, N.Y. 10576

Lambda Legal Defense and Education Fund, 666 Broadway, 12th Fl., New York, N.Y. 10012

Lambda Rising (mail catalog, $2), 1625 Connecticut Ave., N.W., Washington, D.C. 20009

Naiad Press, P.O. Box 1053, Tallahassee, Fla. 32302

National Association of Black and White Men Together, 584 Castro St., San Francisco, Calif. 94114

National Gay and Lesbian Task Force, 1517 U St., N.W., Washington, D.C. 20009

National Gay Rights Advocates, 540 Castro St., San Francisco, Calif. 94114

New York Native (newspaper), P.O. 1475; Church St. Sta., New York, N.Y. 10008

ONE, Inc., 3340 Country Club Drive, Los Angeles, Calif. 90019

Parents and Friends of Lesbians and Gays, Box 20308, Denver, Colo. 80220

RFD (magazine), Rt. 1, Box 127-E, Bakersville, N.C. 28705

Senior Action in a Gay Environment (SAGE), 208 W. 13th St., New York, N.Y. 10011

Sinister Wisdom: A Journal for the Lesbian Imagination in the Arts and Politics, Box 3252, Berkeley, Calif. 94703

Universal Fellowship, Metropolitan Community Churches, 5300 Santa Monica Blvd., Suite 304, Los Angeles, Calif. 90029

Visibilities, P.O. Box 1258 Peter Stuyvesant Sta., New York, N.Y. 10009-1258

Part IV
THE EIGHTH DAY OF CREATION: COMMUNITY

Although many of the earliest European adventurers and settlers in North America had primarily material motives, others hoped to create socially and religiously superior communities. Some of the first Euro-American colonies were consciously established with a sense of collective idealism, whether they were the "wilderness Zion" of the New England "saints" or the "holy experiment" of the Quakers.

This religious heritage of covenental communities may have contributed to or combined with later Enlightenment dreams of planned and rational societies, illustrated by the construction of the United States of America through a written constitution for "a more perfect union."

The United States, then, began with both messianic and rationalist traditions that could be expressed through voluntary communities. Although most of these have been no more radical than Alexis De Tocqueville's special-interest groups, some have been utopian, embodying a comprehensive vision of life that drew upon basic elements of U.S. culture while discarding and adding others.

Today, there are many "ideal communities" in the United States seeking the realization of religious and/or social principles.

In religion, many churches advocate more than the individual salvation of their own members. Catholic communitarianism, for example, is expressed by the over 220,000 sisters and brothers who have taken the ancient vows of poverty, chastity, and obedience. Many Protestant groups have been active in the Social Gospel, applying their beliefs to social problems. Another major religion, Judaism, has many vital communitarian traditions, such as the kibbutz.

Since the first Israeli kibbutz was founded in 1909, tens of thousands of American Jews have visited them, worked in them for extended periods, and sometimes joined them. By the 1980s, there were about 100,000 people in over 200 Israeli kibbutzim. Some of the communes are entirely agricultural; some are industrial (producing items like plastics and electrical goods); some are both. They can be politically ranked from the left all the way to what has been termed "the biblical right wing." In all of them there have been American kibbutzniks, and the U.S. Jewish community is generally conscious of the kibbutzim as a voluntary communal movement that has contributed more than its population share to the agricultural and industrial production of Israel.

Finally, there are new forms of religious communitarianism, such as the devotees of Krishna Consciousness (with their shaved heads, robes, and chants), members of the Unification Church (characterized, in the 1980s, by such books and movies as "Blinded by the Light," *Crazy for God, Moonwebs,* and "Ticket to Heaven"), and supporters of utopian reinterpretations of Christianity. Clarence Jordan, for example, founded the Koinonia community in Georgia in 1942 to provide cooperative work and low-cost housing for whites and blacks. Chapter 8 contains a discussion of some of the militant religious movements for progressive change.

American society also has many political and social voluntary associations that are working to expand democracy, whether through civil liberties lobbying, union activity, self-help, or co-ops. For example, there has been a growing interest in worker-owned and worker-managed businesses, which represent a third way between socialism and capitalism. There are co-ops that farm, build houses, bank, manufacture, and sell groceries. The National Consumer Cooperative Bank had assets of $300 million in 1987, and there were more than 5,000 consumer goods co-ops that had a total of over $1 billion in sales.

As an illustration of a social group that is becoming more conscious of itself as a community, with special interests and needs, I have chosen the elderly, especially the militant elderly. American society has slowly provided minimal pensions and health care, and, as this segment of the population increases, it is likely to exercise ever-growing power.

FIRST PREPARE The GROUND.

All these social and religious groups provide models of community that may clarify our basic assumptions about the ideal society. Do we believe that the individual prospers best by competing against the threats of other competitors, by submitting to the good of the whole, or by developing within a cooperative social order?

SOURCES OF FURTHER INFORMATION

Requests for information should be accompanied by a stamped, self-addressed envelope.
Examples related to religion can be found at the end of Chapter 8.

Academic Council for Kibbutz Studies, 27 W. 20th St., New York, N.Y. 10011

American Institute of Cooperation, 50 F St., N.W., Suite 900, Washington, D.C. 20001

Association of Community Organizations for Reform Now (ACORN), 401 Howard Ave., New Orleans, La. 70130

Changing Work, P.O. Box 261, New Town Branch, Newton, Mass. 02258

Communities, 126 Sun St., Stelle, Ill. 60919

Community Jobs, 1516 P St., N.W., Washington, D.C. 20077-1755

Co-op America, 2100 M St., N.W., Suite 310, Washington, D.C. 20063 ("If the business of America is doing business, let's do it our way.")

Cooperative Housing Federation, 2501 M St., N.W., Suite 450, Washington, D.C. 20037

Cooperative League of the USA, 1401 New York Ave., N.W., Washington, D.C. 20059

Employee Stock Ownership Assoc., 1725 DeSales St., N.W., Washington, D.C. 20036

Federation of Southern Cooperatives, 100 Edgewood Ave., N.E., Suite 1228, Atlanta, Ga. 30303

Industrial Areas Foundation Training Institute, 36 New Hyde Park Rd., Franklin Square, N.Y. 11010 (founded by Saul Alinsky in 1940)

Koinonia Partners, Rt. 2, Americus, Ga. 31704

Labor Research Review, 3411 W. Diversey Ave., Suite 14, Chicago, Ill. 60647

Labor Today, 7917 S. Exchange, Rm. 202, Chicago, Ill. 60617

Midwest Academy, 225 W. Ohio St., Chicago, Ill. 60610

National Association of Housing Cooperatives, 2501 M St., N.W., Washington, D.C. 20037

National Association of Neighborhoods, 1651 Fuller St., N.W., Washington, D.C. 20009

National Center for Employee Ownership, 426 17th St., Suite 650, Oakland, Calif. 94612

National Council of Farmer Cooperatives, 50 F St., N.W., Washington, D.C. 20001

National Historic Communal Societies Association, University of Southern Indiana, Evansville, Ind. 47712

National People's Action, 954 W. Washington Blvd., Chicago, Ill. 60607

New Society Publishers, 4527 Springfield Ave., Philadelphia, Penna. 19143

Rain, 1135 S.E. Salmon, Portland, Ore. 97214

Working Assets, 230 California St., San Francisco, Calif. 94111

Workplace Democracy, 111 Draper Hall, Amherst, Mass. 01003

8

God Is on the Side of the Poor: Prophets and Saints for Our Time

Let justice roll down like a river
and integrity like an unfailing stream.

Amos 5:24

Would Amos have endorsed conservative programs for minimal "trickle-down" aid to the poor? Or is this a political issue that he would have kept separate from religious values?

In practice, religion is not a once-a-week ritual. Even people who are not church members in this society have been shaped by Judeo-Christian concepts. Americans' sense of history as progressive stages of revelation, with individuals as active rather than passive agents, would be different in a Buddhist or a Hindu culture.

This religious heritage is being reinterpreted constantly. In the 1980s such television preachers as Pat Robertson, Jimmy Swaggert, and Jerry Falwell spread their messages through electronic churches. As many as 13 million people watched such televangelists. Greed sometimes tarnished their credibility; take, for example, Oral Roberts's 1987 announcement that God threatened to kill him unless the faithful sent in $8 million, and the escapades of Jim and Tammy Bakker. The Bakker scandal, ridiculed as Godscam, Gospelgate, and Pearlygate, involved salaries and bonuses of $1.9 million for one year, palatial "parsonages" (one with an air-conditioned doghouse), sex with a church secretary, and misappropriation of money from a Christian amusement park and charities. Critics emphasized that none of the ten wealthiest television ministers were among the 350 members of the Evangelical Council for Financial Accountability that had been founded by evangelist Billy Graham in 1979.

The television ministers can be apolitical ("The world doesn't matter; I've got Jesus"), but some preach a gospel of large military spending, small government programs for the poor, praise for individual business success, criticism of women's rights, restrictions on the freedom to choose abortion, and simplistic denunciations of sinister communism.

Other people have condemned this dogma as a conservative limitation of religious justice. They offer alternative models of discipleship. In the past, these models have been called prophetic religion, the Social Gospel, Christian socialism, liberal Christianity, and social evangelicalism. Within the contemporary United States, there are efforts to connect religion with social reform within ethnic groups like blacks, Indians, and Chicanos, and there are caucuses in all major denominations for greater sensitivity to the problems of race, sex, and class. Influences from abroad include various "liberation theologies." These have especially altered the domestic and foreign policy views of some U.S. Catholics, since almost one-half of the world's 840 million Catholics live in Africa, Asia, and Latin America. Conservatives have frequently cursed such domestic and foreign ideals, christening the progressive Catholics the "roamin' Catholics," the liberal New Jewish Agenda the Non-Jewish Agenda, and the Protestant reformers virtual agents of Satan.

In fact, what are the unifying beliefs of most religious reformers? They emphasize love and compassion rather than hatred of the enemy, criticism of deviants, and scorn for the poor. They are likely to portray God as more than a white man, Jesus as more than a European, and angels as more than German or Italian youth. For them, God may be neither male nor female, black nor white. God encompasses all, and a spark of God is within everyone.

This theistic humanism is rooted in the Scriptures: "If any one says 'I love God,' but hates his brother, he is a liar; for one who does not love his brother whom he has seen, cannot love God whom he has not seen" (I John 4:20); "love your neighbor as yourself" (Matthew 22:39); "preach good news to the poor . . . proclaim release to the captives . . . set at liberty those who are oppressed" (Luke 4:18). Religious liberals and radicals characterize oppression as a form of blasphemy against God, who created all persons.

Progressive religions do not accept oppression, but praise rebellion. God did not tell the Jews in Egyptian bondage to be content, work hard, and wait for freedom in heaven. The Old Testament prophets were not shy in criticizing the rulers of the world, including their own.

Christ continued this tradition. He was a poor, long-haired, wandering, impractical extremist who was skeptical about temporal authority and critical of most religious teachers. Jesus would not have been killed if he had praised Rome, applauded the religious elites, and taught a privatistic faith of indi-

REWARD
For Information Leading to the Apprehension of —

JESUS CHRIST

Wanted – for Sedition, Criminal Anarchy - Vagrancy, and Conspiring to Overthrow the Established Government

Dresses poorly. Said to be a carpenter by trade, ill-nourished, has visionary ideas, associates with common working people the unemployed and bums. Alien — beleived to be a Jew Alias : 'Prince of Peace, Son of Man' – 'Light of the World' &c &c Professional agitator Red beard, marks on hands and feet the result of injuries inflicted by an angry mob led by respectable citizens and legal authorities .

vidual conversion. He was executed as a troublemaker. As a black minister
realized, "Jesus was a first-century nigger, lynched on a tree."

Reformers ask, "Who are the saints of our time?" Are they the comfortably
fed clergy in their several-hundred-dollar suits driving in limousines to their
television studios? Are they conservative businessmen dining at prayer
breakfasts? Are they complacent worshipers in air-conditioned, carpeted,
and wood-paneled churches?

Religious progressives believe that many religions have made a Faustian
bargain for money, property, and status. Too many churches and synagogues
have fled to a comfortable captivity—not in Babylon but in suburbia. They
are tribalistic social clubs presided over by resident Pharisees. A modern
prophet who wanted to drive the moneylenders out of the temple would
discover that they had a mortgage on it.

Reformers claim that such institutions are preoccupied with protecting
themselves and the serenity of their members. Even these religious institutions meet various needs, of course. If they didn't, they wouldn't exist. But
other spiritual groups are eager to create communities of godly service. We
see that after Vatican II, every Catholic archdiocese in the world was required to have a commission on social justice and peace. Among Protestant
churches, black congregations have been healing communities from the earliest days, as described by C. Eric Lincoln: "Their church was their school,
their forum, their political arena, their social club, their art gallery, their
conservatory of music. It was their lyceum and gymnasium as well as *sanc-
tum sanctorum*" (Introduction to Gayraud S. Wilmore, *Black Radicalism
and Black Religion*, p. vii). While these early black churches were created
partly because of white racism, they positively merged institutional practice
with prophetic religion. They have often been seven-day-a-week centers for
community life, sustaining fellowship and justice. Martin Luther King, Jr.,
bore the cross in a way unimaginable for the spiritual stars of the electronic
church.

Progressives and conservatives, then, have had differing views on humanity, prophecy, and the bureaucratic church. Their responses to patriotism
constitute a fourth difference. Most churches display a flag, as if the temporal government and the divine were linked.

The Old Testament was wary about such alliances. The prophet Samuel
warned the Jewish people not to create their first king; he predicted a future
of taxation, conscription, exploitation, corruption, unhappiness, and physical
harm: "You will cry out because of your king, whom you have chosen for
yourselves, but the Lord will not answer you in that day" (I Samuel 8:18).
Nonetheless they insisted, and much of the Old Testament does not glorify
the leaders of state.

Christ was offered dominion over the kingdoms of the world during his
temptations in the desert. Satan presumably could grant such authority.
Jesus, however, chose the life of nonpower. He neither supported Rome nor

raised armies against it. Instead, he counseled, "Put up your sword, for those who live by the sword will die by the sword. Do good to those who hate you" (Matthew 26:52). It seems unlikely that Christ would have waved the flag for big military budgets. Indeed, for several centuries after Christ's death, believers refused to serve in the Roman government or armies. In our time, draft card burnings during the war inVietnam may have been equally meaningful. The editors of *Commonweal* compared them to liturgical ceremonies:

[From] the homilies delivered by A. J. Muste and Dorothy Day, through the ritual destruction of the cards, through the closing hymn—"We Shall Overcome"—there ran a quality so frequently missing in the sacred acts of the Church. Here was an act with consequences; not just another manifesto, but a commitment backed by the willingness to risk five years of personal freedom. ("Burning Draft Cards," *Commonweal*, November 19, 1965, p. 203)

Conservatives may respond that America's collective wealth is a sign of divine favor, but radicals ask if the Roman Empire should have been seen in the same light. Jesus, after all, endorsed no earthly kingdom; instead, he urged the wealthy to give all they had to the poor. It is not surprising that comfortable people ignore the uncomfortable maxims that it is better to give than to receive, that it isn't profitable to gain the whole world if you lose your soul, and that it is easier for a camel to pass through the eye of a needle than for a rich man to enter heaven. Material prosperity may lead to congratulatory self-indulgence. Critics pointed to President Reagan's lawyer Edwin Meese, who announced that there was no authentic evidence of poverty in America. When informed of long lines at soup kitchens in Washington, D.C., Meese declared that "people go to soup kitchens because the food is free and that's easier than paying for it."

For the contrasting ideal of Christian compassion, let us turn to Dorothy Day of the Catholic Worker Movement. I should note that I am not a Catholic; most of my ancestors would have suffocated me in my crib if they had known that I would live to say a positive word for Catholicism.

I discuss the Catholic church because it has the longest and most varied organizational history in Western civilization, and because today it is the biggest transnational corporation in the world. Dorothy Day was a significant member because she was an impoverished servant of people's real needs, not a Pharisee.

Day was born in 1899 in Illinois. By the time of her death in 1980, she was known as one of the most ridiculed and revered lay leaders produced by American Catholicism. While a few people steadfastly denied that her Catholicism was genuine, sometimes calling her Moscow Mary and insisting that her movement was a Trojan horse for subverting the faith, many others praised her as the godmother of recent Social Catholicism in the United

States. Over the decades of her work, praise became more common than condemnation. A liberal Protestant journal, *The Christian Century*, lauded her as a progressive voice of conscience, "pushing up needles from the underside of American society"; Father Theodore Hesburgh, president of Notre Dame University, approvingly remarked, "Dorothy Day has been comforting the afflicted and afflicting the comfortable all of her life"; the liberal Catholic *America* bestowed on her the title of "American Catholicism's reigning First Lady"; and social critic Dwight Macdonald, not a Catholic, admired her as a "radical abbess." Many of the Catholic activists of the last decades, such as the young Michael Harrington and the Berrigan brothers, looked to Dorothy Day as a standard-bearer, sometimes to her dismay.

She was not born into Catholicism, but started a painfully slow conversion when she was in her late twenties. Her youthful radicalism included writing for the socialist *Call* and the *Masses*, participating in the activities of the Socialist party and the Industrial Workers of the World, interviewing Leon Trotsky and other militants, friendships with prominent Communists like Elizabeth Gurley Flynn and Mike Gold, a common-law marriage with an anarchist, travel in revolutionary Mexico, and dreams of the revolutionary transformation of the United States. This was an unpromising background for an aggressively devout Catholic.

Yet, after years of uncertainty about the purpose of her life, Day's fascination with the Catholic church grew throughout the 1920s. In 1927 she had her newborn daughter baptized as a Catholic. She revealed in her first autobiography, *From Union Square to Rome*, that she wanted to protect her daughter from "floundering through many years as I had done, doubting and hesitating, undisciplined and amoral." Nonetheless, she resisted committing her own life to the church, although it promised answers to her doubts, a reassuring sense of historical continuity, and a supportive community. These were satisfactions that she found missing in Protestant individualistic America. She still hesitated to join because the Catholic church seemed a reactionary roadblock to progress, despite its moral claims. She could not deny that the church was profoundly conservative, but she was not convinced that this was inherent in Catholicism rather than an accident of history.

ROOTS OF THE MODERN U.S. CATHOLIC LEFT

Today it is clearer than it was to Dorothy Day in the 1920s why American Catholicism had seldom allied itself to reform movements. The first element in its pervasive conservatism was the desire of many Catholics to overcome Protestant hostility toward them as "outsiders," agents of the Vatican, and "un-American" by adopting an ultra-patriotism.

Catholics were a beleaguered minority in a Protestant-dominated society during most of their history in this part of the world. In the colonial period, few settlements allowed Catholics to practice their religion, to vote, or to hold office. Priests and nuns were often outlawed. Popular suspicions about Catholics were heightened by the fact that the enemies of the colonists were usually "Catholic powers" such as France and Spain. Even after the American Revolution, Catholics were given full equality in only five of the original thirteen states.

Many members of the church continued to be viewed as liberty-threatening aliens. In 1834 the Ursuline Convent in Charlestown, Massachusetts, was burned to the ground by a Protestant mob. In 1836 Americans trusted the sensational exposés about life in the nunnery that had been written by Maria Monk, who was actually a fraud. In 1844 Philadelphia rioters burned two Catholic churches and killed thirteen people. In the 1850s, the powerful Know-Nothing party instigated and led riots against Catholics in such cities as Baltimore. Ignorance and violence were manifested by the American Protective Association and the Ku Klux Klan throughout the late 1800s and early 1900s.

In the 1920s Day witnessed bigotry toward the Democratic candidate for the presidency, Al Smith. Since he was a "Papist," he was occasionally greeted by burning crosses. Day also saw Protestant American indifference to the persecution of Catholics in Mexico, attempts to restrict Catholic schools in the United States, misrepresentation in the press, bias in public institutions, and Protestant teachings in the public schools.

American Catholics were understandably defensive. They became partially ghettoized, for religious and ethnic reasons, into an elaborate system of separate schools, separate hospitals, separate orphanages, and separate charitable institutions. Catholics focused upon practical activities among themselves rather than general social reform.

The cultural background of the new immigrants of the late 1800s (constituting 5 million out of the total of 12 million Catholics in 1900) reinforced conservatism. Most of these newcomers had limited education and came from societies with no tradition of vigorous lay participation in church life. Furthermore, ethnic groups that were active inside and outside the church tended to promote their own interests rather than broad democratic reforms. The Irish, for example, worked within political structures to achieve modest gains for themselves.

Third, Day realized that Protestant antagonism was common at all levels of government. Catholics hesitated to increase political powers that might be used against them.

Paradoxically, even liberal trends within American Catholicism stifled the creation of radical tendencies. There were advocates of assimilation ("Americanizers") who insisted that there were no fundamental conflicts between Catholicism and "true Americanism." James Cardinal Gibbons (1834–1921), Archbishop John Ireland (1838–1913), and Bishop John Keane (1839–1918) asserted that the church was not hostile to the dominant values of American society.

Each of these factors was essentially conservative, and collectively they were magnified by the essential conservatism of the popes of the 1800s and early 1900s. While acts of charity might be emphasized, social justice was not.

Day recognized, however, that the church was not a monolith. Although she was unaware of the full dimensions of earlier Catholic radicalism and reform, she was familiar with the work of John A. Ryan and the editors of *Commonweal* (founded in 1924). Since most Catholics were urban industrial workers, the church and Catholic newspapers could not entirely ignore the problems of capitalist society, if only to provide a Catholic alternative to "atheistic socialism."

In 1928 Day overcame her doubts that she could be both a Catholic and a radical. She formally joined what seemed to her a church of the poor with a deep concern for the entire community, unlike most Protestant churches. Although she had satisfied her hunger for meaning, she grieved over the reactions of her friends. As she remembered decades later:

It was such a betrayal of them, they thought. One who had yearned to walk in the footsteps of a Mother Jones and an Emma Goldman seemingly had turned her back on the entire radical movement and found shelter in that great, corrupt Holy Roman Church, right hand of the Oppressor, the State, rich and heartless, a traitor to her beginnings. ("Reminiscences at 75," *Commonweal,* August 10, 1973, p. 424)

Within a few years, however, the Great Depression transformed the attitudes of many inside (and outside) the church and created a larger audience and constituency for those who were working for social change on the basis of Catholic principles, such as Father John A. Ryan. In 1932 there were as many as 15 million unemployed, "Hoovervilles" (shantytowns) outside many cities, and no comprehensive welfare system to cushion this human misery. Some members of the church urgently called upon it to assume leadership in constructing a fairer society.

In December 1932, after returning from a hunger march in Washington, D.C., Dorothy Day met the social prophet who would coalesce her own vision into a program. Peter Maurin (1877–1949), a French immigrant who viewed himself as a Christian agitator, impressed Day with his message, derived from an education in the De La Salle Brotherhood, Marc Sangnier's *Le Sillon* ("The Furrow"), the social teachings of the church, and the distributist theories of Hillaire Belloc, Eric Gill, and G. K. Chesterton, along with his own hard life as a ditch digger, stone quarrier, construction worker, coal miner, janitor, and wanderer.

Day, with her own diverse background, was prepared to hear this self-described "instigator" and "Apostle on the Bum." He offered a comprehensive system of "cult" (liturgy for the soul), culture (literature for the mind), and cultivation (agriculture and crafts for the body). Day turned his ideas

Peter Maurin, portrayed by Fritz
Eichenberg

into realities by launching the Catholic Worker Movement in 1933. It would
be built upon autonomous cells, with no application forms, no dues, no
records, no budget, and no officers. It would attempt to serve the people by
several means.

First, the *Catholic Worker* newspaper began on May Day, 1933. When
the paper was started, its editors had 92 cents among them. It was written
and planned in a tenement kitchen and on subway platforms. Day's type-
writer was sold to pay the printing bill for the second issue. Beginning with a
tiny edition of 2,500, the *Catholic Worker* had periods of rapid expansion
followed by near collapse, depending upon the fluctuating popular response
to its consistent views. By 1987, more than a half-century after its inaus-
picious beginning, it had a monthly press run of about 90,000. Some of these
copies were never read. Some were read many times.

In each issue, faith and deed were combined in articles on communalism, thoughts on the faith, and comments on contemporary events, such as "Feeling a Draft?" This newspaper, throughout the decades, has been a constant champion of racial equality, unionization, disarmament, and social justice.

Second, the movement has always meant service. This was embodied in about fifty, locally controlled "houses of hospitality" that were scattered throughout the United States by the late 1980s. Catholic Workers live in a house, dress in secondhand clothes, and receive subsistence, while seeking to feed, clothe, and shelter the homeless poor. They purchase food supplies in large lots, and receive leftover food from cafeterias and hospitals, heads and tails from fish markets, and bread that is several days old. For the Catholic Workers, the miracle of the loaves and the fishes is repeated three times a day, throughout the year. But no one is required to be religious to be fed. The food line is a kind of service to God.

Is any of this necessary today, in the era of the welfare state? The Catholic Workers point to many people who are unemployed, underemployed, or ill-paid. Some cannot live on meager pensions from Social Security. Others, despite official aid, remain desperately poor. Day recorded such a case:

The great city of New York just a short month ago came into our door on First Street with a poor little woman who was covered with lice from head to foot from sleeping in filth in broken down buildings, with some loathsome sores and, to be very delicate, a prolapsed rectum, covered with filth, excrement, urine and head-lice and body-lice and they sent her to us—the police, the Brooklyn police. (Quoted in Judith Nies, *Seven Women: Portraits from the American Radical Tradition* [New York: Penguin, 1977], p. 201)

Although Day was accused of romanticizing the poor, it would be difficult to prove this from her stories of impoverished, sick, and often mentally disturbed people. It may be pleasant to think about "saints," but it is another matter to live in cramped quarters, during a sweltering New York summer, in the middle of spitting, coughing, shouting, or sullen women, thieves, drunks, prostitutes, and drug addicts, that the welfare system would deem "the undeserving poor." One Catholic Worker, after surveying this throng, proposed that houses of hospitality be renamed houses of hostility. Day conceded that "to see Christ in these people was a tremendous act of faith."

Day and Maurin urged that every parish maintain a hospice to provide mercy and education for the abused and despised. Hospitality, they said, had become commercialized, and charity too much a thing for "other people" and "institutions" to do. Indeally, mutual aid societies might become the nucleus for a decentralized, cooperative, and federated society.

As another form of service, besides houses of hospitality, movement supporters own small farms. Maurin hoped that they would become rural colonies. In practice, the first in 1935 was so tiny—one acre!—that they called it

Rita Corbin

a "gardening commune." While the later Maryfarm, Holy Family Farm, and Tivoli provided temporary havens from the city, they never realized Maurin's vision of "agronomic universities" that would combine religious life with manual labor and intellectual work to exemplify a healthy society of production for use rather than for profit. Day, however, was not an agrarian mystic like Maurin. Even if she occasionally compared the "clean dirt" of the country with "man's filth," she reminded her followers that heaven was portrayed as a city, the spiritual Jerusalem, not as an agricultural retreat.

THE RELIGIOUS RADICALISM OF DOROTHY DAY

Day's critics were often bewildered by her militant appeal to ancient Catholic beliefs. Capitalists might dismiss her as a Communist; Communists might label her a capitalist; and both generally considered her a crank. In fact, her movement represented a third way, although some of its characteristics defied common sense.

First, the Catholic Workers never had elaborate blueprints, but a set of basic values that they sought to apply to everyday life. Day was skeptical about intellectuals and their neat worlds. She said of her two years at the

University of Illinois, "To this day I haven't the slightest idea of what I learned in class." Or consider her dismissal of one conversation between the famous writers Kenneth Burke, Malcolm Cowley, and John Dos Passos: "It stood out in my memory because I could not understand a word of it." Catholic Worker beliefs have been compared to a Mulligan stew with bits of potato and carrot floating in it.

Second, it would not have worried Day and her coworkers to be told that their moral vision was unrealizable. They sustained it as the best goal nonetheless, just as the church upheld its own "impossible faith." Day affirmed that it was better to devote one's life to a splendid ideal and fall short than to achieve less than what could be. Early Christians, after all, were not told to be practical, but to be "a spectacle unto the world," "fools for Christ's sake" (I Corinthians 4:9–15). What is immediately workable may not call for self-sacrifice, service, and dedication, and thus fail to realize some potential within humanity. For Day, most people were too adjusted to the realities of society. They needed to be jolted, shocked, and confronted by "the folly of the cross."

Day was confident that everyone was capable of reaching for higher standards. She dismissed those who said that they were too weak, whereas she was a saint: "When they start calling you a saint it just means they've decided not to take you seriously." Instead of such excuses for mediocrity, everyone should attempt to develop the heroic within themselves.

In this effort, the individual need not be alone. The Catholic church represented a community that could nurture the divinity within each person. Established by Christ, it symbolized that Christ was recrucified every day in the lost potential of humanity. Her church was not one of corporate investments and buildings but of concern for the squandered preciousness of life.

She knew that the real church was far from her ideal church, just as St. Augustine had concluded that the perfect City of God and the imperfect City of Man can never be fully one. While she loved the church, she was painfully aware of its faults:

The scandal of businesslike priests, of collective wealth, the lack of a sense of responsibility for the poor, the worker, the Negro, the Mexican, the Filipino, and even the oppression of these, and the consenting to the oppression of these by our industrial-capitalist order—these made me feel that priests were more like Cain than Abel. (Day, *The Long Loneliness*, pp. 145–46)

Imperfections are part of human life, even if they should not be lightly tolerated. She remembered Christ's metaphor that the church was a wide net cast into the sea, drawing in all varieties of people. (For Day, it brought in too many sharks and blowfish.) She quoted Christ that "the worst enemies will be those of your own household," giving the examples of the betrayal by Judas and Peter's denial of Christ before the crucifixion. She admitted that there were modern Pharisees, and too many members in bondage to the powers and values of earthly empire, but she insisted that while the church may be "a harlot at times, she is our Mother."

Day was an obedient, if angry, daughter of the church. Conventional radicals were appalled by her submission to church authority. She agreed that "if the Chancery ordered us to stop publishing the *Catholic Worker* tomorrow, I would." She replied to many questions with the simple statement "I follow the Pope." She referred to even Pius XII, who gave public support to Mussolini, as "Our Dear Sweet Christ on Earth."

On the other hand, progressives realized that this public obedience encouraged support within the church. Although a cardinal who read the *Catholic Worker* once informed Day that "we never studied these things in the seminary," there was no real effort to restrain her. In the 1930s the archdiocese had a chaplain in the New York house of hospitality, but he was a quiet man. The movement was rebuked only twice by his successors, once for urging draft refusal, a federal crime. Perhaps some church officials believed that Day was just a warm-hearted woman, while others admired her movement's charity. Cardinal Spellman confided to Day, "You'll find that many of the bishops are on your side." In any case, she avoided open

Fritz Eichenberg, in the *Catholic Worker*

challenges within the church. As she told Dwight Macdonald, "There are ways of getting around a cardinal."

She maneuvered around some clerics, because her allegiance to the church had not diminished her social radicalism; rather, it gave it a new justification. After 1933 she looked to the social encyclicals for a way to translate Christian commitments into social action. Particularly important were Leo XIII's "The Condition of Labor" (1891) and Pius XI's "On the Reconstruction of the Social Order" (1931). While Leo XIII criticized socialism, he had condemned the business treatment of labor as a commodity. Pius XI concurred that "raw materials went into the factory and came out ennobled and man went in and came out degraded," but he was more explicit than Leo XIII about a replacement. His encyclical talked about three basic principles:

(A) Personalism .. that the state and society must develop the God-given potential of the individual;

(B) Subsidiarity .. that organizations should avoid largeness, but be the smallest possible unit;

(C) Pluralism .... that there must be intermediate groups between the individual and the state. Direct relations between the state and the individual inevitably reduce the individual to a condition of pathetic dependence if not slavery.

Day was convinced that the nation-state was the worst form of contemporary idolatry and the worst threat to honest religion. Christianity must come before citizenship. Even a limited state diminishes personal responsibility. Individuals should act directly rather than waiting for the state to do something for them. The whining question of Cain, "Am I my brother's keeper?" is the ethic of surrendering one's conscience, whether to the capitalist welfare state or to a socialist agency. The New Testament says, "See how they love one another," not "See how they pass the buck." While the ideal church is the mystical Body of Christ (representing the Christ in each person), the state belittles the dignity and duties of the individual. Secular bureaucracies reduce the needy person to a "client" or a "case." The person giving aid is "the caseworker." People are replaced by abstractions.

It is not surprising that Day and her followers consistently opposed many of the policies of the state. Over the years, they refused to pay federal taxes, rejected tax-exempt status for their religious institutions, condemned voting, burned draft cards, poured blood on draft records, and were arrested for picketing. They did not wait for popular votes, conferences, reports, and "proper channels" to authorize their actions.

The state, on the other hand, retaliated sometimes by harassing Catholic Worker dwellings as "flophouses," slumlord "hotels," and overly congested "places of assembly." The government enforced health laws suited to institutions far different from those of the Catholic Workers. The latter, being unincorporated, were legally planted in the air.

The Catholic Worker conscience has been no less hostile to capitalism. Everyone has heard biblical quotations about greed without thinking about what they might mean in this society. How many today live by this standard: "Having food and raiment, let us be therewith content, for the love of money is the root of all evil." As Christ's Sermon on the Mount urged the faithful:

Lay not up for yourselves treasures upon earth, where moth and rust doth corrupt, and where thieves break through and steal: But lay up for yourselves treasures in heaven, where neither moth nor rust doth corrupt, and where thieves do not break through and steal: For where your treasure is, there will your heart be also. (Matthew 6:19–21)

Early Christian social ethics, based upon spiritual goods and love, are not capitalistic. Day interpreted capitalism as a selfish and predatory system of organized greed that taught people to prey upon one another. It sinned against society by rewarding competition and conflict rather than community.

While Day believed that a society organized entirely by capitalist principles would be a "materialist jungle," she did not plead for the abolition of private property. She preferred limited property, drawing upon St. Thomas Aquinas, who felt that some private ownership was useful. Even so, she publicly honored a few Communists for their moral commitments, saying that their love of humanity surpassed that of most Christians.

As one alternative to capitalist and socialist materialism, Day urged the ideal of voluntary poverty. Although the Bible counsels that we should render unto Caesar that which is Caesar's, Day reasonably noted that the less of Caesar's that we have, the less we have to render. People should say "no" to the spiritually unsatisfying quest for more possessions and form communities to maintain their basic needs.

Catholic Worker communities have attracted idealists because they are democratically managed (essentially by consensus, although one person may have deference because of his or her experience), and because the money donated to the Catholic Worker is actually spent on the poor. This compares favorably with the administrative costs of most charities. Maurin complained that ministration was swamped by administration in both the church and the state. Among the Catholic Workers, however, there is face-to-face help, as among the early believers. This contrasts with the impersonality of both professional charity and the welfare state. The Catholic Worker program provides food, companionship, and shelter (community) along with ideology (meaning and hope).

How shall we measure the success of Day and the Catholic Workers? Have they failed because they do not own brick and marble buildings with stained-glass windows, manage no huge budgets, and lack an organizational chart? These are not the goals that they have set for themselves. Rather, they have sought, by the witness of a small band of activists, to arouse the indignation of others against injustice and to awaken their imaginations to a

Graphics by Ade Bethune

vision of Christian love. In Day's words, "Love is indeed a brash and dreadful thing to ask of us, but it is the only answer."

This love, manifested through years of painful struggle, has disturbed the consciences and lives of many people. Some have formed or joined Catholic Worker groups or contributed to other organizations that represent her interests in pacifism, such as the Catholic Peace Fellowship. The Catholic Worker life-style of communitarian resistance was reproduced by organizations such as Jonah House in Baltimore, the Skidrow Justice Center in Los Angeles, and the Community for Creative Nonviolence in Washington, D.C. Radical Catholics of the 1960s and 1970s drew inspiration from Dorothy Day while working in the East Coast Conspiracy to Save Lives, We the People, the Planetary People's Offensive, the Flower City Conspiracy, and the New and Improved East Coast Conspiracy. For them, the Catholic Worker Movement was "the cradle of Catholic radicalism in this country."

But is the Catholic Worker less relevant today, since the world has changed so much since 1933? A Catholic was elected president of the United States in 1960. The closed windows of the church were opened with Vatican II. Official Catholicism is more willing to insist that "no one is justified in keeping for his exclusive use what he does not need, when others lack necessities" ("The Development of Peoples," 1967). Catholics have been prominent in the sanctuary movement to provide asylum for Central American refugees, protests against U.S. aid to wealthy elites in Central America, and social justice programs compatible with the pope's advice in 1986, "Instructions on Christian Freedom and Liberation." Also in 1986, the National Council of Catholic Bishops issued a rousing pastoral letter that was printed as *Economic Justice for All*. The bishops urged voluntary limits on profits, some worker ownership of the means of production, and "new forms of partnership between workers and managers." Church leaders have voiced their opposition to massive arms spending and nuclear proliferation.

But institutions, as institutions, are usually conservative. Despite progressive leaders within the church, and some progressive actions, Catholicism is known mainly for its official opposition to most liberation theology, its second-rate treatment of women, pronouncements against all forms of "artificial" birth control, rigid sanctions against abortion under any circumstances, hostility toward divorce reform, negative comments about homosexuality (despite the major presence of gay priests and nuns), and attempts to silence such critics as Archbishop Hunthausen of Seattle and Father Charles Curran of Washington, D.C. But the critics within the church have not been silenced. As one asserted, American Catholicism has reached "the last of the trained-seals' generation."

The prophetic religion of Dorothy Day and other religious radicals will not be outmoded unless there is a final revolution where "the postindustrial capitalist," "the new socialist man," or "the scientific humanist" is free from imperfection, no one venerates or worships secular deities, and no one is a member of a rationalist church with its own liturgies and eschatologies of explanation and justification. Until then, the "maximum program" of Christian love and the critique of the idolatry of power will be living principles.

SOURCES OF FURTHER INFORMATION

Books and Articles

This is a modest selection from an intimidatingly vast literature. It stays near the main roads rather than wandering off toward cults, marginal phenomena (such as feminist mother goddess groups or gay caucuses within established churches), meditation, yoga, personal growth, and Eastern spiritual consciousness.

Aman, Kenneth, ed. *Border Regions of Faith: An Anthology of Religion and Social Change.* Maryknoll, N.Y.: Orbis Books, 1987.

Berrigan, Daniel. *To Dwell in Peace: An Autobiography.* New York: Harper & Row, 1987.

Berryman, Phillip. *Liberation Theology: Essential Facts about the Revolutionary Religious Movement in Latin America and Beyond.* New York: Pantheon Books, 1987.

Cohn-Sherbok, Dan. *On Earth as It Is in Heaven: Jews, Christians, and Liberation Theology.* Maryknoll, N.Y.: Orbis Books, 1987.

Coles, Robert. *Dorothy Day: A Radical Devotion.* Reading, Mass.: Addison-Wesley, 1987.

Cone, James H. *A Black Theology of Liberation,* 2d ed. Maryknoll, N.Y.: Orbis Books, 1986.

——. *Speaking the Truth: Ecumenism, Liberation, and Black Theology.* Grand Rapids, Mich.: Eerdmans Publishing Company, 1986.

Cox, Harvey. *Religion in the Secular City: Toward a Postmodern Theology.* New York: Simon & Schuster, 1984.

Day, Dorothy. *By Little and by Little: The Selected Writings of Dorothy Day,* ed. Robert Ellsberg. New York: Knopf, 1983.

——. *The Long Loneliness: The Autobiography of Dorothy Day,* intr. by Daniel Berrigan. New York: Harper & Row, 1981.

Dolan, Jay P. *American Catholic Experience: A History from Colonial Times to the Present.* New York: Doubleday, 1987.

Ellis, Marc H. *Toward a Jewish Theology of Liberation.* Maryknoll, N.Y.: Orbis Books, 1987.

Fairclough, Adam. *To Redeem the Soul of America: The Southern Christian Leadership Conference and Martin Luther King, Jr.* Athens: University of Georgia Press, 1987.

Faw, Bob, and Nancy Skelton. *Thunder in America: The Improbable Presidential Campaign of Jesse Jackson*. Austin: Texas Monthly Press, 1986.

Ferm, Deane William. *Third World Liberation Theologies: An Introductory Survey*. Maryknoll, N.Y.: Orbis Books, 1986.

_____, ed. *Third World Liberation Theologies: A Reader*. Maryknoll, N.Y.: Orbis Books, 1986.

Fiorenza, Elizabeth S. *Bread Not Stone: The Challenge of Feminist Biblical Interpretation*. Boston: Beacon Press, 1986.

Forest, Jim. *Love Is the Measure; A Biography of Dorothy Day*. Mahway, N.J.: Paulist Press, 1986.

Franklin, Margaret A., ed. *The Force of the Feminine: Women, Men, and the Church*. Winchester, Mass.: Allen & Unwin, 1986.

Gannon, Thomas S., ed. *The Catholic Challenge to the American Economy: Reflections on the Bishops' Pastoral Letter on Catholic Social Teaching and the U.S. Economy*. New York: Macmillan, 1987.

Gleason, Philip. *Keeping the Faith: American Catholicism Past and Present*. Notre Dame, Ind.: University of Notre Dame Press, 1987.

Kann, Kenneth. *Joe Rapoport: The Life of a Jewish Radical*. Philadelphia: Temple University Press, 1980.

King, Martin Luther, Jr. *A Testament of Hope: The Essential Writings of Martin Luther King, Jr.*, ed. James M. Washington. New York: Harper & Row, 1986.

Lernoux, Penny. *Cry of the People: The Struggle for Human Rights in Latin America—The Catholic Church in Conflict with U.S. Policy*. New York: Penguin, 1982.

Lincoln, C. Eric. *Race, Religion, and the Continuing American Dilemma*. New York: Hill & Wang, 1985.

Link, Eugene P. *Labor-Religion Prophet: The Times and Life of Harry F. Ward*. Boulder, Colo.: Westview Press, 1984.

McDowell, John P. *The Social Gospel in the South*. Baton Rouge: Louisiana State University Press, 1982.

Marty, Martin E. *Pilgrims in Their Own Land: 500 Years of Religion in America*. Boston: Little, Brown, 1984.

Meconis, Charles. *With Clumsy Grace: The American Catholic Left, 1961–1975*. New York: Continuum, 1979.

Miller, William D. *Dorothy Day: A Biography*. New York: Harper & Row, 1984.

Musto, Ronald G. *The Peace Tradition in the Catholic Church: An Annotated Bibliography*. New York: Garland, 1987.

New Jewish Agenda, comp. *The Shalom Seders*. New York: Adama Books, 1984.

Norman, Edward. *The Victorian Christian Socialists*. New York: Cambridge University Press, 1987.

Oates, Stephen B. *Let the Trumpet Sound: The Life of Martin Luther King, Jr*. New York: New American Library, 1985.

Piehl, Mel. *Breaking Bread: The Catholic Worker and the Origin of Catholic Radicalism in America*. Philadelphia: Temple University Press, 1984.

Reddick, Lawrence D. *Crusader without Violence: A Biography of Martin Luther King*. New York: Harper & Row, 1987.

Robinson, Jo Ann Oiman. *Abraham Went Out: A Biography of A. J. Muste*. Philadelphia: Temple University Press, 1982.

Rothman, Stanley, and Robert S. Licther. *Roots of Radicalism: Jews, Christians and the New Left*. New York: Oxford University Press, 1982.

Ruether, Rosemary. *Sexism and God-Talk: Toward a Feminist Theology*. Boston: Beacon Press, 1984.

————, ed. *Womanguides: Readings toward a Feminist Theology*. Boston: Beacon Press, 1986.

Schneider, Susan Weidman. *Jewish and Female: Choices and Changes in Our Lives Today*. New York: Simon & Schuster, 1984.

Sernett, Milton C., ed. *Afro-American Religious History: A Documentary Witness*. Durham, N.C.: Duke University Press, 1985.

"And who is my neighbor?" Jesus made answer and said: "A certain man was going down from Jerusalem to Jericho; and he fell among robbers, who stripped him and beat him, and departed, leaving him half dead. And by chance a certain priest was going down that way; and when he saw him, he passed by on the other side. And in like manner, a Levite also, when he came to the place and saw him, passed by on the other side. But a certain Samaritan, as he journeyed, came where he was; and when he saw him he was moved with compassion, and came to him, and bound up his wounds, pouring on them oil and wine; and he set him on his own beast and brought him to an inn and took care of him. And on the morrow he took out two shillings, and gave them to the host and said: 'Take care of him, and whatsoever thou spendest more, I, when I come back again, will repay.' Which of these three, thinkest thou, proved neighbor to him that fell among the robbers? . . . Go, and do thou likewise!"

Luke 10:29–37

Drawing by Fritz Eichenberg

Sorin, Gerald. *The Prophetic Minority: American Jewish Immigrant Radicals, 1880–1920*. Bloomington: Indiana University Press, 1985.

Stern, Frederick C. *F. O. Matthiessen, Christian Socialist as Critic*. Chapel Hill: University of North Carolina Press, 1981.

Tabb, William K., ed. *Churches in Struggle: Liberation Theologies and Social Change in North America*. New York: Monthly Review Press, 1986.

Wallace, Dewey D., Jr. "Recent Publications in American Religious History: A Bibliographical Essay and Review." *American Studies International* 19 (Spring/Summer 1981): 15–42.

Weisbrot, Robert. *Father Divine*. Boston: Beacon Press, 1984.

Welch, Sharon D. *Communities of Resistance and Solidarity: A Feminist Theology of Liberation*. Maryknoll, N.Y.: Orbis Books, 1985.

West, Cornel. *Prophesy Deliverance! An Afro-American Revolutionary Christianity*. Philadelphia: Westminster Press, 1983.

Wilmore, Gayraud S. *Black Religion and Black Radicalism*, 2d ed., rev. and enl. Maryknoll, N.Y.: Orbis Books, 1983.

Wilmore, Gayraud S., and James H. Cone, eds. *Black Theology: A Documentary History, 1966–1979*. Maryknoll, N.Y.: Orbis Books, 1979.

Organizations and Publications

Requests for information should be accompanied by a stamped, self-addressed envelope.

American Ethical Union, 2 W. 64th St., New York, N.Y. 10023
American Friends Service Committee, 15th and Cherry, Philadelphia, Penna. 19102
American Humanist Association, 7 Harwood Drive, P.O. 146, Amherst, N.Y. 14226-0146
Americans United for Separation of Church and State, 8120 Fenton St., Silver Spring, Md. 20910
Catholic Peace Fellowship, 339 Lafayette St., New York, N.Y. 10012
Catholics for Free Choice, 2008 17th St., N.W., Washington, D.C. 20017
Catholic Worker, 36 E. First St., New York, N.Y. 10003
Center of Concern, 3700 13th St., N.E., Washington, D.C. 20017
Central Committee for Conscientious Objectors, 2208 South St., Philadelphia, Penna. 19146
Christian Century, 5615 W. Cermak Road, Cicero, Ill. 60650
Christianity and Crisis, P.O. Box 1308-C, Fort Lee, N.J. 07204
Commonweal, 15 Dutch St., New York, N.Y. 10038
Clergy and Laity Concerned, 198 Broadway, New York, N.Y. 10038
Cross Currents, Mercy College, Dobbs Ferry, N.Y. 10522
Fellowship of Reconciliation, Box 271, Nyack, N.Y. 10960

Friends Committee on National Legislation, 245 Second St., N.E., Washington, D.C. 20002

Interfaith Center on Corporate Responsibility, 475 Riverside Drive, Rm. 566, New York, N.Y. 10115

Israel Horizons, 150 Fifth Ave., Suite 911, New York, N.Y. 10011

Jewish Currents, 22 E. 17th St., Suite 601, New York, N.Y. 10003

Methodist Federation for Social Action, 76 Clinton Ave., Staten Island, N.Y. 10115

National Council of Churches of Christ in the USA, 475 Riverside Drive, New York, N.Y. 10115

National Interreligious Service Board for Conscientious Objectors, 800 18th St., N.W., Washington, D.C. 20006

Network: A Catholic Social Justice Lobby, 806 Rhode Island Ave., N.E., Washington, D.C. 20018

New Jewish Agenda, 64 Fulton St., Suite 1100, New York, N.Y. 10038

New Oxford Review, 1069 Kains Ave., Rm. 425, Berkeley, Calif. 94706

The Other Side (evangelical), 300 W. Apsley St., Philadelphia, Penna. 19144

Pax Christi, 348 E. 10th St., Erie, Penna. 16503

People for the American Way, 1424 16th St., N.W., Suite 601, Washington, D.C. 20036

People United to Serve Humanity (PUSH), 930 E. 50th St., Chicago, Ill. 60615

Religion and Intellectual Life, College of New Rochelle, New Rochelle, N.Y. 10801

Religious Coalition for Abortion Rights, 100 Maryland Ave., N.E., Washington, D.C. 20002

HOW TO KILL BOLSHEVISM—No. 2.

Denver, Colo. — The Reverend A. Jaw-bunk, a local · minister of prominence, preached an eloquent sermon yesterday on "Bolshevism, The Peril of the Twentieth Century."

He advocates the burning at the stake of all Communists, and for Liberals to be imprisoned for life.

He announced that his sermon next week would answer his critics: "Was Jesus Really Poor and Opposed to Aristocracy?" Mr. Jawbunk has proof that Jesus was an aristocrat and wanted the poor to stay where they belong.

One type of Protestant minister, ca. 1920

Shmate, Box 4228, Berkeley, Calif. 94704

Society of Separationists, P.O. Box 2117, Austin, Tex. 78768 (founder: Madalyn Murray O'Hair; atheist publications)

Sojourners (evangelical), P.O. Box 29272, Washington, D.C. 20017

Southern Christian Leadership Conference, 334 Auburn Ave., N.E., Atlanta, Ga. 30312

Theology in the Americas, 475 Riverside Drive, Rm. 1244-AA, New York, N.Y. 10115

Tikkun: A Bimonthly Jewish Critique of Politics, Culture and Society, 407 State St., Santa Barbara, Calif. 93101-9709 (Tikkun: "to heal, repair and transform the world")

Unitarian-Universalist Service Committee, 78 Beacon St., Boston, Mass. 02108

United States Catholic Conference, Office of International Peace and Justice, 1312 Massachusetts Ave., N.W., Washington, D.C. 20005

War Resisters' League, 339 Lafayette St., New York, N.Y. 10012

Witness (Episcopal), P.O. Box 359, Ambler, Penna. 19002

9

Will You Love Me
When I'm Old and Gray?
The Activist Elderly

There is one minority that most of us hope to join: the elderly. We probably would not have been successful during most of human history. Old age and retirement were rare in the past, and there were not enough elderly to form the social movements that are emerging today. In 1900 the average life expectancy of Americans was forty-six, and only 4 percent of the population lived to be over sixty-five. Pensions, then, were even rarer than old people.

By contrast, most Americans now expect to live to old age and retirement. In 1987 one of every nine Americans was over sixty-five years old. Over 90 percent of those born in the late twentieth century will reach sixty-five. This population will grow from the present 25 million to 35 million by the year 2000 (one of every six Americans), and to 65 million by the year 2030 (one of every five). Furthermore, the number of those eighty-five or older—the old old—will double to 4 million during the next twenty years. This population explosion of older people is without historical precedent. The elderly of today can be called "the new old."

The rapid growth of this aged population could be a time bomb for the American economy, political system, and society. Just as the 1950s saw the beginnings of major civil rights struggles for minorities, the 1960s were noted for youth movements, and the 1970s were the years of the creation of a large women's movement, the 1980s and the 1990s may be distinguished by the popularization of issues related to "the graying of America."

Movements by the activist elderly draw upon earlier achievements. The New Deal saw the passage of the minimal Social Security Act of 1935, partly as a response to the wide appeal of radical proposals by such critics as Dr. Francis Townsend, a retired physician. Out of the 1960s and the 1970s came the Older Americans Act (1965; amended 1973), Medicare (1966), the Age Discrimination in Employment Act (1967; amended 1978), the Employment Retirement Income Security Act (1974), and the Age Discrimination Act

(1975). There are now federal and state agencies to insure basic incomes, health care, food, and housing for the old.

Because of the limitations of these agencies, advocacy organizations have developed that represent millions of members. Some speak for professional interests, such as the Gerontological Society and the National Council on Aging, a confederation of approximately 1,400 public and private social welfare organizations. Some represent the retired members of particular jobs, such as the National Association of Retired Federal Employees. Others have expanded from representing one group, such as retired teachers, into being a mass institution, like the American Association of Retired Persons, (AARP), which claimed 24 million people over the age of fifty in 1988. The largest organizations are moderate lobbying and service-oriented groups, although there are differences between the essentially white professional members of the AARP and the more union-oriented and liberal membership of the National Council of Senior Citizens (with 4 million on the rolls in 1988). In addition to these groups, which are among the largest voluntary associations in American society, there are smaller bands of "wrinkled radicals," such as the Gray Panthers (with 60,000 members).

All these organizations focus on certain major problems. The central problem for most of the aged is money. Retirement often means instant poverty. The average monthly Social Security check in 1985 was for $594, although one-third of the old received less than $4,000 a year in income. Single and widowed old women and minorities were especially likely to end their days in the same inferior status that they had occupied for a lifetime. Single women over the age of sixty-five had an average income of $536 in 1982. Even by the government's 1985 definition of poverty—where a couple was not poor if their combined income was more than $6,503—about one out of every eight old people were poor. It may be questioned also whether the government's definition of poverty is realistic.

The one-fourth of the elderly who have incomes in addition to Social Security may have other problems. Inflation may tarnish the "golden years" of the middle class. The cost of one major illness can destroy the savings of a lifetime. Those who planned carefully for their retirement may outlive their savings. For most people, a long life will mean being poor.

The Census Bureau disputed these gloomy figures in a special report in 1983, as did the President's Council of Economic Advisors in 1985. It was asserted that enormous progress had been made since 1972 when Social

Security increases were tied to rising prices. While the real incomes of many workers had declined during this inflationary period, since wage increases had not matched inflation, the Social Security checks of the aged had grown rapidly. This fact, combined with the monetary worth of food stamps, medical care, housing subsidies, and reduced taxation of the old, meant that they were living comfortably. Many critics of these reports argued that the sums of money involved were low, that housing subsidies were often unavailable, that medical plans did not cover all of the expenses of the aged, and that the reports concealed the class gap between the resources of the aged rich and the aged poor.

Both liberals and conservatives do largely agree, however, that the Social Security system is not as secure as it could be. Although the system now covers 118 million people—90 percent of the workforce—the ratio of those paying in to those who are receiving benefits has been declining steadily. In 1950 there were sixteen workers for every recipient; in 1960, five for every one; and, in 1981, 3.2 for every one. As the number of elderly has grown because of longevity, the birth rate (and the number of youth) has fallen. The system was tottering toward bankruptcy in 1983 when payroll taxes were raised and expenditures were limited. Following these modifications, the pension fund relied upon a contribution of 7.05 percent of the worker's salary up to $37,500, combined with a 7.05 percent contribution from the employer. Although this averted collapse, the long-term solvency of this procedure is in some doubt.

Further changes have been proposed, including the elimination of automatic cost-of-living increases, freezing some planned increases, restricting benefits to those who are poor or disabled, requiring higher taxes of wealthy retirees, and drawing upon general tax revenues. Some critics of Social Security have urged that people be allowed to leave the system to establish their own retirement plans. It is unlikely, however, that most people would contribute over 14 percent of their income (the total for employee and employer), during a period of many years, into some individual retirement account (IRA) or Keogh-type plan. Voluntarism would serve few and could reduce Social Security to the status of a welfare program.

For the millions of people who retire on severely restricted incomes, life presents many problems. If less money comes in, property taxes, utilities, and phone bills may be impossible to pay. It could be necessary to sell the home. Selling can destroy old friendships and habits. The elderly person may not be able to find a comfortable apartment that is affordable, especially because subsidized housing for the elderly is uncommon. A rent increase as small as $10 a week can be crushing to many. The head of the National Council on Aging had this comment: "Many of the elderly repeat month by month the miracle of Chanukah, where one day's oil lasted for eight days." He added, "The poor never saved for rainy days because it rained every day of their lives."

Those with small incomes cannot afford good food. Not surprisingly many committees have documented the consumption of dog food and similar substances by some elderly. Robert Frost of the National Council of Senior Citizens remarked, "They can get two meals out of a can. Where else could they get so much for so little money?" A common diet relies heavily on the starches found in bread, butter, oatmeal, and potatoes. Although this food can make a person look fat, it is not healthy. Reliance on starches can contribute to fatigue, insomnia, irritability, loss of short-term memory, and depression.

Those who have money for good housing and a good diet may still fear impoverishment from medical bills. For those who have long-term chronic illnesses, income and savings may be bled down to nothing by health costs. Even if you had planned carefully, your money would vanish quickly if you got Alzheimer's disease or some other affliction that demanded expensive care.

Government medical programs have not solved these problems. Medicare, for example, does not cover eyeglasses, hearing aids, dental work, or prescription drugs. A deductible must be paid. Many other expenses are covered partially: Medicare usually pays 40 percent of day-to-day care. Some doctors refuse to participate in this program because it doesn't pay them enough, or it inconveniences them. Finally, reimbursement may take months. Other government programs require that an individual spend almost all disposable income to qualify for assistance. Given such choices, an

Shangri-La
NURSING HOME

elderly person might decide to do without dental work, glasses, or medical treatment, and suffer the consequences. The agenda of the 1987 Congress included these issues and the crucial matter of insurance against the costs of "catastropic illnesses."

Many elderly fear that they will end their days in an institution. This is the fate of a relatively small number, totalling 5 percent of those over sixty-five and 10 percent of those over seventy-five. But the growth of the older population and the tendency to institutionalize people who could be taken care of at home will make conditions in these institutions a major issue. About 40 percent of those who are institutionalized are not ill; they have nowhere else to go. They do not have support systems that might allow them to live independently. Other industrial nations have more programs for in-home care, where the elderly are helped with laundry, shopping, cooking, cleaning, repairs, and transportation. The Government Accounting Office estimated, in 1987, that 3.2 million elderly need home nursing or other care to stay at home, but that only 60 percent received this aid. Such programs would be more humane than nursing homes, and they would be less expensive.

Nursing homes are seldom homelike. About 90 percent of the 23,000 homes are profit-making businesses, unlike those in European societies. To make a profit, they hire unskilled staff for low-paying jobs. Only one out of every ten nursing home workers is a trained nurse. As an owner of a nursing home lamented: "This is very hard physical work, and few people want to do it because our society doesn't like to think about, or look at, old age. . . . You can't provide decent care if you make a profit by paying low salaries."

By the year 2000, there will be at least 2 million elderly in nursing homes. Will there be legal standards to guarantee that they receive good food, lodging, physical therapy, health care, entertainment other than television, and genuine concern by a competent staff? Today, there are few standards, and they are often not enforced. The General Accounting Office estimates that over one-half of all nursing homes do not meet minimal federal guidelines. Militant groups are justified in comparing many nursing homes to "concentration camps" for the elderly, human warehouses, gray ghettoes, and "open graves." People in custodial care frequently lose interest in life, refuse to talk, eat little, become bedridden, and soon die. A major cause of their death was their environment.

All of these problems of poverty, bad housing, poor food, and wretched medical care are worse for minorities and women. The typical black man born in 1985 will pay approximately $60,000 to Social Security, but will die before he is old enough to collect anything. The average black woman lives to retirement, but lives seven years less than the average white woman. For black men and women who live to retirement age, almost 40 percent are below the official poverty line.

Much the same is true of the rural poor, other minorities such as Indians, and most women. All are likely to have low-paying jobs, to die earlier because of stress, or to end up with minuscule pensions. In 1980 over 12 percent of all whites were over sixty-five, compared to 7.9 percent of all blacks and 4.8 percent of all Hispanics. The latter groups all suffer from the problems of a lifetime, as do women, who constitute three-fourths of all elderly poor. While 19.8 percent of all people under the age of 65, and 23.7 percent of old people overall, are officially poor, the figure is 51.6 percent for elderly black couples and 65.1 percent for elderly black women. For all of these groups, conditions have not improved fundamentally during the last decade. Reaganism, for example, has not put money into these people's pockets, nor improved the way they live.

Let us say that an elderly person tries to overcome these difficulties by keeping his or her job. That person notes that workers do not cease to be productive at some clearly established time, and that mandatory retirement is blatant discrimination. A retirement age of sixty-five was first set by the chancellor of Germany in 1889 when the life span of the average German was thirty-seven and few people expected to live to retirement. Times have changed dramatically.

This is a vital concern. Even if a person dislikes his or her job, it provides a meaningful identity, as well as money. Anyone who is not a worker and a major consumer may be considered a social leech, with devastating consequences for self-esteem. Retirement can become a kind of slow death sentence.

This issue began to receive legal recognition in 1967 in the Age Discrimination Act. This forbade discrimination against workers on the basis of age during the years forty-five to sixty-five. In 1982 over 13,000 complaints of age discrimination were filed with the Equal Employment Opportunity Commission.

In 1986 Congress eliminated mandatory retirement for most workers as age discrimination. Representative Claude Pepper, who sponsored this legislation in the House, idealistically commented that "at long last we will have eliminated ageism as we have previously eliminated sexism and racism as a basis for discrimination in this country, and we will be putting a new emphasis on human rights."

What will these regulations mean in practice? The government has not publicized them, nor has it energetically prosecuted cases. Also, if older workers hang on, this threatens the hiring of the young and the promotion of the middle-aged. On the other hand, there are many workers who want to retire as soon as possible. As the chairman of the Federal Council on Aging said, "If you talk to a black laundry worker about the 'privilege' of continuing work after 65, she'll spit in your eye." Most workers at General Motors retire at about age fifty-eight. They could work until age sixty-eight, but only 2 percent do. At Exxon only 20 percent work until sixty-five. But what about white-collar professional jobs like business managers, people in government bureaucracies, and college administrators and faculty?

One proposed solution is competency tests for those who want to continue their jobs. Few employers favor this, however, since they are hesitant to judge an associate as less than competent. They may wish to use the automatic method of age retirement to ensure opportunities for younger employees and a turnover of expensive top jobs to stimulate creativity and savings.

A second possibility is gradual retirement. "Gliding out" of full employment is more common among European professionals. In the United States a person is likely to be an employed and productive worker one day and completely retired the next. But American employers are apprehensive that flexibility may tangle them in personnel problems.

Finally, there are part-time jobs. A 1981 national Harris Poll indicated that 79 percent of workers approaching the age of sixty-five did not want to cease working totally. But employers prefer to use older people with marketable skills as volunteers. Those who get part-time jobs find that promotional opportunities are minimal. And there are few job-training programs for the elderly. It is particularly difficult for older women to find good jobs, since they may be reserved for younger and more "attractive" women. The skills and talents of old people are a wasted national resource.

A final concern is "ageism." Ageism is like racism and sexism: a person is treated certain ways solely because of his or her age, just as people are stereotyped because of skin color or sex. Age assumptions govern the acceptable behavior of children, adolescents, adults, and the elderly. Age stereotypes are implied in the command, "Act your age!" Although these categories may limit the individual humanity of all, they are especially cruel to the old, who may be characterized broadly as worn out and worthless.

Everyone has learned the fictions of ageism. When a young person is forgetful, that is natural. But when a sixty-five-year-old forgets, it may be quickly labeled senility. Or when a working man applies for credit, he gets it because he is drawing a salary. When a retiree asks for credit, he may be turned down even though his pension or Social Security checks are just as regular as another person's wages. In medicine, doctors don't like treating the elderly because they are trained usually to cure illness, not to treat chronic and long-term afflictions. If a person has a pain in one knee, that's because he's old, although the other knee is just as old! In television com-

mercials, the young are enjoying themselves, while the old are fussing over iron pills, laxatives, headaches, and constipation, since illness is generally equated with old age. Sharon Curtin talked about these stereotypes in her book *Nobody Ever Died of Old Age:*

If your hair grays, you must dye it. If your physical condition deteriorates—as it must—you will enter an institution. If you stop to watch children playing, you're suspected of being a dirty old pervert. . . . If someone wishes to pay you tribute, they say you're young—considering your age. That is as grievous an insult as telling a woman she "thinks like a man."

The aged, by and large, are powerless people that other Americans are embarrassed about, just as we frequently don't know what to "do about" our grandparents. The elderly are often depicted as senile old men or silly old women. The old are encouraged to stay in geriatric ghettoes, whether they are golden ghettoes like Sun City and Leisure World, or the old-age ghettoes of nursing homes. Although many of the old prefer the company of their peers, such thorough age segregation may not be in either their best interests or those of society.

This ageism affects women more than men. Much of our culture's appreciation of women is physical, and physical beauty tends to be short-lived. It is a common joke that women lie about their age. Of course, everyone tends to worry about aging, since this society does not value age. This has been called "gerontophobia," the fear of growing old, which is usually ironic since most people also hope for a long life. Men are less fearful about age because they are less drastically influenced by physical roles.

Suppose, for example, that a husband and a wife who are in their late forties decide to divorce. The husband has an excellent chance of getting married again, probably to a younger woman. His ex-wife, however, will find it difficult to remarry. Attracting a second husband younger than herself is improbable. Even to find someone her own age may require luck. She is likely to marry a man considerably older than herself. While men are not as socially limited by age, a divorced or widowed woman in later life is likely to be poor and alone.

This is primarily a question of cultural imagery, not of biology. Older women and men are victimized and dehumanized by myths that depict them as inferior. Many of the elderly have accepted these images, or unconsciously incorporated them into their behavior. Some, confronted with the loss of authority or status, may retreat into dreams of earlier times, as a psychological escape from the unpleasant reality of being old in a land of the young. Some decide that suicide is preferable to such a life: one of every four suicides is by someone over sixty-five, far more than their percentage of the general population. Who wants to be considered "used-up," "cast-off," and superfluous?

The economic, social, and psychological plight of the elderly has led some to turn to politics and social organization for solutions. In the past it has not been easy to organize the old. Many feel doubts about their own value, accept personal blame for their problems, are fatalistic ("That's the way it is"), are anxious about losing what little they have by criticizing authorities, or are temporarily comfortable and believe that they are safe from any personal disaster. But as the elderly have become the fastest growing section of the American public, this has changed.

One small but influential example of "gray liberation" is the Gray Panthers, now a network of about 60,000, with over 130 chapters. They were founded by Maggie Kuhn and five other recently retired people in 1970. Kuhn had been forced to retire as the editor of a journal published by the United Presbyterian Church. She was not exhausted at the age of sixty-five, and began the Consultation of Older and Younger Adults for Social Change (originally directed against the war in Vietnam). This was dubbed the Gray Panthers in 1972.

They have a reputation far beyond their numbers, and they are known for more than bingo games and shuffleboard. Kuhn asserted, "I wouldn't mind being called a 'senior citizen' if I actually got any seniority rights, but as it is, people can damn well call me old. It's going to happen to them, so they'd better get used to the word."

The national program of the Gray Panthers stresses health, housing, and hunger, along with a call for a "new economic system," a New Deal for the old. The Gray Panthers have vigorously complained that Medicare does not cover routine physical exams, preventive medicine, dental care, and optical service, nor problems related to hearing, feet, and certain other maladies. Also, Medicare pays only part of the bills in most cases. Medicaid, which is supposed to solve many of these problems, is too complicated and confusing. As an alternative, the Panthers endorsed the plan by Representative Ron Dellums for a no-fee national health service that would be locally controlled. Dellums criticized the Congress: "Very few of my colleagues will turn down socialized medicine at Walter Reed or Bethesda, or attendance by the House physician, which they're entitled to as Congressmen. Why shouldn't every American have such care available?"

The United States is the only major industrial nation without a comprehensive national health care system. If every city and locality had a few centralized health facilities, everything from medical laundries to laboratories might be more efficient and inexpensive. A medical system that is more humane, just, and accessible is not impossible, although some will cry "socialism!" In practice, even the conservative Reagan did not scorn medical treatment for himself at government expense, despite his status as a millionaire.

The final medical issue is, of course, death. Should terminally ill people be kept alive by enormously complex and expensive methods? In 1984 Governor Richard Lamm of Colorado publicly declared that such people had "a duty to die and get out of the way." The expense of maintaining them was called a burden on the economic health of the United States. Furthermore, their useful lives had ended, and their suffering was being increased.

These comments provoked widespread outrage, but they did highlight the use of exotic technology to force life into people who would otherwise be dead. One-third of Medicare costs are now for those with less than one year left to live. Few want to spend their last days being fed through a tube, heavily sedated, on a respirator, and, perhaps, in a vegetative condition. To delay death, under these circumstances, is not much of a life.

Groups like the Gray Panthers emphasize that the choice should be the individual's. By 1987 thirty-five states recognized the legality of a "living will," in which a person states that he or she does not wish to be kept alive by extraordinary means. In other states, doctors feel compelled to use life-prolonging equipment or risk lawsuits from the patient's relatives. The "right to die" could be regarded as one aspect of self-determination.

A second focus of the Gray Panthers is one of the central concerns of the living: decent housing. The Panthers have publicized the difficulty of finding

and keeping affordable housing for those on pensions. They have urged more public projects for the elderly, property tax limitations, and consideration of such innovations as Share-a-Home "families" of the elderly, resembling communes run by a manager. They have sought strict regulation of nursing homes and retirement centers, comparing many of the present ones to trash cans into which the old are dumped.

Third, hunger. The Gray Panthers would like to see automatic cost-of-living raises for all pensions so that the "golden years" are not haunted by inflation and financial doubt. They support extension of nutrition programs under the Department of Health and Human Services, such as Meals on Wheels, which feeds some of the homebound elderly in 2,000 communities. By contrast, the Reagan administration in 1987 urged that the age requirement be raised from 60 years to 70 years old, that a means test be instituted, and that funds be cut. Congress disagreed, as supporters of the program documented that many cases of apparent senility are caused by bad diets and psychological depression; they are not the inevitable results of aging.

Locally, Panther chapters have worked for reduced transit fare for the aged, elimination of age stereotypes in the media, improved social services, elderly day-care centers, easy ride vans, and "resource fairs" that encourage the old to reemploy their skills in paid or volunteer jobs.

It is often said that the old are naturally conservative and resistant to change. It is possible that the elderly of the present and of the future will be compelled to act as a major force for change in some of the basic institutions of our society. Although the politically screened and packed White House Conference on Aging in 1981 proclaimed that the United States has "the wealthiest, best-fed, best-housed, healthiest, and most self-reliant older population in our history," many people think that more could be done for

the majority of the old. Since they already constitute 15 percent of the voting-age population, are more likely to vote than the young, and are concentrated in various cities and states, organizing could bring them decisive influence. In addition, as the baby boomers mature into their later years, it is not likely that they will accept poverty without complaints. It may be the young and the middle-aged, threatened by increased taxes and job competition, who will then prove to be more conservative.

SOURCES OF FURTHER INFORMATION

Books and Articles

Achenbaum, W. Andrew. *Old Age in the New Land*. Baltimore: Johns Hopkins University Press, 1978.

————. *Shades of Gray: Old Age, American Values, and Federal Policies Since 1920*. Boston: Little, Brown, 1983.

————. *Social Security: Visions and Revisions*. New York: Cambridge University Press, 1986.

"The Aging Society" (entire issue), *Daedalus* 115 (Winter 1986).

Berkowitz, Edward D., ed. *Social Security after Fifty: Successes and Failures*. Westport, Conn.: Greenwood Press, 1987.

"The Black Elderly" (entire issue), *Black Scholar* 13 (January-February 1982).

Borenstein, Audrey. *Chimes of Change and Hours: Views of Older Women in Twentieth-Century America*. Rutherford, N.J.: Fairleigh Dickinson University Press, 1983.

Callahan, Daniel. *Setting Limits: Medical Goals in an Aging Society*. New York: Simon & Schuster, 1987.

Cole, Thomas R., and Sally A. Gadow, eds. *What Does It Mean to Grow Old? Reflections from the Humanities*. Durham, N.C.: Duke University Press, 1986.

David, Sheri. *With Dignity: The Search for Medicare and Medicaid*. Westport, Conn.: Greenwood Press, 1985.

Davis, Richard H., and James A. Davis. *TV's Image of the Elderly: A Practical Guide for Change*. Lexington, Mass.: D. C. Heath, 1985.

Doress, Paula Brown, Diana Laskin Siegal, and the Midlife and Older Woman Project. *Ourselves, Growing Older*. New York: Simon & Schuster, 1987.

"The Elderly in America" (articles by Albert Rosenfeld, Timothy M. James, and W. Andrew Achenbaum), *Wilson Quarterly* 9, no. 1 (1985), pp. 96–139.

Fischer, David Hackett. *Growing Old in America*. New York: Oxford University Press, 1978.

Golant, Stephen M. *A Place to Grow Old: The Meaning of Environment in Old Age*. New York: Columbia University Press, 1986.

Gold, Margaret. *The Consumers Union Guide to Housing Alternatives for the Older Citizen*, rev. ed. Mount Vernon, N.Y.: Consumer Reports, 1986.

Graebner, William. *A History of Retirement: The Meaning and Function of an American Institution, 1885–1978*. New Haven, Conn.: Yale University Press, 1984.

Haber, Carole. *Beyond Sixty-Five: The Dilemma of Old Age in America*. New York: Cambridge University Press, 1985.

Hendricks, Jon, and C. Davis Hendricks. *Aging in a Mass Society: Myths and Realities*, 3d ed. Boston: Little, Brown, 1986.

Hess, Beth B. *Growing Old in America*, 2d ed. New Brunswick, N.J.: Transaction Books, 1980.

Kaufman, Sharon R. *The Ageless Self: Sources of Meaning in Late Life*. New York: New American Library, 1987.

Keith, Jennie. *Old People as People: Social and Cultural Influences on Aging and Old Age*. Boston: Little, Brown, 1982.

Koehler, Barbara, and Yvonne Lev, eds. *Encyclopedia of Senior Citizens Information Sources*. Detroit: Gale Research Company, 1987.

Kübler-Ross, Elisabeth. *Death: The Final Stage of Growth*. New York: Simon & Schuster, 1986.

Longman, Philip. *Born to Pay: The New Politics of Aging in America*. Boston: Houghton Mifflin, 1987.

Markides, Kyriakos S., and Charles S. Mindel. *Aging and Ethnicity*. Newbury Park, Calif.: Sage Publications, 1987.

Pifer, Alan, and Lydia Bronte, eds. *Our Aging Society: Paradox and Promise*. New York: Norton, 1986.

Rosenwaike, Ira, and Barbara Logue. *The Extreme Aged in America*. Westport, Conn.: Greenwood Press, 1986.

Rubinstein, Robert L. *Singular Paths: Old Men Living Alone*. New York: Columbia University Press, 1986.

Salver, Eva. *Don't Send Me Flowers When I'm Dead: Voices of Rural Elderly*. Durham, N.C.: Duke University Press, 1983.

Silverman, Philip, ed. *Modern Pioneers: An Interdisciplinary View of the Aged*. Bloomington: Indiana University Press, 1987.

Stannard, David E., ed. *Death in America*. Philadelphia: University of Pennsylvania Press, 1975.

Stearns, Peter N., ed. *Old Age in Preindustrial Society*. New York: Holmes & Meier, 1983.

Stokell, Marjorie, and Bonnie Kennedy. *The Senior Citizen Handbook: A Self-Help and Resource Guide*. Englewood Cliffs, N.J.: Prentice-Hall, 1985.

Tedrick, Ted, ed. *Aging: Issues and Policies for the 1980s*. New York: Praeger, 1985.

Van Tassel, David D., ed. *Aging, Death, and the Completion of Being*. Philadelphia: University of Pennsylvania Press, 1979.

Van Tassel, David D., and Peter N. Stearns, eds. *Old Age in a Bureaucratic Society: The Elderly, the Experts, and the State in American Society*. Westport, Conn.: Greenwood Press, 1986.

Work in America Institute, Inc. *The Future of Older Workers in America: New Options for an Extended Work Life*. Elmsford, N.Y.: Pergamon Press, 1982.

Worth, Richard. *You'll Be Old Someday, Too*. Danbury, Conn.: Franklin Watts, 1986.

Organizations and Publications

Requests for information should be accompanied by a stamped, self-addressed envelope.

ACTION (federal volunteer programs), 806 Connecticut Ave., N.W., Washington, D.C. 20525

Administration on Aging, Department of Health and Human Services, 300 Independence Ave., S.W., Washington, D.C. 20201

Ageing and Society, Cambridge University Press, 32 E. 57th St., New York, N.Y. 10022

Aging, Superintendent of Documents, GPO, Washington, D.C. 20402-9371 (produced by the Office of Human Development Services of the Department of Health and Human Services)

American Association for International Aging, 1511 K St., N.W., Suite 1028, Washington, D.C. 20005

American Association of Homes for the Aging, 1129 20th St., N.W., Suite 400, Washington, D.C. 20036

American Association of Retired Persons, 1909 K St., N.W., Washington, D.C. 20049

Federal Council on Aging, Department of Health and Human Services, 300 Independence Ave., Washington, D.C. 20201

Gray Panthers, 311 S. Juniper, Suite 601, Philadelphia, Penna. 19107

Institute of Gerontology, University of Michigan, 300 N. Ingalls, Ann Arbor, Mich. 48109-2007

International Federation on Aging, 1909 K St., N.W., Washington, D.C. 20049

JASA (Jewish Association for Services for the Aged), 40 W. 68th St., New York, N.Y. 10023

Journal of Aging Studies, Department of Sociology, University of Florida, Gainesville, Fla. 32611

National Alliance of Senior Citizens, 2525 Wilson Blvd., Arlington, Va. 22201

National Association of Retired Federal Employees, 1522 New Hampshire Ave., Washington, D.C. 20034

National Caucus and Center on Black Aged, Inc., 1424 K St., N.W., Suite 500, Washington, D.C. 20005

National Citizens Coalition for Nursing Home Reform, 1424 16th St., N.W., Suite I2, Washington, D.C. 20036

National Council of Senior Citizens, 925 15th St., N.W., Washington, D.C. 20005

National Council on the Aging, 600 Maryland Ave., S.W., West Wing 100, Washington, D.C. 20024

National Hispanic Council on Aging, 2713 Ontario Rd., N.W., Suite 200, Washington, D.C. 20009

National Institute on Aging, Information Center, 2209 Distribution Circle, Silver Spring, Md. 20910

National Senior Citizens' Law Center, 2025 M St., N.W., Washington, D.C. 20036

Older Women's League (OWL), 1325 G St., N.W., Lower Level B, Washington, D.C. 20005

Select Committee on Aging, United States House of Representatives, Washington, D.C. 20515

Senate Special Committee on Aging, United States Senate, Washington, D.C. 20510
Senior Action in a Gay Environment (SAGE), 208 W. 13th St., New York, N.Y.
   10011
United Seniors Health Cooperative, 1334 G St., N.W., Washington, D.C. 20005

**"The best effect of
any book is that it
excites the reader to
self activity."**
—Thomas Carlyle

Our Future from Our Past?

We the people of the United States, in order to form a more perfect union, establish justice, insure domestic tranquility, provide for the common defense, promote the general welfare, and secure the blessings of liberty to ourselves and our posterity, do ordain and establish this Constitution for the United States of America.

From the Preamble to the United States Constitution, 1787

We are maturing as a nation. Born in violence in the late 1700s, our first national state was a failure. George Washington scorned the Articles of Confederation for producing "a half-starved, limping government, always moving on crutches and tottering at every step." Our second "united states" emerged from the Constitution written in 1787. It was a patchwork of compromises, and it was widely criticized. Popular fears quickly led to the addition of ten amendments, forming the Bill of Rights. Our national capital was moved several times before settling within an artificially created District of Columbia. Thomas Jefferson once described the location as little more than "an Indian swamp in the wilderness."

The United States began like many Third World agricultural countries: weak, divided, and disorganized. "We the people" did not include most Americans, such as women and blacks. Only after a civil war killed 600,000 people was black citizenship written into the Constitution. It required eight decades of struggle for women to receive the national right to vote in 1920. Our evolution toward "a more perfect union" has been accomplished by great sacrifices and pain. Our Constitution has become the oldest such document among large nations because it is not a rigid code; it lives through constant reinterpretation.

Today, the federal government acts in many ways to insure "the general welfare." There are limits on the selfish ravaging of the earth and the poisoning of our air, water, and food. The silent danger of nuclear energy is monitored. Women and racial minorities have some protections from open discrimination. The elderly are not abandoned to their individual fates. The lives of most people have improved since the early days of our society.

As we Americans enter the third century of our national life, some people claim that this progress has ended and that we must accept a future of scarcity and stagnation for the average person. They say that "the public interest" must take precedence over the well-being of "special interests." These "special interests" include the vast majority of our population. There are two minorities, however, who may be dangerous to the general public. These two groups are handled gently by almost all politicians and the mass media. They are the wealthy and the military. How compatible are their interests with those of most Americans?

The first group, the wealthy, are getting richer while the numbers of the poor are growing and those of the middle class are shrinking. In 1986, .5 percent of American households had assets of more than $2.5 million, controlling 35.1 percent of the total net worth of the United States. (In 1963, the figure had been 25.4 percent.) This uppermost elite included, in 1987, 49 billionaires. The next .5 percent of households, with assets of $1.4 million to $2.5 million, controlled another 6.7 percent. (In 1963, it was 7.4 percent.) The following 9 percent, with $206,340 to $1.4 million, had 29.9 percent, compared to 32.3 percent in 1963. Everyone else—90 percent—controlled 28.2 percent of the worth of the United States, with some other assets owned by foreigners. These embarrassing figures from the Federal Reserve Board have been disputed. Some critics argue that they exaggerate the concentration of wealth in the United States, while other people conclude that they underestimate that concentration since the figures do not include the wealthiest, such as members of the Forbes 400. These 400 people had a net worth, in 1987, of $220 billion. While the stock market crash of October 1987 may have diminished their worth, few probably are standing on street corners selling pencils. In all likelihood, the basic structure of wealth remains the same as that outlined in a 1986 report by the Joint Economic Committee of the U.S. Congress entitled *Concentration of Wealth in the United States*. The wealthiest .5 percent of the population owned 35.6 percent of all private real estate, 46.5 percent of corporate stocks, 43.6 percent of bonds, and 58.2 percent of corporate assets. The top 10 percent controlled, respectively, 77.8 percent, 89.3 percent, 90.4 percent, and 93.6 percent. These are the superrich who run the show.

About one-half of the wealthiest people inherited their money. This reminds one of a cartoon in *Playboy* where an older man gives his son this advice: "Here's a million dollars. Don't lose it." The head of the Seagram's fortune once observed that it was hard to turn $100 into $110, but it was almost automatic to turn $100 million into $110 million. It is a cliché that the

United States is a middle-class nation, but, in fact, a hereditary class system dominates. Not everyone is in the same boat; some are in yachts.

Many of the largest earned incomes in the 1980s came from stock speculation. In 1987 *Financial World* listed the top 100 incomes on Wall Street. At the head of this list was one individual who received $125 million in 1986. The average for the top ten people was $68.1 million, compared to $51.1 million in 1985.

Incomes among chief executive officers of corporations have been at less exalted levels, but they are still the highest among the twenty largest industrial nations. A 1987 report by the international consulting firm of Towers, Perrin, Forster and Crosby ranked our CEOs as getting more money, more bonuses, and more benefits, while generally paying fewer taxes and having greater purchasing power, than the business executives of the other nineteen countries. While Japanese executives were fourth on the income list, they were sixteenth after taxes and a consideration of their actual purchasing power. American executives are also more likely to have such corporate perks as cars, country club memberships, credit cards, medical care, and dining and entertainment costs—usually as tax-free "business expenses." Such executive benefits come at the same time as many corporations are calling for sacrifices by their workers.

This growing economic inequality raises questions about the inordinate political and social power of tiny elites within a democratic society. Many people have agreed with the view of Louis Brandeis, a Supreme Court justice, that "we can either have democracy in this country or we can have great wealth concentrated in the hands of a few, but we can't have both." Furthermore, there is a threat to economic stability when the consuming power of masses of people is depressed. In the past, financial and political turmoil have intervened to reduce gross inequality.

The investment practices of elite money may again lead to such chaos. It has been seldom used to rebuild our outmoded steel furnaces, old car factories, and decaying industrial plants. Instead, most of it has gone into quick-profit schemes in real estate and stocks. The "merger mania" of the 1980s meant huge fortunes from shuffling papers, while corporate debt grew to $1.5 trillion in 1986. Stock prices rose steadily under the pressures of what some called "casino capitalism," including the insider trading for which one individual, Ivan Boesky, was fined $100 million in 1986, and more than a dozen traders submitted guilty pleas in 1987. Such activity was profitable for a few, but it did not create real products that could be sold on domestic and international markets. These circumstances, along with the public's annoyance at gouging corporate managers and "runaway" businesses to foreign countries, contributed to a Lou Harris poll in 1986 that showed that only 35 percent of Americans had a favorable view of corporate leaders, down from 69 percent in 1979.

The tax "reforms" of the 1980s were an additional slight to much of the public. The 1981 revisions, which added enormously to the deficits of later years, gave families making $50,000 a year an average gain of more than $2,000 a year, whereas families in the $18,000 range got a tax decrease of $100. Furthermore, these tiny gains at the lower incomes tended to be consumed by increases in Social Security taxes. The progressive income tax was virtually rejected in 1986; the top rate had fallen from 70 percent in 1980 to 28 percent. The highest rate applied whether you were a middle-class homeowner earning $40,000 or someone bringing in $40 million. We now have the lowest tax rates of all industrialized Western nations. It is a system in which the wealthiest have the lightest financial burdens for maintaining American society. Our income distribution is already the worst in the advanced industrial world. As former Speaker of the U.S. House of Representatives Tip O'Neill said in his 1987 autobiography: "[Reagan's program] made the rich richer and the poor poorer, and it did nothing for the middle class. On the contrary: it took from the truly needy and gave to the truly greedy."

Many of the lower middle classes and the poor suffered further in the 1980s from reductions in government programs for school lunches, job training, college education, Medicare, Medicaid, and income supplements. Senator Larry Pressler, a Republican from South Dakota, noted:

In 1987 the College Work Study program was funded at nearly $600 million. The 1988 request is zero. The Supplemental Educational Opportunity Grant Program received $412 million in 1987. In the 1988 request—zero. The National Student Direct Loan Program received $188 million in 1987—zero for 1988. The State Student Incentive Grant Program received $76 million in 1987—zero for 1988.

What kind of society is unwilling to invest in the future of its youth? Or was the future represented by the Reaganite goal of increasing the $535 million spent in 1987 for the Reserve Officer Training Corps on U.S. campuses?

Many of the social and tax policies of recent governments, along with those of corporate America, have not benefited the average American. While 46 percent of American households earned $15,000 to $35,000 in 1970, only about 39 percent got the same number of constant dollars in 1985. Meanwhile, the number of people that the federal government defined as poor grew from 9 percent in the mid-1970s to 14 percent in 1987. The U.S. Bureau of the Census reported in 1983 that 55 percent of all households had no net financial assets after subtracting debts. That is, over one-half of all American households had either zero net worth or a negative net worth. Such families are unlikely to save money to improve their lives, or to advance the hopes of their children.

What about the 33.7 million who were defined officially as poor in 1987? Were they loafing welfare parasites? About 11.5 million were children under the age of fifteen (about 25 percent of U.S. children are in poverty); 9.1 million worked for pay; 2.1 million were retired; 2.7 million were disabled or ill; 4.1 million were mothers who had no access to day care or training; 2.3 million were full-time students; 1.4 million were looking actively for work; and some of the remainder were unemployable. Many of these people, and others within the middle class, have gone heavily into debt to maintain themselves. Installment debt reached a half-trillion dollars in 1987.

Most new jobs during this period have involved low-wage "hamburger" labor in retail trade or services. During 1979–1984, 55 percent of new employment was in these "McJobs" that paid $7,000 or less in 1984 dollars. This compared to 19.9 percent of new jobs during 1973–1979. The better jobs are closed to many people because they cannot afford the necessary training. While federal support for higher education grew 200 percent in the 1970s, it declined over 20 percent during 1981–1985, with the severest cuts in vocational education and job training. At the same time, the costs of education were increasing.

Senator Tom Harkin of Iowa has understood this growing class problem: "We've come to the point where too few people have too much and the rest of us have too little." The parable of Lazarus and the rich man can be seen in all of our cities. These and other areas may become a Third World within our borders. While almost 34 million Americans are below the official poverty level, a few people are grotesquely wealthy.

A second "special interest" that gets more than its fair share, other than the indecently rich, is the military. The United States became a global power by the end of World War II, when other major nations were either defeated or exhausted. In 1945 the United States was 40 percent of the world economy. There were predictions of an American Century. That world, however, is already dead. The U.S. share of the world economy is now less than one-half that of 1945. Nevertheless, the United States continues to maintain a vast network of military support for friendly nations and financial aid for our international welfare clients.

The enemy, a supposedly monolithic communism directed from Moscow, has been replaced by a communist world divided by ideology, economics, and nationalism. The Soviet Union has major internal problems, and its foreign "successes," such as maintaining Cuba, supressing Solidarity in Poland, or propping up a government in Afghanistan, have been economic and political burdens. Too many of these successes would weaken the Soviet state. The U.S. military, on the other hand, prevented neither the crushing of Solidarity, nor the Russian war in Afghanistan. The U.S. has agreed not to invade Cuba, while blockading it economically, although a flood of American tourists might undermine communism more rapidly than unused American weapons. Russian power, as a global inspiration or as a threat, has been in overall decline for decades.

American power is also in decline. Many other capitalist nations, such as

Japan and West Germany, are major powers in their own right. Nuclear weapons are no longer controlled by just the United States and the Soviet Union; they are becoming dangerously common. Expensive equipment like nuclear aircraft carriers may be industrial dinosaurs vulnerable to modern "smart" missiles. Other smaller weapons have not been effective against terrorism. What are we getting for the money that we spend?

The United States has more than a half-million troops outside its borders. They are scattered throughout the world, on ships and in countries like Japan, South Korea, the Philippines, Egypt, Saudi Arabia, Panama, Cuba (at Guantánamo Bay), Spain, Italy, and the United Kingdom. The United States has more than 350 military bases in over 40 countries and spent $2 trillion between 1980 and 1985. Meanwhile, the Japanese commit about 1 percent of their gross national product to defense while benefiting from American soldiers. We cut programs for our citizens while spending, in 1987, $85 billion to protect West Germans; this amounted to 28 percent of our "national defense" budget. We are draining our society because of adolescent illusions about our power in the world. Is this required "to provide for the common defense"?

Americans may have been educated by the excesses of recent years. The United States does not have the power to be the policeman of the world. It is a role that is both ineffective and despised. Power must be shared with

genuine allies, not servants, and competing systems must be dealt with realistically. Our government talks about "the evil empire" of communism, but the truth is that American banks loan money to communists and American companies do an enthusiastic trade, such as the sale of 4 million tons of wheat to the Soviet Union in 1987. We live in an interdependent world, full of many peoples with their own long histories and cultures.

Americans need to ask whether the money that we spent meddling in Lebanon, El Salvador, and Nicaragua should have been invested in America. Americans should think about Barry Goldwater's plan to close or consolidate "at least thirty" U.S. military bases. Americans might listen to George Kennan's call for a 50 percent cut in all nuclear weapons. Superman and Rambo belong in comic books, not in foreign policies.

Most of us are going to pay, eventually, for the indulgences of these two special interests. In 1980 Ronald Reagan promised to increase military spending, cut taxes and social programs, and balance the budget. George Bush called this "voodoo economics," and Representative John Anderson said it could only be done with mirrors. They were right, and bad policies can no longer be concealed by a presidential grin. Reagan has been responsible for larger deficits than all previous presidents. During his years of power, the national debt tripled to over $2.3 trillion by the summer of 1987. (This is 41 percent of the gross national product; it was 26 percent in 1980.) American citizens now pay $140 billion a year in interest on this debt. About 50 percent of this money goes to the top 1 percent of U.S. income earners, who hold these bonds. Another large sum goes to the foreign controllers of $340 billion in U.S. treasury notes, especially to the Japanese. Until 1982 the United States was the largest creditor nation in the world. By 1987 it was the largest debtor nation in the world, with over one-half of the debt of 1986 being funded by foreign sources. How long can we live on borrowed money before the bill becomes due? "Special interests" have benefited from Reaganite policies, but not the majority of the American people.

It is difficult to believe that most of us will agree that the rich own America and can do whatever they want with both the land and its inhabitants. Although we have been shaped by the past, our history is not that of a fatalistic people. Where do we go from here? Will our future include an imperial military and a reduced democracy? Trade wars? The bankruptcy of the banking system? A distribution of wealth that resembles the Third World?

Past solutions are not likely to work. In the nineteenth century America grew through territorial expansion, industrialization, and the development of the railroads. In the twentieth century, there was the invigoration of the Spanish-American War, World War I, World War II, Korea, and Vietnam, along with the economic stimulus of automobile production and sales and the construction of a highway system. Today, large wars are too dangerous, and technology—even computers and superconductivity—does not offer the promise of massive employment and sales. Expansion covered up many problems in American society and allowed only those reforms that did not involve basic structural changes. There have been eight recessions since World War II. The average unemployment rate has risen steadily from 4.5 percent in the 1950s to 4.8 percent in the 1960s, 6.2 percent in the 1970s, and about 7 percent in the 1980s. What is now called a recovery would be considered a recession in the 1950s. Moreover, the growth of the GNP has slowed from 4.2 percent in the 1960s to 3.2 percent in the 1970s and 2.5 percent in the 1980s. Productivity has declined continuously as money has been spent in speculative schemes or, in the case of the government budget, to pay for the wasted research of scientists and engineers whose talents have been applied to useless military projects. Two-thirds of government research money is now spent on the military, and only .4 percent on increasing industrial productivity.

The Reagan administration attempted such radical solutions as supply-side economics (tax cuts for the rich and budget cuts for the poor), extravagant military spending to pump up the economy, and devaluation of the dollar to stimulate foreign purchases of U.S. goods. These strategies have harmed everyone except the rich.

We do have other traditions that we could rely upon for our future. President Franklin D. Roosevelt expressed our democratic aspirations when he presented his 1944 State of the Union message to the Congress:

We have come to a clear realization of the fact that true individual freedom cannot exist without economic security. . . .

We have accepted, so to speak, a second bill of rights under which a new basis of security and prosperity can be established for all, regardless of station, race, or creed. Among these are:

The right to a useful and remunerative job in the industries or shops or mines of the nation.

The right of every farmer to raise and sell his products that will give him and his family a decent living.

The right of every businessman, large or small, to trade in an atmosphere of freedom from unfair competition and domination by monopolies at home and abroad.

The right of every family to a decent home.

The right to adequate medical care and the opportunity to achieve and enjoy good health.

The right to adequate protection from the economic fears of old age, sickness, accident and unemployment.

The right to a good education.

These goals have not been achieved. An Economic Bill of Rights may require fundamental alterations in American society. If so, it is time for radical thoughts, radical plans, and radical actions. Conservatism will only mean decay.

Above all, we must understand how the present society limits our opportunities in life. What is our place in the system? As John Maynard Keynes once observed: "Practical men, who believe themselves quite exempt from any intellectual influence, are usually the slaves of some defunct economist." Americans need a more mature view of life. This is not a classless society; our national interests are not the same as those of corporate and social elites. We need a class-conscious politics for the majority. This suggestion is not socialistic or communistic, but realistic. The wealthiest 10 percent, in most cases, already have an accurate knowledge of their class interests, and they control most politicians. Too many Americans still have their heads clogged by business ideology and illusions. Alice Rivlin, formerly of the Congressional Budget Office, once noted that if the average person was told that "Our system is totally rigged, with an elite at the top that has tremendous advantages over everybody else," that person's response was likely to be "How can I get my kid into the elite?" rather than "How can I change the system?" Individual success, even if possible, will not improve American life.

Many alternatives to this selfish individualism have been promoted in the 1980s. Martin Carnoy, Derek Shearer, and Russell Rumberger composed *A New Social Contract* (1983) that emphasized economic democracy; Gar Alperovitz and Jeff Faux outlined proposals in *Rebuilding America* (1984); Samuel Bowles, David Gordon, and Thomas Weisskopf developed their own Economic Bill of Rights in *Beyond the Waste Land;* and Irving Howe edited a collection entitled *Alternatives: Proposals for America from the Democratic Left* (1984). These and other critics have sought to use our existing federal system to promote local and state innovations, regional cooperation, federal block grants, and national encouragement for democratically controlled companies such as municipal utilities and cooperatives.

Although our national government is empowered to "promote the general welfare, and secure the blessings of liberty to ourselves and our posterity," some people may claim that fundamental justice is impossible because there is no money for it. In fact, most of the political battles of the Reagan era were over social programs that represent less than 1 percent of our GNP. Most of the vast private wealth of this country has been sheltered from social use. The basic problem is not American poverty but the lack of popular will to redistribute wealth and reorganize our spending priorities. This would require more than "quick fix" reforms; it would require reconstruction.

Wealth could be redistributed by a return to the progressive income tax (where those who benefit the most from American life pay the most), an annual tax on accumulated wealth, and inheritance taxes. In 1972, for example, Senator George McGovern proposed an inheritance limit of $500,000. By contrast, in 1987, there was no federal inheritance tax paid by those who received bequests and an estate tax of 1 percent on the largest estates (which brought in $6 billion to the U.S. treasury). Today, the whole game is pre-determined in favor of a few.

And what about the money that the government already has? The largest forms of welfare waste can be found in the military. Only 5 percent of Pentagon procurement dollars are spent through competitive bids. There are many dubious projects, such as the MX missile, the Trident II missile, Star Wars planning, NATO troops in Europe, aircraft carriers, and the $30 billion spent in 1987 on *first*-strike nuclear bombs. Also, some of those who receive our aid—such as the Japanese, whose sea-lanes we protect—can afford to pay the costs. American money should be spent first on the American people and on the infrastructure of this society.

With the proper use of our resources, our future would not be one of austerity but of expansion. Let us begin with our children. There has been a 25.6 percent increase in the number of children living in poverty since 1979. About one in five white children are growing up in impoverished homes, and over two out of every five Hispanic and black children. Conservatives talk about being pro-family, but the United States has the shabbiest record among the major industrial nations for prenatal care, maternal leave, family allowances, child care, medical care, and supplemental food programs. The Dodd-Schroeder Family and Medical Leave Bill, to be debated in 1988, would be a step toward reform. Representative Pat Schroeder (D.–Colorado) commented that "If you look at American families, they are in as much trouble as the stock market. . . . All we have given them is rhetoric." It would be possible, furthermore, to expand Title XX Social Services Grants to encourage child care for working mothers.

When our children are old enough for school, our schools are often inferior. Our 180-day school year contrasts with one that is 240 days long in Japan. Our lack of vocational and apprenticeship programs, along with job training, compares sadly with West Germany. Over one-third of our adult population has not finished high school, and many Americans are functionally illiterate. What future will these people—and our country—have?

The general physical environment could be improved by greater state expenditures for airports, bridges, highways, transit, ports, and water and sewage systems. In the late 1960s, 2.3 percent of the GNP was spent for public investment. Today, it is less than .4 percent. Public spending is also needed for a national health service (about 40 million Americans have no health insurance), and for research on high-tech projects involving such areas as energy efficiency, high-speed rail, and waste treatment. Without these short-term expenses, we are going to become more and more backward compared to much of the rest of the world. Long-term gains are not possible without investment today.

Full employment should be a national goal. If private jobs are not available, Senator Paul Simon (D.–Illinois) has urged the guarantee of four days of work per week for anyone who wants to work. Federal funds can be provided to local government for public building projects, child care, and conservation.

For those employed, there must be a reasonable minimum wage (the present standard has not changed since 1981, despite an overall inflation rate of 22 percent). Real wages have not grown for most workers since 1973. Reductions in the length of the workday and the workweek might be considered. Federal agencies for health, safety, and equal opportunity could cease their pro-corporate bias. Violators of OSHA standards, for example, have seldom been inconvenienced by small fines, and no businessman has ever been thrown in jail for wrongdoing. Government could also encourage unionization as a counterbalance to corporate power.

Individuals and small businesses cannot easily challenge corporations. About 200 corporations dominate the U.S. economy. In addition, the U.S. Office of Technology has estimated that by the year 2000, 75 percent of the nation's farm production will come from 50,000 of the largest farms. It may be useful to revive the antitrust laws, which have been ignored in recent years. Further, the government might protect family farms (which often take better care of the land than agricultural corporations), and promote cooperatives and publicly owned businesses, such as the utilities that produce one-fourth of our electricity. If a big corporation relocates abroad, it should be treated as a public enemy and forced to pay stiff penalties and all of the costs of its local disruptions.

Our national government, beyond promoting the renovation of American society, could favor unions, democracy, and higher standards of living abroad rather than cynically support military and property-holding elites. Dictatorships may insure cheap raw materials and cheap labor for American businesses, but they provide limited markets and the likelihood of a future of revolution and hatred against the United States. The best assurance of peace and prosperity is justice.

These are not utopian dreams. A 1987 poll by *Time* magazine found that 78 percent would spend more on federal health care for the poor and the old, 73 percent would spend more on the environment, and more than 75 percent wanted an increasingly active government. When they were asked to choose between further military spending or more for social programs, 69 percent favored social programs. And more than 60 percent were willing to raise their taxes to pay for such progress. Most sensible people understand that America will not be "number one" with nickel and dime budgets for education, environmental protection, health, and safety. Quality is expensive, and it should be paid for by those who can afford to pay.

What movements will pressure these changes? Many of them have been discussed in this book. Will they overcome their present single-issue isolation and form broader networks? Will they understand their possibilities and limitations within the new world of international corporations and markets? The AFL-CIO, for example, returned to the International Confederation of

Free Trade Unions in 1981, urging the unionization and improvement of foreign workers as an alternative to American workers being reduced, let us say, to the status of South African labor. The Rev. Jesse Jackson has urged labor unions and civil rights groups like the NAACP to be actively concerned about the rights of foreign workers and minorities, and to emphasize that "our jobs are not being taken by South Koreans and Taiwanese; our jobs are being taken by U.S. companies with tax incentives."

These movements may develop some unifying ideology, such as "neo-liberalism", liberalism, "kick-ass populism" (as described by the Texas politician Jim Hightower), democratic socialism, or some other alternative future. The dominant goals may be for incremental change, a step at a time, or for basic reconstruction.

Nothing human lasts forever. Has the United States reached a dead end? This would be a premature conclusion. As Emerson observed, "The two parties which divide the state, the party of Conservatism and the party of Innovation, are very old, and have disputed the possession of the world ever since it was made. . . . Innovation is the salient energy; Conservatism the pause on the last movement." Perhaps it is once again time to move.

SOURCES OF FURTHER INFORMATION

Books and Articles

Bagdikian, Ben H. *The Media Monopoly*. 2d ed. Boston: Beacon Press, 1987.
Batra, Ravi. *The Great Depression of 1990*. New York: Simon & Schuster, 1987.
Bellah, Robert, et al. *Habits of the Heart: Individualism and Commitment in American Life*. New York: Perennial, 1986.
Block, Fred, et al., eds. *The Mean Season: The Attack on the Welfare State*. New York: Pantheon Books, 1987.

Bookchin, Murray. *The Rise of Urbanization and the Decline of Citizenship*. San Francisco: Sierra Club Books, 1987.

Bouchier, David. *Radical Citizenship: The New American Activism*. New York: Schocken Books, 1987.

Bowles, Samuel, and Herbert Gintis. *Democracy and Capitalism: Property, Community and the Contradictions of Modern Social Thought*. New York: Basic Books, 1986.

Boyte, Harry, and Frank Riesman, eds. *The New Populism: The Politics of Empowerment*. Philadelphia: Temple University Press, 1986.

Boyte, Harry, Heather Booth, and Steve Max. *Citizen Action and the New American Populism*. Philadelphia: Temple University Press, 1986.

Bremner, Robert, Gary W. Reichard, and Richard J. Hopkins, eds. *American Choices: Social Dilemmas and Public Policy since 1960*. Columbus: Ohio State University Press, 1986.

Brown, J. Larry, and H. F. Pizer. *Living Hungry in America*. New York: Macmillan, 1987.

Calleo, David P. *Beyond American Hegemony: The Future of the Western Alliance*. New York: Twentieth Century Fund/Basic Books, 1987.

Chambers, Clarke A. "Toward a Redefinition of Welfare History," *Journal of American History* 73 (September 1986): 407–33.

Chomsky, Noam. *The Chomsky Reader*, Jim Peck, ed. New York: Pantheon Books, 1987.

Cohen, Stephen S., and John Zysman. *Manufacturing Matters: The Myth of the Post-Industrial Economy*. New York: Basic Books, 1987.

Cooney, Robert, and Helen Michalowski, eds. *The Power of the People: Active Nonviolence in the United States*, 2d ed. Philadelphia: New Society Publishers, 1987.

Cottrell, Robert. "Twentieth-Century American Radicalism: A Bibliographical Essay," *The History Teacher* 20 (November 1986): 27–49.

Danziger, Sheldon H., and Daniel H. Weinberger. *Fighting Poverty: What Works and What Doesn't*. Cambridge: Harvard University Press, 1986.

Davis, Mike. *Prisoners of the American Dream: Politics and Economy in the History of the U.S. Working Class*. New York: Schocken Books, 1986.

Davis, Mike, et al., eds. *The Year Left 2: Toward a Rainbow Socialism: Essays on Race, Ethnicity, Class and Gender*. London: Verso/New Left Books, 1987.

DeBenedetti, Charles, ed. *Peace Heroes in Twentieth-Century America*. Bloomington: Indiana University Press, 1986.

Dubofsky, Melvyn, and Warren Van Tine, eds. *American Labor Leaders*. Urbana: University of Illinois Press, 1987.

Edelman, Marian Wright. *Families in Peril: An Agenda for Social Change*. Cambridge: Harvard University Press, 1987.

Evans, Sarah, and Harry Boyte. *Free Spaces: The Sources of Democratic Change in America*. New York: Harper & Row, 1986.

Ezorsky, Gertrude, ed. *Moral Rights in the Workplace*. Albany: State University of New York Press, 1986.

Ferguson, Thomas, and Joel Rogers. *Right Turn: The Decline of the Democrats and the Future of American Politics*. New York: Hill & Wang, 1987.

274

EVERYTHING IS CHANGING

Gaddis, John Lewis. *The Long Peace: Inquiries into the History of the Cold War.* New York: Oxford University Press, 1987.

Galbraith, John Kenneth. *Economics in Perspective: A Critical History.* Boston: Houghton Mifflin, 1987.

Gardner, Lloyd C., ed. *Redefining the Past: Essays in Diplomatic History in Honor of William Appleman Williams.* Corvallis: Oregon State University Press, 1986.

Gillies, Archibald, et al. *Post-Reagan America.* Washington, D.C.: World Policy Institute, 1987.

Ginsberg, Benjamin. *The Captive Public: How Mass Opinion Promotes State Power.* New York: Basic Books, 1987.

Gitlin, Todd. *The Sixties: Years of Hope, Days of Rage.* New York: Bantam Books, 1987.

Greenberg, Edward S. *Workplace Democracy: The Political Effects of Participation.* Ithaca, N.Y.: Cornell University Press, 1986.

Harrington, Michael. *The Next Left: The History of a Future.* New York: Henry Holt, 1987.

Hirsch, E. D., Jr. *Cultural Literacy.* Boston: Houghton Mifflin, 1987.

Jacoby, Russell. *The Last Intellectuals: American Culture in the Age of Academe.* New York: Basic Books, 1987.

Katz, Michael B. *In the Shadow of the Poorhouse: A Social History of Welfare in America.* New York: Basic Books, 1986.

Kidron, Michael, and Ronald Siegal. *What You Need to Know about Business, Money and Power.* New York: Simon & Schuster, 1987.

Kolko, Gabriel. *Anatomy of a War: Vietnam, the United States and the Modern Historical Experience.* New York: Pantheon Books, 1986.

Kuttner, Robert. *The Life of the Party: Democratic Prospects in 1988.* New York: Viking, 1987.

Kwitney, Jonathan. *Endless Enemies: The Making of an Unfriendly World.* New York: Penguin, 1987.

Lekachman, Robert. *Visions and Nightmares: America after Reagan.* New York: Macmillan, 1987.

Lens, Sidney. *Permanent War: The Militarization of America.* New York: Schocken Books, 1987.

Levy, Frank. *Dollars and Dreams: The Changing American Income Distribution.* New York: Russell Sage Foundation/Basic Books, 1987.

Lipnack, Jessica, and Jeffrey Stamps. *The Networking Book.* New York: Routledge & Kegan Paul, 1986.

Loeb, Paul Rogat. *Hope in Hard Times: The American Peace Movement and the Reagan Era.* Lexington, Mass.: Lexington Books, 1987.

McCann, Michael W. *Taking Reform Seriously: Perspectives on Public Interest Liberalism.* Ithaca, N.Y.: Cornell University Press, 1986.

Malabre, Alfred L., Jr. *Beyond Our Means: How America's Long Years of Debt, Deficits and Reckless Borrowing Now Threaten to Overwhelm Us.* New York: Random House, 1987.

Malkin, Lawrence. *The National Debt.* New York: Henry Holt, 1987.

Miliband, Ralph, Leo Panitch, and John Saville, eds. *Socialist Register 1987.* London: Merlin, 1987.

Miller, James. *"Democracy Is in the Streets": From Port Huron to the Siege of Chicago*. New York: Simon & Schuster, 1987.

Nader, Ralph, and Griffin Kelley. *More Action for a Change: Students Serving the Public Interest*. New York: Dembner Books, 1987.

Nader, Ralph, and William Taylor. *The Big Boys: Power and Position in American Business*. New York: Pantheon Books, 1986.

Ollman, Bertell, and Edward Vernoff, eds. *The Left Academy: Marxist Scholarship on American Campuses*, vol. 3. New York: Praeger, 1987.

Parenti, Michael. *Inventing Reality: Politics and the Mass Media*. New York: St. Martin's Press, 1987.

Reich, Robert B. *Tales of a New America*. New York: Times Books, 1987.

Richards, Eugene. *Below the Line: Living Poor in America*. Mt. Vernon, N.Y.: Consumers Union, 1987.

Rodgers, Daniel T. *Contested Truths: Keywords in American Politics since Independence*. New York: Basic Books, 1987.

Rose, Stephen J. *The American Economy Poster and Fact Book*. New York: Pantheon Books, 1987.

———. *The American Profile Poster: Who Owns What, Who Makes How Much, Who Works Where, and Who Lives with Whom*. New York: Pantheon Books, 1986.

Schlesinger, Arthur M., Jr. *The Cycles of American History*. Boston: Houghton Mifflin, 1986.

Schorr, Alvin L. *Common Decency: Domestic Policies after Reagan*. New Haven, Conn.: Yale University Press, 1986.

Schwartz, Michael, ed. *The Structure of Power in America: The Corporate Elite as a Ruling Class*. New York: Holmes & Meier, 1987.

Schwarz, John E. *America's Hidden Success: A Reassessment of Public Policy from Kennedy to Reagan*. Rev. ed. New York: Norton, 1988.

Stares, Paul B. *The Militarization of Space: U.S. Policy, 1945–84*. Ithaca, N.Y.: Cornell University Press, 1987.

Treverton, Gregory. *Covert Action: The Limits of Intervention in the Postwar World*. New York: Basic Books, 1987.

Walker, Robert H. "Reform in America: A Bibliographical Outline," *American Studies International* 24 (April 1986): 2–28.

Williams, William Appleman. *The Tragedy of American Diplomacy*, rev. 2d ed. New York: Dell, 1986.

Wills, Garry. *Reagan's America: Innocents at Home*. New York: Doubleday, 1987.

Woodward, Bob. *Veil*. New York: Simon & Schuster, 1987.

Yates, Michael. *The Labor Law Handbook*. Boston: South End Press, 1987.

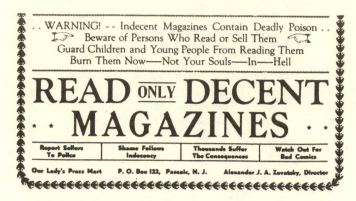

A conservative ad, used by the Alternative Press Center as a
virtual satire on rigidly conservative people.

Organizations and Publications

Requests for information should be accompanied by a stamped, self-addressed
envelope.

Decentralist

Great Atlantic Radio Conspiracy (tapes), 2743 Maryland Ave., Baltimore, Md. 21218
   (Also address for the journal *Social Anarchism*)
Libertarian Party, 301 W. 21st St., Houston, Tex. 77008
Our Generation, University of Toronto Press, Journal Dept., 5201 Dufferin St.,
   Downsview, Ontario, Canada M3H 5T8
Peace and Freedom Party, P.O. Box 42644, San Francisco, Calif. 94142
Reason, P.O. Box 27977, San Diego, Calif. 92128

Democratic Socialist

Charles H. Kerr Publishing, 1740 W. Greenleaf Ave., Chicago, Ill. 60626
Democratic Socialists of America, 15 Dutch St., Suite 500, New York, N.Y.
   10038-3705
Dissent, 521 Fifth Ave., New York, N.Y. 10017
Institute for Policy Studies, 1901 Q St., N.W., Washington, D.C. 20009
In These Times (newspaper), 1912 Debs Ave., Mt. Morris, Ill. 61054
New Politics, P.O. Box 98, Brooklyn, N.Y. 11231 (1961–1978; revived 1986)
Social Democrats, USA, 815 15th St., N.W., Suite 511, Washington, D.C. 20005
Socialist Party, USA, 516 West 25 St., New York, N.Y. 10001
South End Press, 116 St. Botolph, Boston, Mass. 02118

Liberal and General Left

Alternative Press Center, P.O. Box 33109, Baltimore, Md. 21218-0401 (publishers of
   the *Alternative Press Index* since 1969)

American Civil Liberties Union, Membership Dept., 132 W. 43rd St., New York, N.Y. 10036

Americans for Democratic Action, 815 15th St., N.W., Suite 711, Washington, D.C. 20005

Amnesty International, USA, 322 8th Ave., New York, N.Y. 10001

Cineaste, P.O. Box 2242, New York, N.Y. 10009

Common Cause, 2030 M St., N.W., Washington, D.C. 20036

Covert Action Information Bulletin, P.O. Box 50272, Washington, D.C. 20004

Democracy Project, 215 Park Ave., S., Suite 1814, New York, N.Y. 10003

Folkways Records, 180 Alexander Rd., Princeton, N.J. 08540

Modern Times Bookstore (catalog), 968 Valencia St., San Francisco, Calif. 94110

Mother Jones, 1886 Haymarket Square, Marion, Ohio 43305

Nation, Box 1953, Marion, Ohio 43305

National Center for Policy Alternatives, 2000 Florida Ave., Washington, D.C. 20009

National Emergency Civil Liberties Committee, 175 Fifth Ave., New York, N.Y. 10010

National Lawyers Guild, 853 Broadway, Rm. 1705, New York, N.Y. 10003

National Public Radio, Cassette Catalog, 2025 M St., N.W., Washington, D.C. 20036

New Options (newsletter), P.O. Box 19324, Washington, D.C. 20036

New Republic, Subscription Service, P.O. Box 56515, Boulder, Colo. 80322

New York Review of Books, P.O. Box 940, Farmingdale, N.Y. 11737

Paredon Records, Box 11266, Oakland, Calif. 94611

People for the American Way, 1424 16th St., N.W., #601, Washington, D.C. 20036

Progressive, Box 54615, 1909 LaFollette Lane, Boulder, Colo. 80321-4615

Public Citizen, 2000 P St., N.W., Washington, D.C. 20036

Sing out!, P.O. Box 1071, Easton, Penna. 18042

Utne Reader: The Best of the Alternative Press, P.O. Box 1974, Marion, Ohio 43305

Village Voice, Voice Subscriptions, P.O. Box 1905, Marion, Ohio 43302

Marxism: Not Affiliated with a Party

Dollars and Sense, 1 Summer St., Somerville, Mass. 02143

Guardian, 33 W. 17th St., New York, N.Y. 10011

Monthly Review/Monthly Review Press, 122 W. 27th St., New York, N.Y. 10001

New Left Review (English), c/o U.S. distributor, Bernard de Boer, 113 E. Centre, Nutley, N.J. 07110

Radical America, 38 Union Square, Somerville, Mass. 02143

Radical History Review, Bernard de Boer, Distributor, 113 E. Centre, Nutley, N.J. 07110

Review of Radical Political Economics, 155 W. 23rd St., 12th Fl., New York, N.Y. 10011

Science and Society, Rm. 4331, John Jay College, 445 W. 59th St., New York, N.Y. 10019

Socialist Review, 3202 Adeline St., Berkeley, Calif. 94703

Marxism Tied to Programs

China Books and Periodicals, 2929 24th St., San Francisco, Calif. 94110

Communist Party, USA, 235 W. 23rd St., New York, N.Y. 10011-2388

International Publishers, 381 Park Ave., S., Rm. 1301, New York, N.Y. 10016
Militant/Pathfinder Press, 410 West St., New York, N.Y. 10014 (Related to the
   Socialist Workers Party, a Trotskyist group)
People's Daily World, 239 W. 23rd St., 3rd Fl, New York, N.Y. 10011
U.S.-China Peoples Friendship Association, 2025 I St., N.W., Washington, D.C.
   20006 (not Marxist, per se)

"*They're going to make slaves of the Russian People.*"

A 1920s cartoon by Art Young

Illustration Credits

137. Graphic from a 1973 flyer. **157.** Margaret Sanger advertisement, 1915. **166.** Advertisements, ca. 1916. **170.** Cartoon by Fred Wright in *UE News* reprinted by permission of Fred Wright and the United Electrical, Radio, and Machine Workers of America. **186.** Graphic reprinted by permission of Mattachine Society, Inc. **188,190.** Illustrations reprinted by permission of ONE, Inc. **192.** Illustrations from the now-defunct Daughters of Bilitis. **197.** Artist: Rick Fiala. Courtesy of *Christopher Street*. **200.** Cartoon from *Inter-Change*, 1973 (now defunct). **205.** Beth Ahavah advertisement reprinted by permission. **205.** Graphic reprinted by permission of Dignity. **206.** Advertisement reprinted by permission of Integrity/Washington, Inc. Integrity/Washington, Inc., is a local chapter of Integrity, Inc., the international organization of gay and lesbian Episcopalians and their friends. **206.** Logo of the Universal Fellowship of Metropolitan Community Churches (UFMCC) reprinted by permission. **212.** The corporate name of the now-defunct Outright Books of Key West, Florida.

219. Co-op America logo reprinted by permission. **220.** Graphic from the National Historic Communal Societies Association. **221.** Drawing from the now-defunct *New Abolitionist*. **223.** Illustration by Art Young, ca. 1912. **229.** Illustration by Fritz Eichenberg in the *Catholic Worker*. (This and subsequent illustrations from *Catholic Worker* have been reprinted, by permission, from Peter Maurin, *Easy Essays* [Chicago: Franciscan Herald Press, n.d.].) **231.** Drawing by Rita Corbin in *Catholic Worker*. **232.** Reprinted by permission from *The Progressive*. Copyright © 1977, The Progressive, Inc. **234.** Eichenberg illustration in *Catholic Worker*. **236.** Graphics by Ade Bethune in *Catholic Worker*. **238.** *Catholic Worker* logo. **240.** Drawing by Fritz Eichenberg in *Catholic Worker*. **241.** Logos of the New Jewish Agenda, the Unitarian-Universalist Service Association, and the American Humanist Association reprinted by permission. **246.** National Council of Senior Citizens. Reprinted by permission. **248.** Cartoon by Cindy Fredrick, Liberation News Service. **252.** Cartoon by Fred Wright in *UE News* reprinted by permission of Fred Wright and the United Electrical, Radio, and Machine Workers of America.

266. Gary Huck, *UE News*, Huck-Konopacki Labor Cartoons. Reprinted by permission. **278.** "Capitalism" by Peg Averill, Liberation News Service.

Every reasonable effort has been made to trace the owners of copyright materials used in this book, but in some instances this has proven impossible. The publishers will be glad to receive information leading to more complete acknowledgments in subsequent printings of this book, and in the meantime extend their apologies for any omissions.

Index

Nation of Islam, 101
New Deal, 18–19, 74, 245
New Left, 195
Newton, Huey, 195–96
Nixon, Richard, 25
North American Conference of Homophile Organizations, 194, 199
Nuclear power: alternatives to, 50–53; opposition to, 41–44; use in war, 47–50; wastes from, 28, 44, 45; weapons using, 36–41
Nuclear Regulatory Commission, 40, 43
Nursing homes, 249

Olmsted, Frederick Law, 7
ONE, Inc., 188–91, 196, 205
O'Neill, Thomas P. (Tip), 264
Oppenheimer, J. Robert, 36–37
OSHA (Occupational Safety and Health Administration), 24, 271

Partido Nuevo Progresista, 129
Partido Popular Democrático, 128–29
Partido Socialista Puertorriqueño, 129–30
Pepper, Claude, 250
Perry, Rev. Troy, 206
Pinchot, Gifford, 14, 16, 27
Pius XI, 234
Plessy v. Ferguson, 94
Pressler, Larry, 264
Puerto Ricans, 124–31

Racism: against blacks, 85; against Chicanos, 113; general, 59–60; against Indians, 66–67
Radical, definition of, xiv–xv
Radioactivity, 35
Randolph, A. Philip, 98
Ranke, Leopold von, xvi
Reagan, Ronald, 23, 26, 123, 153, 160, 164, 225, 254, 264, 266, 267, 268, 269
Reform, xiv
Religion, radical, 221–43
Rivlin, Alice, 269
Roe v. Wade, 160

Roosevelt, Franklin Delano, 37, 268
Roosevelt, Theodore, 14–16, 67, 122

SANE (National Committee for a Sane Nuclear Policy), 39
Sanger, Margaret, 155–58
Schroeder, Patricia, 270
Schurz, Carl, 9
Seneca Falls (N.Y.), xv, 142, 147
Sex roles, xi, 137–38, 196–97
Sierra Club, 13, 19, 26, 39
Silkwood, Karen, 42
Simon, Paul, 270
SIR (Society for Individual Rights), 193–94
Slavery, introduction of, to the New World, 85–86, 88
Social Security, 245, 246, 247, 251
Sociobiology, 3–4
Solar energy, 52
Soviet Union, 265
Stanton, Elizabeth Cady, 141, 142, 146
Stone, Lucy, 147
Stonewall riot, 194, 195, 196
Student Nonviolent Coordinating Committee, 100, 152

Taft, William Howard, 16
Television evangelists, 222
Thoreau, Henry David, xii, 1, 7, 13, 20
Three Mile Island (Penna.), 42–43
Tijerina, Reies López, 120
Times Beach (Mo.), 27–28
Tolstoy, Leo, xvi
Tourgee, Albion, 88
Truman, Harry, 38
Truth, Sojourner, 139, 143, 147
Tubman, Harriet, 143, 144

Urban League, 97, 99

Vietnam War, 21
Voting Rights Act of 1965, 99

Walker, David, 96
Walker, Jimmy, xiv
Washington, Booker T., 97–98
Washington, George, 70, 261

About the Author

DAVID De LEON, Associate Professor of History at Howard University, is the author of *The American as Anarchist: Reflections on Indigenous Radicalism*, and coeditor of *Reinventing Anarchy: Or, What Are Anarchists Thinking Today?* His articles have appeared in *American Quarterly, Labor History*, and other journals.